"Andrew Root is one of our leadir
has carved out a space within wh
sophical inquiry are merged into practical strategies that are illuminating and
often fascinating. In this new book he continues his ongoing dialogue with
Charles Taylor, providing us with a fascinating and timely exploration of
time, church, and culture. Time is something we tend to take for granted. But
it is a crucial dimension of social and ecclesial life. In this book Root clearly
lays out the implications of thinking about time and speed and the ways in
which we build communities, think about theology, and ultimately become
more faithful disciples. This is a book well worth reading."

—**John Swinton**, University of Aberdeen

"Root serves as a guide for current congregations often lost in the time and
space of the wilderness of high modernity. He deftly leads his readers on an
adventure through historical, philosophical, and theological perspectives,
providing an eternal compass of resonance toward our True North. The experience of reading this book is what I imagined it was like to witness Moses
parting the Red Sea. Just as Moses created a passage for Israel from Egypt,
Root shows us how to suspend the relentless rush of time and points the church
toward a path from our present captivity in the rat race of modernity to the
life-giving vitality of the love of God. This book is required reading for the
next generation of Christian leaders. Root provides a clear and resounding
perspective on why and how the church matters in a secular age."

—**Pamela Ebstyne King**, Thrive Center for Human Development,
Fuller Theological Seminary

"On a secular view of the world, we are thrown into an existence in which our
time is running out. The pressure is on to accomplish as much as we can, as
quickly as we can, which generates a constant anxiety that fuels depression.
Not only does this pressure terrorize the secular world, it also menaces the
many congregations that are fighting for survival in the so-called secular age.
In response to this situation, Andrew Root offers a fierce remedy. As someone
to whom this book really speaks, I could feel a weight being lifted off my
shoulders, page by page. Why? Because this book offers a fresh, timely, and
powerful reminder of the hope of all hopes—the one true hope—to which
the gospel witnesses. As such, it made me a happier person, authentically so!"

—**Andrew Torrance**, University of St. Andrews

"Root is an expert reader of contemporary church life. He deftly distills
complex philosophical, historical, and sociological scholarship and delivers

what his readers need to know. And Root's constructive proposals challenge churches and individuals to rethink their relationship to time and busyness. *The Congregation in a Secular Age* will leave many readers wondering just how Root knows them and their congregations so well. This book is a valuable resource to anyone who has the nagging feeling that there's never enough time."

—**Ryan McAnnally-Linz**, Yale Center for Faith and Culture

the
congregation
in a secular age

the congregation in a secular age

Keeping Sacred Time against the Speed of Modern Life

MINISTRY IN A SECULAR AGE,
VOLUME THREE

Andrew Root

Baker Academic
a division of Baker Publishing Group
Grand Rapids, Michigan

Published by Baker Academic
a division of Baker Publishing Group
PO Box 6287, Grand Rapids, MI 49516-6287
www.bakeracademic.com

Printed in the United States of America

Library of Congress Cataloging-in-Publication Data
Names: Root, Andrew, 1974– author.
Title: The Congregation in a secular age : keeping sacred time against the speed of modern life / Andrew Root.
Description: Grand Rapids, Michigan : Baker Academic, a division of Baker Publishing Group, 2021. | Series: Ministry in a secular age ; volume three | Includes index.
Identifiers: LCCN 2020027155 | ISBN 9780801098482 (paperback) | ISBN 9781540963949 (casebound)
Subjects: LCSH: Church renewal. | Change—Religious aspects—Christianity. | Christianity and culture.
Classification: LCC BV600.3 .R66 2021 | DDC 253—dc23
LC record available at https://lccn.loc.gov/2020027155

The characters in this book are fictional, but they are based on real people and interactions, trimmed and adjusted to fit this context. Some names and identifying details have been changed to protect the privacy of the individuals involved.

21 22 23 24 25 26 27   7 6 5 4 3 2 1

To Maisy Root
A person of resonance, a true delight

contents

preface

While in the middle of writing this book I had a return flight from Amsterdam to Minneapolis. I've taken this Delta flight many times. Usually, around hour six of eight it becomes painfully too long. I just want it to end. Those last two hours are the worst. When this occurs, I'm usually on movie four and my body aches and thirsts to climb out of the metal tube I'm stuck in going 600 miles an hour.

Yet this particular day I decided to do something outside my nature. I decided to pass on TV. I made the choice to format footnotes in this manuscript instead of watching *The Avengers*. As you'll notice from paging through this book, there are a lot of footnotes. Too many—I apologize for that! I'm a little bit addicted to footnotes. But that's not my point. This isn't a call for a footnote intervention. My editor has already initiated those procedures.

My point is this: for the first time, my experience of flying between Amsterdam and Minneapolis was quick. It felt nothing like eight hours. If asked to guess (and unable to see the moving flight map in front of me), I would've assumed it took us only two or three hours to get home. I would have believed it if the pilot had said over the intercom, "Folks, bad news and good news. The bad first: it appears we slid into a wormhole (we have no idea what this will do to your being long-term). But good news: it just so happens that this wormhole got us to Minneapolis in a scant two hours and forty-five minutes." It was honestly the best international flight of my life (because the wormhole was only in my imagination).

It was *best* because I experienced time in a very different way. The hours seemed to melt away. I even found myself wishing for more time, as I poured myself into this project of creative love. (Okay, I understand that footnote formatting is not the height of creativity, but needing to reread and rewrite sections as I placed notes met some threshold of creativity for me, at least on this day, impacting my experience of time.)

Ironically or not, the question that has driven all three of these volumes revolves around time. In the preface to volume 1, I started with a story about the change in time through the adoption of the Gregorian Calendar. Each of these volumes has asked, What time are we in?

We've answered, following Charles Taylor, that our time is a secular one. But to call it secular is to say something complicated. I've tried in each of the volumes to turn Taylor's brilliant interpretation lose on particular issues confronting Protestantism—specifically, faith formation and pastoral identity. I've tried to respond to this dialogue with my own theological construction.

In this final volume I'll do the same, but now giving even more attention to time itself. The driving question in this volume will be, *What time are local congregations in?* How is our secular age impacting them? What will be unique about this volume is that I'll explore this time but focus on *time itself*. To assert that we're in a secular age is to assert that time itself has been reimagined. Like on my flight, our cultural experiences impact our feel of time. Then, in this work, I'll continue my conversation with Charles Taylor. But I'll also, as seems appropriate in this final volume, step beyond him. I'll turn to one of his best and most constructive interpreters, German social theorist Hartmut Rosa.

Rosa is no simple commentator on Taylor. He is a world-class scholar, constructively developing his own unique and rich project. Inspired by Taylor's thought and building on parts of it, Rosa has offered a stunning articulation of modernity in and through time. He believes that what it means to be living in a modern age (in modernity) is to have our lives continually and constantly accelerated. This acceleration has the effect of stripping the sacred out of time.

My argument in the pages below is that this accelerating of time has had a huge impact on the congregation. I even assert that congregations are struck with *depression* because they can't keep up with the speed. When we call them to change, we ask them to speed up, and many, as I'll show, simply can't. This leads to burnout and depression. This final volume will provide a full-blown theory of modernity in direct conversation with congregational life. This book will explore the congregation in a secular age, an age of accelerated time, wherein the sacred has been replaced by a drive to innovate and grow. Faithfulness has been replaced with a drive for vitality.

Each of the three volumes of this series has sought to be timely, confronting what I imagine are misguided conceptions of the time we're in. I continue that—very directly—in this volume. In the last handful of years many denominational leaders, consultants, and others have called the congregation to move into processes of innovation, my own seminary making innovation central to its mission statement. I contend in the pages below that if we're not very careful, this attention to innovation will be detrimental to congregations trying to find their way in a secular age. So following Rosa, and his building off of Taylor, I'll offer a view that names the tensions and possibilities for the congregation inside a robust articulation of modernity itself.

This book seeks to be concrete, inspiring your imagination and encouraging your practical engagement in ministry. But also like the others, it seeks to provide a more cultural and then theological vision than it does direct practice. There will be ample stories and examples, but there is no bullet-point list of what your congregation can do. I only hope to give you a sense of the time we're in and how God can be imagined to act within it, that it might inspire greater and more concrete practices for your own context than I could imagine.

That said, I have written complementary books that flesh out more directly the issues I raise in volumes 1 and 2. For instance, I get much more practical (though still no bullet points) on the implications of *Faith Formation in a Secular Age* and *The Pastor in a Secular Age* in my books *Exploding Stars, Dead Dinosaurs, and Zombies: Youth Ministry in the Age of Science* (Minneapolis: Fortress, 2018) and *The End of Youth Ministry? Why Parents Don't Really Care about Youth Groups and What Youth Workers Should Do about It* (Grand Rapids: Baker Academic, 2020).

This book too will call for something similar. However, what might need to follow is not a more practice-based book but a direct ecclesiology in discourse with Rosa's conception of resonance. What you have in your hands is not a full ecclesiology but an important catalyst for transitioning from a cultural theological dialogue to this needed ecclesiology. So in some sense, like all good projects, this end is only the beginning of a new path to something else. Next up, more than likely, will be a full-blown ecclesiology. This is not that full-blown ecclesiology; this is a cultural and theological discussion of the congregation. My focus is not on the very complicated definition of the church but only on its expression as local congregations.

There have been many people who have supported me on the path of these three volumes. Especially I would like to thank Bob Hosack, Eric Salo, and Mason Slater at Baker Academic. I'm also thankful to Luther Seminary and its board for giving me a sabbatical the school year of 2018–19 to write this final volume. Gratitude to Wes Ellis, Jon Wasson, Blair Bertrand, Alan Padgett, Carla Dahl, and Theresa Latini for reading the whole of this manuscript, giving me very valuable feedback.

I also need to thank the Sir John Templeton Foundation and especially Paul Wason. In the final stages of volume 2, and into this volume, David Wood and I were awarded a small grant called "Purpose, the Pastor, and Charles Taylor." The goal of the grant was to become clearer on the challenges and possibilities that pastors and their congregations face. The grant supported a good deal of the research for this volume. Most directly, it made it possible for David and me to meet with both Charles Taylor and Hartmut Rosa. We had a wonderful conversation with Professor Taylor in a café in Montreal, and a very rich discussion with Professor Rosa in his office at the University of Jena in Germany. These conversations were invaluable. I'd like, then, also to thank David Wood for reading the manuscript and the encouragement he's given me in its pursuits.

Finally, as always, I'd like to thank Rev. Kara Root for reading and editing this manuscript. On each line she kept me honest and made it more readable. I'm blessed to have her mind and heart in my life.

Andrew Root
In Ordinary Time
May 31, 2019

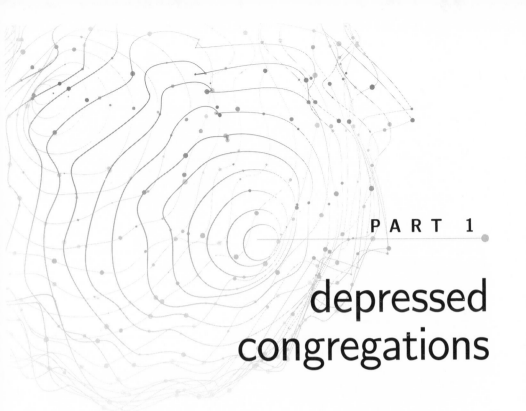

PART 1

depressed congregations

1

the church and the depressing speed of change

In a restaurant in North Dakota, I found myself sitting across from a pastor I had met just hours earlier.

"I don't know how to explain it," he said to me. "It's something more than apathy. It's not that they don't care. It's just that my church, maybe the whole denomination, seems depressed. I know that sounds weird, but that's how it feels. I've battled depression myself for years. I know it from the inside. This feels like church-wide depression. Like we're stuck in mud or trapped under water, and we just don't have the energy to face it."

"Face what?" I asked.

"Anything at all," he returned quickly. Sighing deeply, he said, "Maybe even the energy to be the church at all."

This was too big of a statement for me to process. I tried to step back. "What's the depression over?"

"That's the thing," he continued. "It's like depression usually does: it doesn't have a clear cause. You don't know why, but you just can't find the get-up. The world feels silent and bland. And you don't know why. There may be something that triggers it, but it's just a current pulling you to the bottom, making you too tired to fight to get to the surface."

I'm in his North Dakota town to speak to a large gathering of young Methodist people. I arrived one day early to meet with some local pastors. His church hosted the conversation. He met me at the door, taking me on

3

a tour of his church building. By any measure, it's beautiful, wearing every mark of vibrancy.

We started in the brand-new wing, opened just months earlier. After peeking into the shiny youth room, we moved across the hall to a warm fireside room with leather couches and a decked-out kitchenette. Then we moved to the gym, lit by the late-October sunshine spilling in from a dozen large windows.

The gym echoed with the laughter of about two dozen four-year-olds. They were slowly placing a large parachute on the ground, finishing their game. As the parachute gently hit the floor, they all rushed past us, beelining for the wall behind us, searching for water bottles covered in cartoon characters to quench their little thirsts. Running past us, as though we were invisible, a little girl said, as much to the universe as to anyone, "Now that was *great!*" We laughed with delight. We stood there a few seconds in silence just absorbing the joy and energy of all the little ones before moving on with our tour.

We passed more classrooms filled with more three and four-year-olds. I was told that the congregation ran the largest preschool in town. The walls of the spacious narthex were filled with posters and information sheets of trips, programs, and outings. We looked through the window into the enormous sanctuary. The pastor told me that their worship attendance was about five hundred a week. At the end of the tour, moving toward the pastor's office, we passed through a narrow hallway filled with office doors. I read the name plaques on the doors: Associate Pastor, Director of Children's Ministry, Youth Director, Minister of Music, and even another Associate Pastor.

Hours later, sitting across from this pastor over lunch, I'm shocked that he would describe this seemingly vibrant church as depressed. There was no deferred maintenance, no budget shortage, no lack of young families or staff. And yet he used the word "depressed."

Here at Cowboy Cal's Steakhouse in North Dakota, there was no mistaking it for Manhattan or any coastal city. The bright orange vests on half the customers and the talk of pheasant hunts signaled quickly that this was flyover country, far from the coasts, in a place red enough to burn, where guns and civic religion are both loved.

Yet this North Dakota congregation, insulated from the supposed liberal ethos that undercuts the civic importance of religion, was as depressed as any declining city church in Philadelphia, according to its pastor.

"But you worship with five hundred people a week?" I said, a little incredulous.

"True, but three years ago, when we started the capital campaign for that new addition, it was over six hundred. We're still raising the last 10 percent of that project."

We paused as our sandwiches arrived.

"But that's not really the issue," he continued. "For the most part, people still show up on Sunday morning. But to get them to care or invest in anything else is impossible. We've tried everything."

"Prozac?" I responded, reminding myself to keep my sarcastic sense of humor in check. Luckily he laughed.

"Wow, that would be perfect: congregational Prozac!" he said. "I wonder if they could drip it into our coffeemakers."

I was now sure we could be good friends.

"I only laugh to keep from crying," he continued. "Personally, Prozac probably saved my life. But I've tried the equivalent of congregational Prozac. I've tested all sorts of meds on this church. We've done the small group discipleship thing, the family thing, the church movement thing—we started a new church across town that we can no longer fund—and even the missional thing. As the political climate changed I even did the prophetic justice thing. I felt like I had to, my conscience called for it. That wasn't easy in this community. But I couldn't keep up. I'm not even sure what I was trying to keep up with, but I couldn't. People in my church feel it too. We talk about falling behind, about needing change—it's all we discuss at our regional meetings—but no one seems to know what that change needs to be. And worse, I'm convinced no one has the energy. To be honest, I'm not sure if the lack of knowing what to do creates the depression or if the depression creates the inability to do anything."

He was on a roll now.

"I mean, these should be exciting times. Everyone knows we need change. But instead of creating energy, it creates depression."

The silence that now fell between the two of us felt much different than it did in the church gym among the joy of the children. That silence in the gym was full and open. This one was dull and confusing.

"All of those approaches were helpful. But in the end we'd just slide back into this depressive state, this inability to be any more than a church that shows up on Sunday morning. This congregation is essentially a country club, and I can't break that mentality. I don't think it's because these are bad or selfish people. They're lovely. As a church, we're just depressed."

Depression's Backstory

Parisian sociologist Alain Ehrenberg made a provocative argument in his late 1990s book *La fatigue d'être soi: Dépression et société*, which was mostly unknown in the English-speaking world until it was translated and published in 2016 under the title *The Weariness of the Self: Diagnosing the History of Depression in the Contemporary Age*. In this book, the sociologist argues that depression is an ailment of speed, the feeling of not being able to keep up.

Like Charles Taylor's *A Secular Age*, Ehrenberg's project is a genealogy. As we've seen in the first two volumes of this Ministry in a Secular Age series, Taylor's genealogy traces modernity's movement into unbelief. Exploring our cultural history, Taylor shows how it was possible for us to produce a world in which God is assumed to be absent, unbelief is easy, and the transcendent song of existence is deafeningly quiet. Taylor shows us the genes that produce this kind of world.

Ehrenberg is also interested in tracing our cultural history. Particularly, he's interested in how modernity's unfolding has produced distinct forms of mental illness. Ehrenberg wants to show us how these distinct forms tell us something important about modernity itself. Mental illness isn't an oddity in the project of modernity, something completely disconnected and periphery to its pursuits. Mental ailments and the way we diagnose and treat them unveil something central about the pursuits of modernity itself. Mental ailments are the canary in the mineshaft of modernity.

The story Ehrenberg traces is how each of the three stages of modernity— early (broadly the eighteenth century), high (nineteenth century into the first half of the twentieth), and late (the second half of the twentieth century)—has produced its own ailments. We've shifted from madness to hysteria to despondency. In early modernity, our pursuits for reason led to a radical redefinition of the odd. The socially esoteric, those shouting warnings and living under bridges, were no longer demoniacs or secret sages, or even angels or Jesus himself, whom we owe alms. In the medieval era (premodern, pre-1500s), such people had a place in the economy of salvation and the pursuit of virtue. But not in modernity. Rather, the blessed poor were now mad, overtaken by madness, unable to keep pace with reason.

In high modernity this shifted. The mad could still be spotted, but now the hysterical revealed something important about modernity. The need for the duties of politeness, manners, and all things proper was heavy. Even the death of a child, for the elite class, shouldn't upend your proper appearances. The proper was now tied to a speed engine, a modern economy. The need to order a happy private life so one could compete in a public arena of commerce was essential. Trying to hold everything together amid the pain of loss cracked many, leading to episodes of hysteria, frantic crying, screaming, or trancelike muttering. The hysterical person needed direct treatment because that person's breakdown spilled from the private space into the public. The treatment for such bouts was hospitalization—being placed in a private, enclosed institution away from the rush of public life. The hysterical needed to go away, even away from the private home, to get well. Whether madness or hysteria, it was now assumed to be a sickness. The hope was that you could treat hysteria like you could a broken leg.[1]

Psychology as we know it—particularly its Freudian or post-Freudian veins—has its origin in the diagnoses and treatments of mainly "hysterical" women. The nineteenth century, with its sexist disposition, seemed to do something to the human psyche, causing especially women to go into fits of hysteria. In hospitals in Paris, mostly women were admitted for being hysterical. Young Freud, in Paris training to be a doctor, was assigned these patients as part of his rounds. He discovered, to state it simply, that it was often the hidden obsessions that afflicted the hysterical. These obsessions weighed them down, producing a psychosis that kept them from reaching the speed of normal modern life, being able to marry and work, being a proper wife and keeper of the private space. Psychoanalysis had both its birth and its heyday in dealing with how the conditions of high modernity created hysteria. Psychiatry, on the other hand, would have its golden era in our late-modern times.

The Fatigue to Be Me

The pressure that produced hysteria gave way to something else in late modernity. Ehrenberg shows convincingly that while there were antecedents, such as melancholy (something Luther battled), it wasn't until the 1970s that hysteria was replaced by the late-modern mental ailment of depression. In high modernity the anxiety produced by the modern world could crack you, leading to bouts of hysterical crying and screaming. Sometimes it looked like madness. But in late modernity the issue became despondency, a feeling that you just couldn't find the energy to keep pace.

The title of Ehrenberg's book, *La fatigue d'être soi*, translates as "the fatigue of being yourself." Depression in late modernity is a fatigue with no direct outward cause. It is the feeling, born within yourself, that you just don't have the energy to be yourself. If it gets too heavy, you can become too fatigued to *be* at all. Suicide is no longer an act solely done under the shadow of lost societal esteem. For example, a person's bold action loses people's hard-earned fortunes in a crashing stock market. The failure of this bold action leads to another bold act, convincing that person to leap from a bridge

---

1. This transition plays its own part in bringing forth the immanent frame (a world presumed to be totally and completely natural as opposed to supernatural). Taylor discusses this transition from sin to sickness in *A Secular Age* (Cambridge, MA: Belknap, 2007), 618–20.

in the shame of failure. Bold action causes a bold act. In late modernity, what pushes someone into suicidal ideation has largely shifted. Most often it's not the feeling of a failed bold action but rather a sense that none of your actions matter at all, that any action you take is meaningless. It's not about paying for a bold action with a bold action but about a wish to disappear, to end the painful fatigue of feeling the burden, not necessarily the burden of your decision as much as the burden of being your self.[2]

Psychiatric therapies outstrip psychoanalytic ones in late modernity because often depression has no real narrative source. That's what's so scary about it. It feels like there is no reason for it coming. It arrives like a dark cloud that, painfully, won't lift. For instance, depressed people can have bad childhoods or not, experience abuse or not, feel unaccepted or not, feel guilty for masturbating or not. Depressed churches can have big budgets or not, be in the suburbs or not, have a full-time paid children's minister or not.[3]

Depression is so haunting because, for some, you can have everything you want, seemingly possessing all the sources to be a happy self, and yet you're sad. But not so much a hysterical sad, crying until daybreak—that would be a relief, those tears at least acknowledging that you feel something. What's worse is just feeling nothing, unable to garner the energy to feel even hysterical. Without analyzable narrative sources, it becomes much easier—even logically presumed—to make it a chemical issue, making pills the best treatment for it. Enter the world of Prozac, which Ehrenberg richly delves into.[4]

But it isn't as though depression completely has no source. Rather, Ehrenberg argues that its source is late modernity's demand to create and continue to curate your own self. This task is taxing and deeply fatiguing. The speed of late modernity, its frantic pace of life imposed on us by the blitzing social and technological change since the 1970s, makes life a raging river. In this raging river you need to not only create your own identity but also reach out into the world to receive recognition for that identity, swimming like hell to keep up in the breakneck currents.[5] It is your individual job in a constantly mov-

2. Pankaj Mishra discusses something similar in *Age of Anger: A History of the Present* (New York: Picador, 2017), 27–30.

3. Peter L. Steinke uses the concept of depressed congregations in his introduction to *Healthy Congregations: A Systems Approach*, 2nd ed. (Herndon, VA: Alban Institute, 2006).

4. This is different from Luther's conception of his own melancholy. For Luther, this internal despondency wasn't a sickness or chemical imbalance that a pill could correct but the tempting and haunting of the demonic. See Roland H. Bainton, *Here I Stand: A Life of Martin Luther* (Nashville: Abingdon, 1990), chap. 2.

5. Charles Taylor calls this "the politics of recognition." See Taylor, *Multiculturalism* (Princeton: Princeton University Press, 1994), 25–75.

ing environment to be a self in the always-increasing pace of late modernity. And you need to be not just some generic, bland self but a happy, successful, recognized self who's not spitting out water but riding the rapids, maybe even with style. Needing to swim yourself to the crest of the current means that the self in late modernity can never rest. To be this kind of self requires constant navigating. This self constantly rushes to keep up.

Ehrenberg believes depression is not necessarily a response to some objective disappointment outside of you but a response to the fatigue of failing to keep up, to over and over and over again create and curate a distinct self.[6] It is *la fatigue d'être soi*: depression is the fatigue of being yourself.[7] When this fatigue becomes too much, when we can't find the energy to keep going into the water, creating and curating our self, we feel stuck. We feel sucked back by the current, passed over (a potent nightmare in our late-modern secular age). Everything else is moving so fast, changing and adapting every minute, and we just don't have it in us. Perhaps we even feel something overtaking us that just won't allow us to ever catch up. "I just can't be the parent, employee, spouse, friend I should be. I should try harder, but I just don't have the energy." I have every invitation to change and change again and then change more. But I don't have the energy to meet this demand. If I had the energy, the openness of identity construction would be exciting. But without it, the choice and openness is depressing. According to Ehrenberg, this is the source of my depression.[8]

When Authenticity Leads to Performance

In volume 1 (*Faith Formation in a Secular Age*) we traced the history of the age of authenticity. Charles Taylor told us that the pursuit of authenticity as a high good, as an essential piece—even the foundation—of a good life, was

6. Ehrenberg explains, "Depression presents itself as an illness of responsibility in which the dominant feeling is that of failure. The depressed individual is unable to measure up; he is tired of having to become himself. . . . If neurosis is the tragedy of guilt, depression is the tragedy of inadequacy. It is the familiar shadow of a person without a guide, tired of going forward to achieve the self and tempted to sustain himself through products and behaviours." *The Weariness of the Self: Diagnosing the History of Depression in the Contemporary Age* (Montreal: McGill-Queen's University Press, 2016), 4, 11.

7. Christopher Bollas, in *Meaning and Melancholia: Life in the Age of Bewilderment* (New York: Routledge, 2018), 59–61, discusses how depression and speed are connected.

8. This form of depressive despondency is also connected to the rise of anxiety. Anxiety is a legitimate response to the need to speed up one's identity curating. Hartmut Rosa discusses this in *Resonance: A Sociology of Our Relationship to the World* (Medford, MA: Polity, 2019), chap. 4, sec. 1.

only a minority report back in early and high modernity.[9] It was only small enclaves in Paris, Berlin, London, and New York that sought to be authentic. For most, duty was king. Duty delivered a good life. Duty as a high good— for instance, being proper and put together, always in control in public and orderly in private—made hysteria the core mental ailment of high modernity. To connect Taylor with Ehrenberg, what modernity considers to be a mental ailment is always connected to its ethic, to its assertion of what is good. In high modernity, the weight of duty was disproportionately shared, often leaving women with fewer release valves for the pressure, making them more susceptible to hysteria. When duty's weight acutely pressed in on the psyche, women had few places to go for release.[10]

The age of authenticity ended the strict days of duty by shifting the imagination of what makes a life good. For a handful of reasons, duty was perceived as oppressive, in no small part because its burdens were not mutually shared by all. Women bore much more of the weight, or at least were restricted from blowing off the steam that would keep hysteria from rearing its head.[11]

A new ethic was needed to usher in a new age. The age of authenticity dawned through a new ethic and a new sense of what made for a good life (and what is good).[12] This is the ethic of authenticity that Taylor has famously and lucidly described.[13] This ethic asserts that every human being

9. Taylor does not use the terms "early modernity" and "high modernity." He does use "late modernity" often. However, I'm imposing these categories on him as a way of leaning back into critical theory. In earlier books like *The Promise of Despair* (Nashville: Abingdon, 2010), I entered directly into critical and social theory, particularly in conversation with mainly sociologists such as Anthony Giddens, Zygmunt Bauman, Urlich Beck, and others. I've since turned more directly to philosophy, particularly the cultural philosophies of Taylor and others. This project signals a return to social theory, but now in full conversation with a cultural philosophy. The work of Hartmut Rosa serves as a link for these two fields of conversation. Rosa is a sociologist but wrote his dissertation on Taylor. Following Rosa, I'm bringing the early and high modernity language to my reading of Taylor.

10. Men had forms of sexual expression and adventure—like in war, gambling, etc.—to release the pressure of duty, even spaces like the golf course, casinos, bars, etc. These were often perceived as no place for women.

11. A tracing of feminism is beyond my abilities, but it clearly has its moment here. The women's movement sought liberation from the 1950s suburbs and the cage of private/proper life that seemed to be strangling women. Some wanted access to opportunities, seeking a good life outside the orbit of babies and picket fences. Others, particularly the young, wanted freedom from social mores, wanting the right to blow off steam like men could.

12. Taylor's point, which I affirm and explore more fully in *The End of Youth Ministry?* (Grand Rapids: Baker Academic, 2020), is that all human action is based in some sense of the good life. People are moved by the good, even ranking goods. See Taylor's discussion of hypergood in *Sources of the Self: The Making of Modern Identity* (Cambridge, MA: Harvard University Press, 1989), 10–40.

13. See Taylor, *The Ethics of Authenticity* (Cambridge, MA: Harvard University Press, 1991).

has the right to define for him*self* or her*self* what it means for him or her to be human.

The conforming pressure of duty was now completely upended, conformity itself now the enemy. The rampant rash of hysteria cases subsided. High modernity was over; its ethic of duty, which created the conditions for hysteria, was finished. The age of authenticity gives freedom but only in the logic of late modernity itself—only within acceleration. Duty is discarded in major part because it's too slow. For a few years—like maybe one—we could live in the warm glow of the Age of Aquarius, in the utopia of free love. But, again connecting Taylor and Ehrenberg, by the 1970s, even this new ethic of authenticity, this newly sought good, had created its own mental ailment.

Depression is the shadow side of authenticity. The ethic of authenticity frees you to be whomever you want to be. We should embrace, even celebrate, this, but not without recognizing its shadow side. In the field cleared by authenticity, there stands only you. This is exciting but daunting. All other sources that in earlier times, for good or ill, imposed on you and shaped your identity were over. Now you, and supposedly you alone, get to create and freely articulate your own self.

In the West, the sources of religion, family, clan, and even country could no longer tell you who you are. You decide. But once you decide, to truly have chosen, you can't just sit on your hands, resting quietly in the glow of your chosen identity. That's not how this "freedom" works. This "freedom" calls for constant motion. And this need for constant motion, amped by the new ethic of authenticity, opens the door wide to despondency as the new mental ailment, broadly speaking.

The necessity to perform your identity is plagued with unease. Inside this freely chosen identity, you implicitly or explicitly know that you could be performing another identity. With a quick but intense stab of nausea, you wonder if your performance is the right one. Is this really you? Are you really being authentic?

The only way to know for sure is to perform it, not to correlate it with other sources—like a sacred text or family tradition. Through this performance, you're trying to accomplish what all performances seek: recognition. There are no outside sources for your identity, only your choice. Nevertheless, because this is a performance, you need an audience. You have no identity without some kind of audience to recognize the identity you're performing. Of course, this performance has to feel right to you (it must not violate the ethic of authenticity), but you can only really feel it as you perform it, and you can only really perform it in front of others who recognize it.

As high modernity gives way to late modernity, the high-modern ethic of duty cannot contain the new acceleration of technology, social change, and the pace of life. The speed increase from high to late modernity throws off duty like a loosely worn baseball cap on a roller coaster. You're now free to have whatever identity you wish, but you can't sit idly on it, because that's not how late modernity and its ethic of authenticity work. To have this "free" identity, you must correlate, not with a tradition or sacred text, but with speed itself, by embracing the logic of acceleration. The vehicle for identity to meet the speed of late modernity is performance. You're free to have whatever identity feels most authentic to you, but to really possess that identity, you must meet the speed of modernity, not be free of it. Not coincidentally, those who seem the most authentic are those moving fastest, those with the most Instagram followers, those who most directly perform their identities to win recognition.

In this cleared field of self-chosen identity, wherein you no longer need to measure up to family, religion, clan, or country, you nevertheless must perform, again and again, your "freely" chosen identity. The more you perform it, the better you perform it, the more authentic you appear. You quickly discover (maybe seventh or eighth grade, if not earlier) that you only truly have this identity *as* you perform it. You can be, for the most part, whomever you wish, but you only really have this identity if others recognize and respond to it. Therefore, to secure this identity you must shape this identity for speed. You must perform it in such a way that it can be broadcast.

The pull to perform your identity never ceases, even if you're confident that this is indeed your right identity. You're always aware in this cleared field of authenticity that you could be performing this identity better. You're exposed to so many exemplars on Instagram who seem to be performing their chosen identities better than you are, with so much more authenticity. They're in better shape, reading better books, watching better movies, and better understanding current events. The fatigue to be yourself is real.

Back to Depressed Churches[14]

As I drove the streets of that North Dakota town, passing strip malls and pickup trucks, I couldn't shake my lunchtime conversation with that pastor.

14. This pastor, as well as a number of other characters, will show up throughout the rest of the book. The reasons for this are both stylistic and substantive to the argument. In volumes 1 and 2, I embedded my argument in narrative. For instance, in volume 2, I shared stories of paradigmatic pastors through the ages. Following both Taylor's narrative focus and my commitments to personalism, I have made story central here. These stories are not historical, as they were in volume 2, but experiential. I've reworked them, but these are encounters I've had

Was Ehrenberg's genealogy applicable to the church? Had the church, more broadly, moved from madness to hysteria to despondency? At the dawn of modernity, Luther contended that the church and its pope had gone mad. For the next 450 years after the Reformation, episodes of hysteria seemed to spring up over and over again, right in the middle of Protestantism's production of order, manners, and politeness. Societies built on the Protestant legacy of mutual regard and peace nevertheless produced fierce and ugly divides in churches and denominations. But now, at least in Protestantism, it appears the church has shifted into despondency.

Heretic hunters and church splits can still be found. But it appears that local congregations like this one in North Dakota are mostly depressed. They're lacking energy right when it's needed, unable to garner vigor when the opportunity for change is most ripe.

Without the help of Ehrenberg, I might have thought this was just bad timing. Right when congregations need to change, many are too depressed to grasp firmly with both hands their destiny. What a shame! It's like finding yourself with a terrible flu on the very day you hold front-row tickets to see your favorite band. It's so disappointing, such a lost opportunity, but the concert's arrival and the ailment are unrelated. Therefore, you can only chalk it up to bad luck, or blame yourself for not taking better care of yourself. But you would never think to blame the concert for the flu.

Yet this is exactly Ehrenberg's point. The conditions for change are what push us into depression. Depression is *la fatigue d'être soi*; it's the fatigue to be yourself. It's the openness, the broad horizon stretched before us, that demands we create and curate our own self, which then boomerangs on us. Depression breeds within the freedom to change and then change again and again, but this freedom never delivers on the promise that this change will produce the good life we seek and the meaning we need. Depression is us facing this horizon and realizing that we don't have the energy or time to reach it. It's the need for change itself, the openness to be and do anything (which is supposed to be exciting), that turns on the congregation, giving us *la fatigue d'être eglise*, the fatigue of being the church. This is exactly what this pastor told me over sandwiches.

The Great Change Challenge

Being too fatigued to be the church is a challenge. Its most popular solution is change. Perhaps change is needed, but the pursuit of change, the need to

---

with concrete persons engaging congregations. Stylistically, I hope these stories illustrate for the reader how these ideas connect with real life.

recast an identity, runs the ever-present risk of producing depression. If we fail to keep up, finding ourselves falling behind, depression will meet us. This fashions in us the very opposite disposition than what is needed to meet the challenges brought by changes in our culture.

For church consultants and denominational leaders to call congregations to change is to risk something significant. It opens them to communal depression, producing the opposite of what they need to meet their challenge: despondency. Church consultants risk moving the congregation into a vicious cycle that is too often misunderstood as a straight line. The consultant is often called in when a congregation either has fallen behind or is too obdurate to meet the challenges of a changing world. The consultant leads the congregation in a process of speeding up, offering new models to speed them up to meet change. And then leaves, moving on to another congregation needing change. That feels like a straight line.

Point A: the church is stuck

Point B: give it the strategies to get unstuck

Point C: so that it can meet the speed of change

Point D: move on (and return periodically to tweak the strategies, asking the congregation to speed up further, then move on again)

But once the congregation is up to speed, it needs to forever maintain that speed, but also continually increase the speed year after year.

Modernity is the constant process of speeding things up. Modernity demands that things increase speed. If we're not careful, to diagnose the church's issue as the need for change is to cover it in the core commitments of late modernity itself. If the consultant raises the church to a new speed, this yokes the congregation to always be speeding up to meet the never-ending change that will *always* remain on the horizon, a carrot forever out of reach. Speed is the supposed gift of late modernity that can quickly turn into a depressive curse.

Change is almost always considered to be some kind of growth, and in late modernity that which grows must continually grow. Modernity is about change because it is about growth. It takes a lot of work, and a whole different imagination, to disconnect change from growth. Untying the two leads to something completely different: transformation in the Spirit. Being the church is about *transformation*, not *change*. Though on first blush these seem synonymous, transformation and change are quite different.

Transformation, in the Christian tradition, comes from outside the self, relating to the self with an energy beyond the self. Because transformation comes from an energy outside the self, it invites the self into the new as a gift, as grace. It demands no increase for continuation, no energy investment to receive it. Transformation is the invitation into grace; it comes with an arriving word, "Peace be with you" (John 20:19). Transformation is not the necessity to speed up but the need to open up and receive. Change, on the other hand, comes from within the self. Change makes the self into something new, using the power and the effort of the self: it is produced by the energy of the self.

Transformation and change have significantly different relationships to time. Change seeks to catch up to and possess time. Transformation is an experience of encountering the fullness of time. It is to feel a resonance, not speeding up to change but remaining open to transcendence. Transformation feels something like the full moment of the four-year-old saying to no one in particular, but instead as a proclamation of her existence, "That was *great!*" That felt full, it was good, I felt connected and moved, and yet at rest. She wasn't racing to catch up to change but instead fully relating to the world as a gift.

When we push for change, if we're not careful, we impose modernity's pursuit of growth, which risks congregational depression by thrusting it into a vicious cycle we don't often recognize. The vicious cycle is endemic to modernity itself. Modernity, at its core, asserts that all pursuits must be primed, mathematically speaking. The equation is always something like $M + C = M^2$, money plus commodity equals money prime, meaning money increased. You don't invest money to lose it; the point is to get more. This is how late modernity is structured. The same equation works with the modern research university, where knowledge plus research equals knowledge grown $(K + R = K^2)$.[15] The point of learning, in late modernity, is not to encounter a mysterious world unveiled by that learning. Rather, the point is to prime knowledge. It's to create more and therefore to advance. Those who publish fastest win.

If modernity were a computer, the code driving the system would be the algorithm $X + Y = X^2$. Everything must be primed, and as quickly as possible so that it can be primed again (it's little coincidence that Amazon Prime has mastered the market by mastering speed). Our models of exemplary congregations fit the equation. They are exemplars because we see them through the lens of late modernity. They are the few congregations that have mastered prime. Megachurches like Saddleback, Eagle Brook, and North Point function

15. I'm taking this equation and therefore the overall point from Rosa, "Two Versions of the Good Life and Two Forms of Fear: Dynamic Stabilization and the Resonance Conception of the Good Life," paper presented at the Yale Center for Faith and Culture conference on Joy, Security, and Fear, New Haven, CT, November 8–9, 2017.

with an equation of $M + P = M^2$, members plus programs equals members prime. Here's an example quote from one church consultant: "The leadership summit answers two questions. . . . *Were we successful last year? What will it take to be more successful next year?*"[16] If, like Apple or Amazon, you can return back again through the equation, you can prime your objective again and again. But every time you prime—to be able to prime at all—you must speed up the enterprise, find a way not to become friends of time but to possess and master time.[17] Tim Suttle shares the story of a megachurch that raised $5 million to fund a new overpass to the freeway so that the departure time from their large parking lot could be cut to less than twenty minutes.[18] They knew that in order to prime the M (members), they would need to control the time. The faster you prime, and prime again, the faster you win, increase, and grow.

Modernity promises that if you can get to the speed of change, you'll find purpose and significance. But this purpose and significance won't deliver the goods of contentment, peace, or rest; instead, they only open new horizons inviting more change upon the change you've just met. Speeding up to meet change, late modernity pushes us inevitably to reach for another gear, to speed up further. Speeding up to meet change after new change only promises to create the necessity for more change. This *may be* good for corporations, like Apple and Amazon, competing in markets and seeking new products. But it's much less so for persons seeking a good life, and communities of faith seeking the communion of the Holy Spirit through the crucified Christ felt as the *shalom* of God the Father.

Even if the congregation follows the consultant's advice and reaches for a new missional, parish-based, or movement strategy that spurs them toward change, pushing them to a new speed, a new unavoidable demand to increase

16. Thomas G. Bandy, *Strategic Thinking: How to Sustain Effective Ministry* (Nashville: Abingdon, 2017), 103.

17. "Becoming friends of time" is to quote the title of John Swinton's award-winning book *Becoming Friends of Time: Disability, Timefullness, and Gentle Discipleship* (Waco: Baylor University Press, 2017). Swinton's work is a stunning example of the difference between transformation and change, and how being ministered to by and ministering with those with disabilities can free us from modernity's traps. It is no coincidence that when Henri Nouwen joined L'Arche, he did so because he was depressed and exhausted from the speed of academic life. In being ministered to by disabled people, Nouwen found not so much a slowdown as a resonance, a gift of transformation, and therefore a new relationship to time, experiencing it as full. The world now moved at the speed of a conversation—it spoke to Nouwen, beautifully and paradoxically through a man unable to speak at all. See Henri Nouwen, *Adam: God's Beloved* (New York: Orbis Books, 2012).

18. Suttle, *Shrink: Faithful Ministry in a Church-Growth Culture* (Grand Rapids: Zondervan, 2014), 59.

that speed is thrust upon the congregation.[19] The excitement of reaching a speed that allows for change quickly reveals that exponential amounts of energy will be required in order to keep going. It is more than daunting to realize that change requires change requires change. Ehrenberg says poignantly, "Depression appeared not as a pathology of unhappiness but more as a pathology of change."[20]

Revving the engine to get up to speed to meet every new change over every new horizon produces the fumes of depression. These fumes gather as you realize that the tanks are too low to continue at this speed (let alone to meet the demand necessitated by speeding up further). Or, instead of a slow gathering of fumes, depression arrives like a brick wall: speeding faster and faster, you derail and crash.

It's no coincidence that the founders of megachurches, the ultimate example of a congregation and its leader who meet the ever-increasing speed of change, are so susceptible to affairs, money laundering, and all sorts of other brick-wall crashes that precede (or are produced by) their depression. The indiscretion is the only way out. Burnout is a depression imposed by the inability to keep pace.[21]

To show how this is happening to American congregations, we'll need to examine modernity at a large scale. Congregations are never hermetically sealed; the people in them are affected by many relationships and institutions. Their sense of the good is shaped by the culture, and so too the congregation's sense. As we proceed, I will keep stepping back to look at the larger culture (and how it shapes our individual and corporate sense of the self). This stepping back will help us grasp the great challenge congregations face and the specific situation in which congregations now find themselves. In the chapters that follow, we'll look at broad cultural realities, zooming out from the congregation. Then we'll zoom in and look specifically at the church and how speed sickness is infecting congregations today.

---

19. Ed Stetzer and Warren Bird push hard for pastors to accelerate by growing not just a church but a whole movement of churches. This is acceleration on steroids. Of course, the authors' drive for multiplication is taken from a certain reading of the Great Commission, but it doesn't account for the fact that Jesus wasn't speaking in modernity. "[The apostolic leader is] an initiator who plants churches that in turn plant more churches. . . . The person with apostolic gifting doesn't just want to plant an individual church and be its pastor. That person wants to plant a movement." *Viral Churches: Helping Church Planters Become Movement Makers* (San Francisco: Jossey-Bass, 2010), 18. At the end of the book, they state boldly, "This book can be summarized in two words: multiply everything" (201).

20. Ehrenberg, *Weariness of the Self*, 12.

21. "Burnout—the word implies that our energy is gone. We cannot summon the energy to do what needs to be done." William Willimon, *Clergy and Laity Burnout* (Nashville: Abingdon, 1989), 21.

I've personally seen speed sickness at my seminary. We had gone through a financial crisis in 2012. We entered a faculty meeting believing everything was green lights and growth. Twenty-five minutes later we learned that we were actually millions of dollars in the hole. Every meeting after that was worse, the negative millions increasing. Soon administrators were let go as faculty, staff, and students watched, shell-shocked. Over the next few months, more than a little hysteria could be spotted in all sorts of odd behavior. But after a while, something else set in, particularly among the faculty: depression.

The seminary we had known was gone, and many of us grieved its passing. But what moved us as a whole into depression was the lack of energy to envision something new. The board and new administration looked to the faculty, telling us that we needed to create the seminary's new identity, to forge our new way of being. But the thought of creating a new identity through new actions in this fast-paced environment, with everything else also shifting at a faster pace (denominational structures, financial models, prospective students' desires, donor commitments, and more), caused us to shut down.

When the crisis hit, the administration and board told us to get to work, speed up, reach a new pace, grow, advance. We were told that embracing this change with speed could be the best thing for us. But not having the energy to get to speed instead produced a depression that lasted for years, and in some sense is still with us.

We didn't want to shut down. No one wants, or even chooses, to be depressed. No one desires to do nothing. But we stopped fighting, our ailment coming out less and less as hysteria or madness. The thought of the task of change itself, and the experience that our actions couldn't promise change anyhow, produced despondency. We didn't know what to do, but worse (what really produced the depression) was that we didn't know *who to be*. We suffered *la fatigue d'être séminaire*, the fatigue of being a seminary.

But, honestly, who could be fatigued if they had $1.6 billion?!

2

speeding to the good life, crashing into guilt

why $1.6 billion isn't as good as you think

Ten days after my time in North Dakota, I prepared to board another flight, this time to Kansas City to present to a group of pastors. It's a short flight from Minneapolis, just five hundred miles.

Of course, to say "just" is dependent on your speed. Five hundred miles is a long way to walk or run. If you ran one marathon a day, it would take you about nineteen days. Driving it would make your knees and back ache, but not make you throb in pain or risk kidney failure, like a nineteen-day run would. Using the freeway, you could drive to Kansas City from Minneapolis in just over six hours, but bathroom breaks and lunch would make it closer to eight. On an airplane, you could leave after lunch and still make it to Kansas City for an early dinner.

That was my plan. My forty-seven-minute flight, wheels up to wheels down, departed at 4:00 p.m. and landed in Kansas City at 5:20 p.m. I'm no math major, but that's longer than forty-seven minutes. The airline has to plan in slowdowns, ironically because of how rapidly we'll be speeding up. Our incredible speed means we need to slow down for safety precautions, double-checking equipment and lining up in a slow taxi queue to hit this massive speed.

When we arrive in Kansas City we'll have to do another slow taxi. Having traveled so fast across five hundred miles, we will stand still for what feels like forever as the jet bridge is slowly connected to our plane, so that things can continue to move fast. The gate agent running the bridge goes slowly, so things can continue to move fast. When the doors finally open, we'll line up to slowly leave the speed machine.

My forty-seven minutes has now turned into eighty minutes, but measured from my departure from my house, the speed and pace of life turns forty-seven minutes into three and a half hours. Speed does this. Pushing to speed up has a way of slowing things down.[1]

Yet, given the choice, I'd pick three and a half hours over eight, even with all the lines. It's faster, easier on the knees, and includes free Wi-Fi to keep me moving at the speed of light. And Cinnabon!

––––––––––

As I made my way to the gate for my flight, the airport had an unusual buzz. The Mega Millions jackpot had just expanded beyond its name to $1.6 *billion*. As I waited motionless in line, the person ahead of me asked the gate agent if she had bought any jackpot tickets. They both said that neither of them is an ordinary lotto player, but it was just too much money to resist.

The gate agent said, "A group of us pitched in. I threw in my twenty bucks, because if they won, I didn't want to be left behind."

"What would you do with the money if you won?" asked the passenger.

"Well, there are like fifteen of us, so it would only be like a 100 mil each," the gate agent said sarcastically.

They both laughed.

Freeing herself from sarcasm, the gate agent continued, "Honestly, I wouldn't get out of my PJs for six months . . . maybe a year."

This is a common response. I overheard it more than a few times. Their first thought was to use the money *against speed itself*. They longed to mobilize the funds as a firewall against acceleration, to take back time.

"I'd do a whole lot of nothing!" someone else said in the rental-car line.

They imagined they could use the money to shelter themselves from speed, no longer needing to do anything but rest. The money seems to be the perfect solution to the stress of speed, to the fatigue of being yourself. With $1.6 billion, you'd be lord of time, not having time lord over you.

As we'll see below, money and speed are intrinsically connected in modernity. With that much money, the gate agent imagined she could break the link between money and time. Benjamin Franklin implanted in our consciousness

1. Hartmut Rosa discusses this slowing down in *Alienation and Acceleration: Towards a Critical Theory of Late-Modern Temporality* (Malmö, Sweden: NSU Press, 2014), 15–16.

that time is money. The equation time equals money could be deleted from the algorithm of her life if only she had enough money. But in late modernity, it's tricky, nearly impossible, to unlink the meshed connections between money and time.

We think money could free us from speed, which is why in the end we don't really want money at all. What we long for is to rest in time, to find ourselves in a different relationship with time. We have all sorts of dreams about money because we assume it's the path to give us back time. We wonder—and even count—how much money it would take to release us from the acceleration of time.

It makes sense that when people imagine being rich, they picture not just overloading bank vaults with bills, but more importantly, accruing an unlimited excess of time. Needing money to be free from money is an odd logic that exists in all late-modern people. But none of our trading in money for time would work. As many lotto winners have learned, that's not how late modernity is structured. Money doesn't liberate from time, because time is money's enmeshed sibling. If money comes to live in your life, like $1.6 billion taking residence in your bank account, so too comes not a surplus but a speeding up of time. In modernity, time, linked with money, is hyperactive.[2] In modernity, time, linked with money, always seeks acceleration, reaching toward multiplying and priming.

When the lotto money arrives, it will bring its hyper sibling, time. And time, particularly with all that money, will seek acceleration. You'll have to get out of your PJs and figure out what to do with all that money. Deciding how to invest it, choosing how to give some of it away, calculating who is trustworthy to help you oversee it. There will be no time to be in your PJs and to rewatch all the episodes of *The Bachelor*. Instead you'll need two phones and an administrative assistant to manage the time as money accelerates you to a new speed.

No wonder so many lotto winners end up bankrupt. It's not that they can't take the prosperity, it's that they can't take the acceleration of time, the new speed that the millions or billions demand. Even established billionaires, like Mark Cuban or Richard Branson, show that, even if you can handle the speed of billons "well," it won't slow down your life, freeing you for PJs and

2. Rosa states, "Modernity is about the acceleration of time." *Social Acceleration: A New Theory of Modernity* (New York: Columbia University Press, 2015), 14. Michael Allen Gillespie adds, "The term 'modern' and its derivatives come from the Latin *modus* which means 'measure,' and, as a measure of time, 'just now' with the late Latin derivative *modernus*, from which all later forms derive." *The Theological Origins of Modernity* (Chicago: University of Chicago Press, 2008), 2.

chocolate bonbons. Rather, you'll just learn how to make speed work for you, giving you more time to . . . well . . . accelerate faster.

You'll skip the three-and-a-half-hour lines and instead fly privately in a slick forty-seven minutes. At some point during that forty-seven minutes, you'll wonder whether you should buy a new plane or make a bigger donation to the Minneapolis Airports Commission, to trim the flight down to thirty-six minutes. Why? You're not sure. But you know that going faster, trying to possess time, is how you win in late modernity. Money is the scorecard, but the ultimate prize is to create more time.

In our secular age, asking "More time for what?" can cause you to feel the malaise of modernity, to become nauseated by immanence. That's when you notice a sharp stab of meaninglessness and the void of emptiness touching your soul. Better to speed up than to feel that. Time itself, in our secular age, has no aim beyond itself. Time is no longer full (of demons, angels, purpose, meaning, salvation, and damnation).[3] Thus emptied, time is at its maximal weight to be sped up. It's light, so it can be made fast.

Our secular age empties time so that time can be accelerated to meet all our immanent needs for productivity and individual freedom and expression. Emptied and aimed for productivity, freedom, and expression, time only knows how to speed up. Time no longer cares to serve us or any outside aim; it seeks only more acceleration for the sake of acceleration. We become hamsters on a wheel, realizing we were never actually chasing the money but just trying like hell to not fall behind. We have to run faster and always worry that we're falling behind. Behind what?

The good life.

When the Good Life Hits the Need for Speed

Slowing down, staying in your PJs, and eating bonbons while watching reality TV is a description of the good life that mobilized at least some of the fast-moving travelers in the airport. It feels good. It would feel like the good life to cash the check and build a fort out of fifty-dollar bills to hide from the pace of life. But no fort, no matter how fortified by money, could keep the speeding up of time from slipping in. Speed lives inside the structures of society—meaning that using money to build your hideaway would also bring with it institutions and structures like banking laws, financial markets, interest rates, and 1099s for your administrators, making it impossible to use the money to be free of busy concerns about money.

3. Taylor discusses this change in time in *A Secular Age* (Cambridge, MA: Belknap, 2007), 55–60.

This need to speed up also exists in our own moral disposition, in our own sense of being an agent in the world. It exists in how we conceive of a good life. In this fort made out of fifties, even with the means to do nothing at all, we would start to feel the pressure of speed. We'd begin to feel a deep disquiet. Doing nothing, we'd start to feel the uncomfortable unease. Soon we'd recognize it: guilt. But what is the guilt's source?

We'd feel guilty for *wasting time*. We'd worry we were missing a good life.

To be late-modern people living in a secular age is not necessarily to be freed from guilt. In the nineteenth century, it was a high-modern dream to create a world where guilt was as antiquated as the sundial. Bookshelves throughout the twentieth century were filled with all sorts of self-help programs to finally extract that supposedly meaningless little emotion. Yet, to this day, guilt seems to appear again and again in a new guise, often creating depression more than the madness or hysteria of past periods. This is because guilt's source has shifted in our secular age. Luther felt deep stabs of guilt. Yet, for Luther, guilt's object was the Holy God who judges sin. Jonathan Edwards, too, reminded his congregation that they were in the hands of an angry God, guilty of apathy, prone to drifting. These guilts have their source in a transcendent reality.[4]

Our secular age tried but could not bury guilt, not even by minimizing transcendence itself. Even in an immanent frame (a world presumed to be totally and completely natural as opposed to supernatural) guilt rears its head. Even secular heavyweights on the coasts—hedge fund managers in New York and screenwriters in LA—feel as guilty today as Luther did in the monastery. But unlike Luther, the inhabitants of a secular age have no idea to whom they're guilty, confused about the source of their ignominy.

We've escaped the hands of an angry God to live instead within our own selves. Living for ourselves, we find something shocking, something we were told we wouldn't find. We discover that *our very own self condemns us*. We still feel guilty, but not because we're sinners needing to enter a process of restoration and communion (finding mercy and absolution). Rather, our guilt endures because we cannot be the selves we wish we could be. In this free project to create and curate a self, we fall behind. We fail to be who we feel we should be. Our age shifts guilt's source from a transcendent, personal force, whose law we fail to obey, to our own selves. We are guilty to ourselves by our self.

Our ethic is authenticity. It is the highest good to pursue our own uniqueness, to be original, to be one of a kind. We are always striving to be more

---

4. Taylor, *Secular Age*, 222–30, discusses this shift away from needing something outside of us to frame our guilt and free us as the eclipse of grace.

authentic, believing it will make us happy. The ethic of authenticity claims that every human being has a right to define for themselves what it means for them to be human. We should celebrate the gains of this ethic, the way it allows people to voice their experience. But we should also see that it delivers a conundrum we often can't escape. Defining for yourself what it means for you to be you seems, at first blush, to be enhanced freedom. But soon the burden of self-definition opens us to a new form of guilt.

I've let myself down. In the end, only I have the power to forgive myself. The good I violate is my own authenticity. In a secular age, sin is my inability to optimize myself. (The despondency that meets the congregation is its sense that it must optimize *itself* or bear the guilt of not doing so.) My violation that produces guilt exists not necessarily in the world, not even, we imagine, in some interpersonal space between others and us (though I think this isn't quite true). We believe that this guilt is the failure to be a unique self. We are guilty only before the self.[5]

The only one who can forgive me is me—maybe with the help of a therapist or life coach. Ultimately, I'm judge and jury of my own self. Authenticity is an ethic that exerts its maximal demand in the self. It's right for me; it's a high good that I work on myself, that I be unique and authentic. All that matters is that I be loyal to the project of my self. If I fail to meet this good, the same ethical demand that freed me to be me turns on me and condemns me. I can't be the self I want to be; I've failed myself by not being the unique self I should be.

And this is a heavy guilt, not because it bears the weight of heaven but because, within the self, there are no sources to escape the self, to find a grace from outside the self to forgive and free, renew and remake, the self. To be guilty to the self by the self—to not be as special as I think I should be—is to be trapped by being the only one who can forgive myself. It's only the self that can forgive (or condemn) the self. We are caught in another vicious cycle (late modernity is filled with so many).

Forgiveness, too, wears the mark of speed. Forgiving myself by the power of myself is far from a release. In contrast, when there is a source from outside the self that provides grace, the self is redefined and set free. But in late modernity, needing to forgive myself, I have to work harder. I have to speed up to the place of self-consciousness and self-created self-esteem to climb over

---

5. This is how it feels. But this is a misguided cultural anthropology. We actually are the kind of beings that need always to be with others to receive a sense of our selves. But this isn't how we often assume it to be. Feeling guilty for not being authentic is dependent on looking at others or having others interact with us in a certain way. But we imagine this as really just a feeling we have, locked inside our own sense of our self.

or beyond my guilty feelings. I need to work hard to remake my stories or forget them, finding new strategies and interests that move me in a new direction toward a new authenticity. And I need to do this all with my own energy.

Against the background of this ethic of authenticity, we can find ourselves overwhelmed by the guilt of not having reached this ideal of uniqueness and self-definition. We have not given ourselves enough time to curate a truly special self that matches the freedom given to us by the age of authenticity. We've wasted the freedom of our own expression. We've failed to be unique, to make a true mark, to live a life worthy of the authenticity we're free to pursue. We sense that we've failed to curate the self in a way that would truly make us happy. We fear—we anxiously worry, producing a depression—that we've wasted something important.

We have squandered the time needed to create a good life, to be an authentic self. The violation has been done not to a Holy God, not even to a community of practice and shared life, but to the project of the self. We feel guilty that we're not the person we should be or, worse, could have been. We feel guilty because we've blown the opportunity to be a different, more interesting, more meaningful self. There were so many paths available to the self, and we worry we've chosen the wrong ones. This gives birth to the common cultural mantra (perhaps even an absolution), "It's never too late." This warms us in the cold winter of our guilt, though we also wonder if it's really true.

Guilty to Time

Perhaps saying we are guilty as a result of this drive to be unique may sound extreme and misrepresent the object of our guilt. Few of the orange-vested hunters in North Dakota—or even suburbanites in Sydney or Christchurch—would claim that they felt guilty for not being special, for not being unique and truly authentic. As a matter of fact, it's in places like the rural Dakotas where the ethic of authenticity finds its most direct opposition. People passively (or not so passively) punish uniqueness that is outside of certain codes. But even those who strive for authenticity, regardless of geographical location, are more realistic. Nobody assumes they can reach the summit of uniqueness, winning all the chips of authenticity.

It wouldn't be quite accurate to say that we feel guilty for not rising to the top of uniqueness. Most people recognize that this isn't really possible. It would be like the gate agent blaming herself for not winning the lottery. Few get to be purely unique and authentic. But even those who look askance at the drive for authenticity live under its ethical strictures. Authenticity produces a certain type of freedom (the freedom to be me), but it's not our inability to be unique that condemns us. Rather, what condemns us is that, within the freedom of authenticity, we have wasted time.

It's the lost, wasted, or misspent time that is the source of our guilt. We are guilty for not being able to keep up with time's acceleration. The good life seems to be always speeding up, always bringing change, and we are falling behind. Keeping up would make me satisfied with the uniqueness of myself, happy with myself. Maybe I'd actually be living, instead of chasing, the good life. If only I had more time and had not wasted all the time I had.

Time, and its constant speeding up, judges us. We feel guilty because we've failed to keep up, allowing time to accelerate and pass by, leaving us reaching after the departed opportunity for a good life. Even upwardly mobile people of great financial privilege feel in debt to time. We imagine that a good life would be the ability to keep up, to eat right, to have time to read, to exercise, and to be an attentive partner and parent. But who has the time? We sense that the only way to live a good life is to live a fast life, a life that keeps pace with all the change and opportunity before us.

All the Guilt

Even if you won the lottery and built a fort out of fifties, even if it were possible to use the money to unplug, somehow constraining the structural realities of acceleration, the human need for a good life would get you, and you would be ensnared by the many ways that the late-modern sense of the good life is tied to speed. After binging the eighth season of *The Bachelor* you'd start to feel it. Guilt would creep in and you'd wonder, maybe it isn't right for me to unplug like this; maybe this is a waste.

Right then, the need to catch up would call for you. You'd think, maybe I should take advantage of this time and watch something enriching, like *The Wire* or *BBC World News*. Or better, order Rosetta Stone and learn Spanish. Actually, eating bonbons hasn't been good for my figure; I should work out. But first I should research the best workout. When I get in shape, I'll need to keep up with the workouts or I'll fall behind and gain weight again. That would make me feel guilty. After losing weight, I'll take pride in how I've remade myself, out of the ambition of myself. But regaining the weight, I'll feel so guilty, not so much to the scale as to my sense of self that I wish to possess and present.

Even if I maintain my figure, I don't want to be a dull person. I should read all the Tolstoy novels I never did. Maybe finally get through David Foster

Wallace's *Infinite Jest*. Right now I don't have time; I need to get to the gym. But I'll buy those books, put them on my shelf so others can see that I'm the kind of person who purchases good literature. Every day I'll walk past them, feeling good that I'm the kind of person who owns these books. But that good feeling will be interrupted by guilt: I've never had the time to read them. The guilt will be more intense than just a sense of wasting money; it will feel like hypocrisy in my own being, a violation to myself. I present that I'm a deep person who likes classic lit. That's the self I'm curating, but honestly I've never had the time to read, faking that I know references. My desire to be a certain kind of self, and my inability to keep up with the pace that this self demands, condemns me.

But there's even more that condemns me. I've never been able to get to those books, never past Wallace's first chapter, because I've wanted to be the kind of person who's informed, who knows what's going on in the world. I've never read Tolstoy because I needed to read the *New York Times* or even just the articles on my Facebook news feed. But I couldn't even keep up with the *Times* or Facebook, though the articles are less exhausting and time-consuming than Tolstoy. I was too drained. My friends keep posting *Atlantic* articles. I can't get through the *Times* let alone the *Atlantic*. I feel guilty that I'm not like them, the kind of self who reads and posts *Atlantic* articles.

At least Facebook has connected me with old friends. Yet I feel so guilty that I've lost touch with so many people over the years. Now these people, through social media, rush back into my life like a flood. I soon realize that I have the access but not the time to keep up with hundreds, even thousands, of these friends—which condemns me further. I feel particularly guilty that I'm not the self I wish I were. When a coworker asks, "Have you been following . . . ?" they mean it as a line of conversation, but I first hear it as a condemnation. I haven't! I haven't had time to keep up on election fraud in Wisconsin or environmental corruption in Northern California.

I could be following these current events, but instead I need to read more parenting books. My kids are growing up so fast, and I'm barely hanging on. I'm not being the parent they need. The self I want to be is a good, informed, and diligent parent. Plus, those books can be read fast. The pages turn so much more quickly than Wallace and his footnotes, way less taxing than an *Atlantic* article. I can actually feel good about getting a whole book finished, picking up helpful tips, not getting left behind in parenting, maybe even being more intentional. I'm now able to ask another parent, "Have you read . . . ?" shifting the guilt off me to them.

But truth be told these parenting books and their fast accessibility thrust me into more guilt. They provide me strategies to speed up and be a good parent, reminding me that if I'm not conscious and available at all moments with my kids I'll lose those moments, never getting them back. I'm guilty both for not being the parent I wish I were and, worse, for falling behind time itself. I was supposed to accomplish eight things before my daughter was five, and now she's nine and there are eight more tasks.

Unable to keep up with these parenting books, conferences, and podcasts, I'll release my guilt by following the blog of an irreverent writer. She posts hilarious anecdotes of all her parenting fails, telling her readers to relax. She whimsically reminds her readers that all of us ruin birthday cakes and get drunk at birthday parties for four-year-olds. At one level, reading these posts assuages my guilt (which is why such irreverent bloggers and podcasters are multiplying). But at another level, they too just make me feel more guilt. These irreverent bloggers seem to make even their failures cool, witty, and authentic. They present such interesting selves with such clever references and hip headshots. I'm sure I could never be this kind of cool parent. I doubt I'm this talented, even if they are just like me. Plus, I'll never have the time to try anyhow.

The Morality of Speed

Our guilt shows that our sense of the good life is no less tied to moral conceptions than it was for our ancestors. All forms of the good life, even tacit ways of seeking flourishing in the speed of late modernity, live out of some moral sense. We need some sense of what is right, good, and worthy for our lives. We wouldn't feel guilty if our perception of the good life weren't tied to some moral conception. Our morality, however, has been made lighter, even coming in individualized packages.

Before modernity (and still hanging on in early and high modernity), the good life was fused with substantive traditions and practices that called for duty. In late modernity we're not willing or able to name (beyond for our individual selves) the virtues, the values, or the character traits that make for a good life. We may have some ideas, but describing the substance seems to risk violating the ethic of authenticity. Our moral stance—our sense of what is good and what creates a good life—is authenticity itself. Virtues, values, and character need to concede to the ethic of authenticity. If certain virtues, values, and character traits work for you, good (that's morally right). But if, for whatever reason, they don't, disregard them and find others, whatever will help you be the self *you* wish to be.

The ethic of authenticity gives freedom for expression. As an ethic, it protects the space for you to be you, to be free of any repressive or oppressive moral systems, with their normative virtues, values, and practices, that may hurt your unique self. Through an ethic—a moral stance—authenticity holds this space, but it does so by evacuating any moral substance. The ethic of authenticity provides a crispy moral shell to our lives, but not much substance. This is because authenticity itself serves the freedom of your own individual expressive project.

In late modernity, the substantive content of the good life has been hollowed out, made light (just like time). Keeping it light allows us to move fast, because you need speed to live the good life. We've taken steps to discard morality's substance, no longer concerning ourselves with virtues, values, and character, affirming instead expression, recognition, and uniqueness. These substantive realities of virtues, values, and character are time-consuming and slow. They bog us down. They take time (which is bad enough), but they also make people feel bad about themselves, restricting the freedom and expression of the self (authenticity itself creates its own conditions of condemnation and guilt). We've discarded the substance of morality for a higher moral commitment: to keep up and move fast.[6] As a whole, late modernity is moving too fast for questions about the substance of the good life (we'll explore this more fully in chapters to come). Somewhere deep within, we know that concerning ourselves with substance will slow us down and inconvenience us in our pursuit of the project of the self.

———

The gate agent must have sensed that PJs, bonbons, and *The Bachelor* wouldn't quite do what they promised. The Mega Millions jackpot wouldn't release her from speed. Doing nothing was just the other side of the same coin. Doing nothing offers no distinct moral horizon, no new way of seeking a full life, just a flimsy shelter away from speed.

As she checked in the flight attendants, she turned back to the passenger one last time and said, "I'll tell you what, if I did win that money and had $100 million, there'd be *a lot* fewer homeless and suffering animals."

With genuine intensity, she continued, "That's what I'd really do with the money. I'd make sure all the dogs and cats were taken care of in the Twin Cities."

Doing a whole lot of nothing couldn't provide her with a sense of living a good life. She needed another moral vision. For the gate agent, caring for suffering animals seemed closer to the kind of good life that wouldn't alienate

6. Taylor would call this a hypergood. See *Sources of the Self: The Making of Modern Identity* (Cambridge, MA: Harvard University Press, 1989), 63–65.

her from the world or lock her deeply within herself, making her susceptible to depression. Rather, caring for cats and dogs, she imagined—more like proclaimed—would deliver a full life that would connect her to the world. This connection would mean action—she'd do things, not just sit at home. This kind of doing, reaching out to something other than herself for a good not embedded within herself, would upend the need for speed, giving her a sense of flourishing. She realized she'd need a sense of resonance that would draw her into something beyond herself. She could imagine another moral horizon, a different way into a good life.

This, I realized, would have to be the task of the church.

3

fullness as busyness

why busy churches attract and then lose busy people

If only I could get on the plane and into my seat, I could get to work. I would be stuck, but I would be moving, busy at work, racing to get things done, sliding headfirst into my busyness. I wish everybody would just hurry up. It's a shame I feel this way. I literally have nowhere to go. I admit that, at one level, I hate the rushed feeling of being busy. But at another level it produces in me a sense of fullness.

On the plane (finally!), I plop into my seat, organize my things, and slip on my headphones. I open my email to find nine new messages. Four can be deleted and forgotten immediately. Three are annoying but not arduous: they'll distract me from getting other things done, but what's worse, they'll give me no sense that my busyness is fullness.[1]

The final two emails are very different. One is an invitation to write a chapter for a book. The second is an invitation to speak at an event. To say yes to both would be arduous: it would cause a major acceleration in my busyness. I am not sure how I'll fit them in. But I know right away I'll say yes. That kind of busyness gives me a deep sense of fullness, assuring me that the self I'm

---

1. In using "fullness," I'm drawing on a category Taylor uses as central to his moral philosophy. His contention is that all people and societies seek fullness and act in ways to lead full lives. You can't be human and not have some view—even a misguided one—of fullness. Taylor discusses fullness in *Sources of the Self: The Making of Modern Identity* (Cambridge, MA: Harvard University Press, 1989), 43–45; and *A Secular Age* (Cambridge, MA: Belknap, 2007), 5–20.

curating is in demand. I'm willing to risk the weariness, because it gives me a sense of living a full, good life.

While responding to these two requests, I receive a text message from a college friend who's now a pastor. We had made plans to have dinner when I arrive in Kansas City. The text message says that he just resigned from his congregation today.

Busyness as Fullness

As we discussed in the previous chapter, the good life is assumed to be an accelerating life. We take pride in our lives being saturated, even claiming that we're too busy. The answer to "How are you?" is usually "Busy." This is in part a confession of the weariness imposed by the pace (making us susceptible to depression). But at a more direct level, it signals that though we are stretched, we're in demand, living fast, embracing our opportunities. It signals to other late-modern people that we're flourishing (in the logic of late modernity itself). This flourishing is risky, leading to weariness that can produce despondency. Nevertheless, it signals that we're moving fast, keeping up, and therefore living well. Sayng "busy" means we're accelerating our own being, even our inner lives, to match the pace of modernity itself.

To live the good life is to feel a sense of fullness, which is what all human beings seek. We need to feel ourselves full of, or wrapped in, something good.

To be busy is to feel like your life is full, or has some version of fullness.[2] In late modernity busyness is the quickest but riskiest way to produce this sense of fullness. Vapid people seem to be the busiest. I once eavesdropped on mid-level movie executives eating at In-N-Out in Santa Monica. They were so busy, but their aims seemed so vapid, overwhelmed with consumerism, sex appeal, and all the stupid people at work they should be promoted ahead of. Yet by all appearances they couldn't recognize the vapidness of their sense of the good life because of how busy they were. Being busy gave them a sense of importance, which in turn produced an overall feeling of fullness, but it rendered them unable to spot their own vapidness. This same fullness keeps me from recognizing my own vapid rush to board the plane.

Busy people, whether in Santa Monica or on Wall Street, often have no time for more substantive moral traditions, because those traditions are too slow. The fullness of busyness is a different type of fullness than the fullness

---

2. Judy Wajcman says, "There is the prestige attached to a busy lifestyle that swells the refrain of relentless haste in some quarters." *Pressed for Time: The Acceleration of Life in Digital Capitalism* (Chicago: University of Chicago Press, 2015), 7.

provided by religious practices and substantive moral traditions. Or, to connect this back to the Dakotas, the fullness of busyness is radically different from the fullness of the little girl who proclaimed, "That was *great*!" The pastor and I paused and soaked it up because we encountered something good. Mysteriously, the moment felt blessedly full to the seams.

Yet busyness is more appealing, more apparent, for us late-modern people because it correlates with our moral sense of time. We feel the pull to extract as much out of time as we can, to move fast. Busyness causes us to obsess about time, feeling as if we could master it if only we could keep up; but we forget that time *never* slows, meaning this month's busyness will increase next month. Jeremy Begbie says, "Our culture [has an] inability to live peaceably with time."[3]

In contrast, the sense of fullness in the little girl's proclamation becomes timeless; it gathers time. She felt fullness not because she was mastering time, squeezing interests and resources out of time. Rather, her fullness was bound in interconnection. Playing connected her to the world, moving her beyond herself while completely including herself.[4] The North Dakota pastor and I forgot about time, soaking in the moment, feeling a connection to something that gathers time—which made time about something other than acceleration. This fullness called us to stop and be. It gave us a sense of joy and peace, an experience of resonance with something bigger than us (we'll have much more to say about resonance in the chapters below).

Yet in a secular age, the drive for finding fullness amid busyness is ever calling.[5] We often can't even name why it's good to be busy. Sometimes we curse the pace, but we nevertheless concede that busyness puts us nearer to the good life of late modernity. Not surprisingly, those who still wear the marks of substantive moral traditions—priest in cloaks, women in hijabs— seem slow. The ethic of authenticity asks that we respect them—giving them tolerance. But often the ethic of authenticity will misread the act. We'll be asked to give them tolerance because we shouldn't (it's wrong to) question and belittle someone else's individually chosen project. If a woman wants to wear a hijab or veil, that's her choice, she's free *to do her*.

3. Begbie, *Theology, Music and Time* (London: Cambridge University Press, 2000), 144.
4. The relational is central here. Antje Jackelén, *Time and Eternity: The Question of Time in Church, Science, and Theology* (Philadelphia: Templeton Foundation Press, 2005), has argued for thinking of time and eternity as relationally bound. In this relational connection, eternity breaks forth into time. We sensed this with the little girl. It was a concrete experience of eternity entering time. Hartmut Rosa calls these experiences *Resonanz*, or resonance. What Rosa is touching on in social theory is what Jackelén explains theologically. Experiences of resonance are encounters in which eternity is unveiled in time.
5. Japanese theologian Kosuke Koyama provides insightful comments on busyness as a fullness in *Three Mile an Hour God* (London: SCM, 1979), 115–30.

But ironically, that's not at all how she sees it. She wears the hijab or veil not as a way of living out the project of her individual self. Rather, a larger, deeply substantive moral tradition leads her into a sense of practice, delivering a very different fullness than that of busyness through speed. She wears the hijab not for the expression of herself but to connect to something bigger than herself. She connects with a moral tradition substantive enough to even affect how she dresses. Even those who are willing to be tolerant, letting her be her, will admit that such a moral perspective seems too slow, even leading some to distrust her.[6] From within the hollowed moral stance of the ethic of authenticity, some will wonder how we could even trust someone who would follow any moral tradition that restricts freedom of expression by keeping you from wearing what you want.

Or to give a less geopolitically loaded example, ask young pastors in clerical collars how many odd looks and strange comments they receive. Our secularized world expects a seventy-year-old man in a collar, but the thirty-year-old calls for comment. These young and supposedly fast individuals inhabit the dress of the slow. They should be fully engaged in the light ethic of authenticity, yet they are willing to publicly take on the heavy and slow marks of a moral tradition with a substance that demands the slowness of forging character, practicing virtue, and forming values.

This is why it becomes particularly interesting, even *cool*, for the young pastor in the clerical collar to also don a tattoo sleeve or at least a pompadour haircut with hip, thick-rimmed glasses. This juxtaposition signals that this person is unique, able to balance the fast with the deep, something ever more difficult in late modernity's acceleration.

To most people, in our need to move fast, it doesn't seem like a good idea to be bogged down by moral precepts, practices, and traditions. A good life is no longer necessarily about any particular substance but rather the form, even fashion, of keeping up. Hence we reason, "I'm well. Busy, but well." Those who are moving fastest—without hurting anyone by preventing them from moving fast[7]—seem the closest to living a good life, receiving the fullness of busyness.

Running to Stay in Place

At first glance, authenticity and the free project of the self feels like a way of moving forward, a journey toward a new horizon of a good life. But if we

6. For an example, see Richard Dawkins, *The God Delusion* (Boston: Mariner, 2008).

7. This is the mutual equal regard of the modern moral order that Taylor discusses in *Secular Age*, 198–205. See also my own discussion of this in volume 2, *The Pastor in a Secular Age: Ministry to People Who No Longer Need a God* (Grand Rapids: Baker Academic, 2019), 70–80.

peel things back, we realize that speeding up isn't really about going forward after all. We'll begin to notice that busyness is not the kind of fullness that can connect us to something bigger than us. Rather, busyness asks us to run fast, not in order to move forward but to keep from falling behind.[8] I say yes to the chapter and the lecture even when doing so overwhelms me with busyness, because I fear that I'll fall behind if I don't. Someone else will write the chapter, and I'll be seen as less of an expert. If I say no to the lecture, my book sales and platform will decrease.

The fullness of busyness makes strong claims about what is good. It is good to go fast, to do a lot, to not miss out, to know things and experience them, and to be the kind of self who is full with commitments, interests, and opportunities. Despite all this, we have no direction. There is no telos other than to be a self that is happy with the self, satisfied that you're living well because you're busy.[9]

And the fullness of busyness compels us to move ever faster. When we dare to stop and look, we realize we're going nowhere in particular. We need a sense of moving toward something, but we can discern that busyness can't provide a destination to anything outside of us. It draws us deeper within ourselves. Busyness asks us to run faster, not to go anywhere in particular but just to remain busy so we can feel full, to be the kind of self that is authentically living and not wasting (or missing) opportunities to be a different, better, happier, more interesting self.

On the other hand, substantive moral traditions provide us ways of seeking some aims, reaching for some horizon beyond the self. For example, a Jewish family at Passover says "Next year in Jerusalem" as a sign of their desire to return to the rebuilt city. This is a proclamation of a distinct aim sought through practices, values, and character. It produces a fullness that connects the family to six thousand years of history, taking them outside of themselves by including them in something bigger than themselves. The fullness of busyness, which at first blush seems to move us quickly toward some horizon, is

8. Nate Stucky adds helpful texture to this: "If we or our young people feel busy, the research suggests that in most cases this sense doesn't come from a jam-packed schedule. Notable exceptions exist, but for the majority, the problem of feeling busy appears to stem less from structured time and more from unstructured time and the cultural lauding of busyness. In other words, the research seems to indicate not so much a lack of time, but a loss of our collective ability to track time. We're too busy trying to be busy. We lose time; it slips away; and we're unsure of where it goes or why we feel so frazzled. Perhaps the smartphone in our pocket, the laptop on our desk, and the tablet in our hand hold a clue." *Wrestling with Rest: Inviting Youth to Discover the Gift of Sabbath* (Grand Rapids: Eerdmans, 2019), 52.

9. Nicolas Berdyaev has a beautifully prophetic articulation on the problems with happiness in *The Destiny of Man* (San Rafael, CA: Semantron, 2009), 74–102.

only a mirage. Its frantic pace uses time to harvest resources to curate the self. It draws us back within ourselves, telling us that the core of the good life is being an authentic self. But authenticity is never firmly secured. It is most often measured by keeping up with the authenticity of those around us. We hurry to stay in place, reaching for just a little more authenticity. We're busy trying not to fall behind, not to lose our authenticity, or maybe even to find it in the first place.

Late modernity's radical freedom and individual expression, which produce an ethic of authenticity, become the HD video screen on the treadmill that gives us a sense that we're moving somewhere. But most of us end up running away from, not toward, something. The freedom to chase our dreams turns on us, and soon we're running away from the guilt of being left behind, anxious and worried that the busyness that gave us a sense of fullness will eat us alive.

We fear we're not able to be a self we can live with. Or worse, we fear that in curating the self through all the busyness we'll discover that we've chosen the wrong interests and activities, ending up a dull self who wasted so much time. We're running away from the possibility that we're missing out on a good life, an entirely subjective measurement. There are few outside criteria (other than winning recognition from others) to assure me that I've reached the good of the project of myself. Even the good parts of our lives we now possess—being in shape and healthy, saving for retirement, keeping up on the news, fashion, internet memes, and TV shows, being an attentive parent and connected friend—can all get washed away if we don't keep running and rushing. We have a nagging awareness that we're running faster to stay in the same place.

Back to the Church

It is these fatigued runners who enter our churches on Sunday morning or Wednesday night. It's these fatigued runners who want more from their congregations but who are unable to volunteer because of their busyness. They ask their churches and their pastors to run faster and be busier. The people in these congregations may not be individually depressed, but they are unequivocally busy. Many wear their busyness as a badge of a good and full life. They keep running and running to avoid being tackled by the guilt of not running fast enough (another vicious circle).

Perhaps these people have made it to church because their running to stay in place hasn't amalgamated into depression. They still have time (and energy) for church in their busy, full lives. They still think the church offers something for their lives. But they sit on a razor's edge, demanding that the church offer something that directly adds to their fullness, some kind of relevance for their busyness. And they're not wrong. The church *should* have something to say about fullness!

But when this fullness is in the form of busyness, the congregation finds it hard to offer a moral horizon that encompasses fullness in the kingdom of God, participation in the life of the Trinity, and ministry to the world. Not unlike in the past, people are present in church because they think it is good; they believe it can help them into a good life. Yet, matching the cultural moment, the substance of what the church offers is confused or even unimportant. This is the reason few congregations, especially in the mainline, get overly concerned about theology. Theology mattered greatly in the substantive moral systems the church once offered. We needed to think deeply about what certain practices do to us, both in time and in eternity. We needed to be concerned about which forms, virtues, and character traits draw us near to the divine or toward damnation. Yet, in the fullness that comes from busyness, the congregation is pulled into hollowed-out moral conceptions of attending to the self—in this case, the self of the congregation. We become infatuated with the congregation itself and not how the congregation lives as a servant in heralding God's ministering action in the world. The leadership of the congregation becomes obsessed with questions about what their church is, how it needs to change, how it needs to keep up, and how it must use its resources better.

The congregation, like the late-modern individual, starts running, seeking speed, to go nowhere in particular. Even a sabbatical can be treated as merely a timeout to build energy to return to the rush, rather than as an opportunity to rest to see anew the fullness of God's action. In this widespread logic, the congregation becomes as susceptible as individuals to feeling guilty. *La fatigue d'être soi* becomes *la fatigue d'être eglise.* The church enters, or nears, a state of depression because it is trying to run fast without a vision that calls the congregation beyond its concern for itself. Like a person, the church (which is ultimately a communion of persons finding life—fullness—in the person of Jesus Christ) can have its being only by being pulled outside itself to seek a horizon much bigger than itself.[10]

10. This is why missional church literature has teetered between helpful and problematic. When it pushes the congregation's imagination toward a horizon outside of itself, to the *missio Dei*, it is helpful (see Darrell Guder's work). However, when it becomes just a new strategy (e.g., a new branded version of busyness), it only justifies speeding up, which is a losing option in late modernity.

The Busy Church

Those seeking fullness through busyness, having no sense of a larger horizon, assume that the church needs to be relevant. The church appears relevant when it's able to move within this moral conception of busyness, matching this form of fullness, by meeting the demands of speed. For the church to appear relevant to people seeking fullness through busyness, the congregation too must be busy. The congregation must concede that fullness comes through busyness. This will appear to be the best way to attract and retain members. People spot a relevant or appealing congregation most often through the moral lens through which they see their own lives. If their form of fullness is busyness, then unless that form of fullness is shifted (or theologically speaking, judged and cruci-fied), they'll look for a congregation that makes busyness its form of fullness.

People seeking fullness through busyness will find that slow congregations— those that look like old cathedrals more than community centers, with leaders dressed in robes and not Hawaiian shirts—are downright repulsive or at least cringe-worthy. Those slow congregations repel us because they are operating at a different moral frequency. They seem to be opposing the very form of fullness that the repulsed visitor holds dear.

Inevitably, the busiest congregations will seem to be doing the best, draw-ing busy people who are willing to carve out time from their busy lives for church. It seems odd that busy congregations would draw busy people. Why wouldn't busy people choose a church that would slow them down, giving them a break from the pace? Of course, some people do, wanting the liturgy and pomp of ecclesial order they knew when they were young, finding it pro-vides a break from the speed of late modernity. But these are the exceptions; most want relevance. And relevance (a hard thing to spot and to be sure of) is discerned through busyness itself. Because of how speed is connected to the good life, most people want something different from church than a chance to slow down. To slow down, people would need far more than the encourage-ment to take a break. Taking a break would be a curse, only producing guilt from all the other things people could be doing. Slowing down and seeing the church as inviting us to fundamentally slow down (if that should even be our goal) could only occur if the form of fullness through busyness was met by a different form of fullness. The church would need to offer a different moral vision for a different sense of a good life. Slowing down would need to be placed inside a completely different moral category of what makes life full, rather than slowing down just being a break from the pace of busyness.

Because busyness is a form of fullness, and because human beings are deeply drawn to (even false forms of) fullness, people will seek a congregation that matches their form of fullness. Relevance is inseparable from our sense of what makes a full, good, and flourishing life. We're too busy to go to a boring church; that's just a waste of time—almost immoral. Rather, being busy as a way of seeking fullness, we choose a congregation that is also full in the form in which we understand fullness. Caught up in our own form of fullness through busyness, we pick the congregation that matches our own moral pursuit. It's infinitely easier for busy suburban people to go to a big church than to participate in a slower small church filled with slow, aging people (who seem far from "authentic"). As with my experience of boarding the plane, next to the rush of busyness, such people seem annoyingly slow.

The Church's Form of Busyness

Many see the busy congregation as a congregation that can offer fullness. Of course, thanks to our secular age, this fullness doesn't center on divine action, mystery, or a sacramental ontology (these are perceived as slow realities because their form of fullness is reached within a substantive moral tradition). Rather, the busy congregation connects to the pursuits of curating a self and of finding a way to cope with speed so that the fullness of busyness can be harvested without guilt.

To meet this moral imagination, the congregation must be busy in two ways. First, it must be busy in its offerings: programs, activities, groups, and a full schedule. People seeking fullness from busyness want to be near busyness (even if they don't really want to participate). This is deeply frustrating to pastors, children's ministers, and youth workers but nevertheless an unavoidable result of creating a relevant, busy congregation to reach busy people. Even if such busy people don't have the time to partake themselves, they feel good knowing the church is busy, full with activities. It gives them the assurance that the church can offer them fullness when they finally carve out the time to participate. Thus parents might not have the time to get their thirteen-year-old to youth group, missing every week from October to March because of basketball tournaments; nevertheless they expect the youth group to be vibrant and exciting, complaining by email if it wanes. When such a congregation grows, it does so by adding programs and activities at a much higher rate than participants and new members, putting undue stress on the pastoral staff.

Second, the congregation must be busy in its message, helping busy people find the resources they need to get more fullness out of their busyness. In late modernity, for our own ethical reasons, we've hollowed out the substance of our moral pursuits for the sake of authenticity and speed. Who has time for long confessions, wordy liturgies, and exegetical sermons? We're looking to work on the self, to run fast to harvest the experiences the self needs to be unique, happy, and satisfied. Better, then, to preach sermons, or have small groups, that focus on "How to Handle Discouragement," "How to Survive under Stress," "How to Feel Good about Yourself," "How to Stay Calm in a Crisis," and "How to Keep On Keeping On."[11]

When fullness is sought through busyness and when authenticity hollows out the moral substance for the sake of being light enough to be busier, it becomes very hard for the congregation to know its purpose, other than being busy and helping resource busy people. What is the congregation for? In the slower substantive moral imaginations before the age of authenticity, the church could clearly claim what it was for—keeping you from hell, or providing virtue to flourish now and in eternity, or offering practices and sacraments to thwart temptation and evil. But all these substantive moral conceptions have been evacuated for the sake of speed.

So now what is the church for? The congregations that *seem* to be faring the *best* are those that look (or are) the fastest. They're busy with busyness. The calendar is filled with activities, the building is multiuse, the parking lot is large and kinetic, and the pastor seems like the kind of self that is keeping up with the pace of modernity. He or she seems like a curated self who's up to date on news, parenting techniques, TV shows, viral videos, music, and classic literature.

Losing the Busy

The busy church for busy people opens up another vicious circle. Once the congregation concedes to helping people find fullness through busyness, it sets itself up to lose them. When those using busyness to find fullness hit a fatigue that becomes despondency, they'll stop coming at all. This hair-raising conundrum seems endemic to late-modern American Protestantism. When people feel that busyness has not achieved fullness, but instead has turned on them, producing a deep fatigue that settles in as depression, they'll disappear. Why wouldn't they?

Speed and busyness are the source of their depression, so why darken the door of a congregation trying to resource busy people in their pursuit of fullness through busyness? It just adds to their guilt. It seems counterintuitive that people would claim that a congregation so accommodating to busy

11. These are all real titles of Rick Warren sermons.

people, willing to hollow out its own substantive moral commitments, would feel condemning. It should feel anything but. Nevertheless, people leave when depressed, feeling too guilty to come to church. I'd argue that they leave not because they feel like sinners falling short of some substantive moral commitment. They leave because they can't keep up.

They imagine the congregation is for resourcing busy people, helping them harvest the fullness from busyness. But if they can't handle their own busyness, going to church in a congregation that helps busy people find fullness feels condemning. All these people in the church seem to be able to cope with speed—the church, in its own way, is supporting people's speeding up—but those who can't manage the speed disappear because they feel guilty. The congregation seeking relevance only adds to the people's guilt.

Interpreting this disappearance through the ailment of high modernity, we might think, "They're not doing well, so they're hiding from the community, ashamed that their public life isn't perfect. They don't want us to see that they are hysterical or depressed." We add to this interpretation by turning on the church itself: "The church is supposed to be exactly where they should be. We should be a place where people can be authentic with their struggles, not hiding them from each other." We use the ethic of authenticity to blame the church. The congregation is in a double bind. To be relevant and authentic it must be busy, but being busy, it can't be authentic *enough* to meet those who are struck with the ailment of late modernity's failed grasp at fullness.

This same double bind stretches even deeper, pushing the church itself into depression. Everyone agrees with the pastor, denominational official, council chair, or consultant who heralds that the church needs to change. They can see that the church is not keeping pace with modernity, not as relevant as it should be. It is falling behind. They'd like the church to change, to speed up, to catch up with their own lives, to provide more resources to help them keep pace. The universal reaction is that the church should indeed change.

But this is exactly where the need for change turns from obvious to fatiguing, from desired to depressing. When the church's need for change means you'll personally have to do more and give more, instead of receive more, a collective depression comes over the congregation. People seeking fullness through busyness have an insatiable need to receive resources to cope with speed, but they have no margins to give—especially to give time! When you're running at the pace of late modernity, the last thing you need is something behind you vying for your attention or needing your help. You're just trying to keep up. If the congregation pushes too hard for your attention and resources, it will cross a line. The church will no longer be helping you cope with busyness but adding to it.

The pastor in North Dakota told me that his church was still relatively full on Sunday mornings. His people still had the energy to show up. But beyond showing up, it felt like a depression had set in, not with the individuals but with the congregation as a whole. His people wanted the church to change, to catch up. Once they realized that any change would mean giving (not receiving) resources, *la fatigue d'être eglise* set in. This fatigue led them to wish all the more for the church to change and to assist them in finding resources to keep up. The vicious circle never ends!

––––––––––

As I arrive in Kansas City and jump into my rental car, my friend's text about his resignation is still buzzing in my mind. I suspect there might be some connection with the pastor in North Dakota. As we sit down for dinner, I'm sure of the connection.

"So what happened at the church?"

He allows a pregnant silence and then says, "Things just got stale."

"Stale?" I ask, trying to hide the fact that I think his response is lame.

He breathes in as if to communicate that he doesn't want to get into all this, but here we go.

He finally says, "Okay, I know it sounds superficial. I just felt like everything was lifeless. I was racing to do stuff, to bring the church through a bunch of changes and into new directions. I was the pastor of innovation and the leader of the staff, especially when the senior pastor transitioned to basically just preaching. I was busy, but a different kind of busy. In the past, when I was busy, it made me feel alive. I was tired but I still felt *something*. But all of a sudden, I was busy but not feeling anything. It was frightening. It was like Advent was over before it started. It was moving too fast to even be a space I could live inside. And I was the pastor! It was depressing. This sounds stupid and full of self-pity, but last month when a member of the church was diagnosed with cancer, my first thought was that he was lucky, because he had a way out of the busyness."

He pauses. We're now somewhere very deep. I realize that "stale" is anything but superficial.

"I was just so tired. I thought that was it. When I requested a sabbatical, it was a big deal. Our congregation doesn't do sabbaticals. But I felt *that* desperate. I needed a break to slow down. When I told the leadership team and all the members who were helping with the projects and groups I was leading, they were happy for me, but I could tell they were panicked too. I felt guilty about leaving them on their own for three months. But the worst feeling was that everything had become stale, and no sabbatical was going to fix that.

I didn't even feel like I was really living when I was doing ministry. I mean, that's why I felt called to ministry in the first place, to help people really live, and I felt nothing but staleness."

"So what happened with the sabbatical?" I ask.

"The staleness went away. For a little while. Being able to be with my kids was great. It was tiring and annoying sometimes, but far from stale. I felt alive again being with them."

I smile and nod.

"But something happened at one of my kid's soccer games. I reconnected with a guy who used to be part of our church. About a year ago, he went through a divorce and totally disappeared. Back in pastor mode, and feeling some of that staleness return, I asked him if he wanted to get a coffee sometime. When we met up, we found out that our stories were almost the same. He thought that his life would be worth something if he could become the vice president at his company. But when it happened, he felt that same staleness. He said, 'I didn't have time to feel alive.' That was exactly how I was feeling. I knew right then, having coffee with him, that it was time to leave the church."

We sit silently, his story resting between us.

"So what are you going to do now?" I finally ask.

"Who knows, maybe manage my father-in-law's body shop. Mainly I just want to spend more time with my kids. The sabbatical allowed me to spend such good time with them. It was delightful. That time was a lifesaver, actually."

Time. I kept thinking about time. What is time, and how is it possible that time can speed up? Why does it feel like time moves faster or slower depending on our experience?

Something gets stale because time has gotten to it. Bread becomes stale because time has made it dry, lifeless—the fullness of time has passed it by. My friend felt lifeless because time seemed to be speeding up and passing him by. The fullness of busyness turned on him and sucked the life out of him. Things were going too fast for him to find the space to feel connected.

Or maybe it's better to say that time was moving so fast that it no longer allowed him to have time to enjoy a life of ministry, to savor it, to feel connected to something bigger than himself and the initiatives he was implementing. Busyness gave him a sense of fullness, of being important and in demand. But this fullness was blunted, leading to a sense of lifelessness. It's the lifelessness that the pastor in North Dakota was describing as a congregation-wide depression. Churches that speed up by adding new initiatives of change run the risk that this fullness of busyness will birth lifelessness.

As we prepare to leave, we both feel a tangible connection. We smile back at each other. As we stand to leave, he says, "Back in college, when we were just starting to think about ministry, I would never have imagined the feeling of staleness." We stand for a moment in the warmth of the memory of those past days.

As we walk out, I ask, as a way both to continue my thoughts about time and to transition us to something lighter, "Remember that class Creativity in the Fine Arts?"

"Oh, yeah," he responds, "Remember Christianity in Western Civilization?"

"I do." I laugh and add, "I remember we barely passed both of them."

For some reason, those classes seem imminently connected to this whole discussion.

4

the strip show

when sacred time is no longer the time we keep

At the Christian liberal arts university that my friend and I attended, there were two required courses for every first-year student. These courses were always taught by a team of professors across multiple disciplines. One was a survey of Christianity in Western Culture (aka CWC) taught by philosophers, theologians, and historians. The other was Creativity in the Fine Arts (aka CIFA) (discussed at the beginning of the next chapter). Christianity in Western Culture explored how Christianity developed in the West from the fourth century to today. It was a painfully difficult course for our freshmen minds. Reading Augustine, Descartes, Kant, and Hume was no joke after skipping chapel to watch *The Price Is Right* and playing a few quick games of *Madden '94* on Sega (yeah, I'm old).

I remember vividly, from all those years ago, paging through the assigned binder of essays, spot-reading what I'd be up against over the next thirteen weeks. As I did, I panicked. I barely understood a sentence on any of the pages. My anxiety spiked after the first lecture and my arrival at the first small precept group. I could hide in a lecture, but these small groups of ten students and a professor would out my ignorance for sure.

I felt a slight relief when the professor started by saying, "If you looked through the binder, I bet you felt like you were in the middle of a crisis."

She continued, taking things in a much different direction than I expected. "The history and ideas that move the West are almost always born out of a crisis. For instance, Augustine is writing against the crisis of Pelagianism. And as we get into the Enlightenment and our modern society, crises seem to be everywhere. The binder before you welcomes you into a crisis. And I think understanding these past people's crises will help you face, and even answer, the crises we face today."

I looked around the small room. Everyone else was nodding excitedly. No one else seemed to be sweating and flushed like me. I wanted to raise my hand and ask, "What about the crisis of not understanding a word these dead people are saying?" But instead, I joined the gaggle of gawking head bobbers to hide that I was now deep in the middle of a personal crisis.

Never-Ending Crisis

Modernity is a child born from crisis, and she has never left the lap of her mother. For modern people nursed on reason, it's a normal disposition to worry about some future catastrophe. Since modernity's dawn, we've been touting one threat or another. I suppose this is the backside of progress. We cannot progress without some nightmare of demise. Always leaving something behind and entering something new brings angst for what's been lost and fear for what's next. Because modernity brings speed, and because speed imposes change, modernity is inextricably linked with fears of crisis. Our present day isn't the first time we thought the church was in trouble. This is the collective psychological nausea of constant speed increase. The Germans call it *Zeitkrankheit*, time sickness.[1] As any roller-coaster rider knows, speed has a way of producing heightened senses. For some, it triggers the fight-or-flight mode, moving them to see threats and pending calamities around each bend.

Charles Taylor taught us in volume 2 of this series that the premodern world was a period of great anxiety.[2] Apocalyptic plagues of death, which could wipe out high percentages of whole villages and towns, have a way of doing that. In Thomas Becket's day (1119–70) people lived in constant fear of agents of death like devils and demons. They even worried that taking the Eucharist for anything other than its church-sanctioned purpose bore such

---

1. Carl Honoré explains that we have something similar in America. "In 1982 Larry Dossey, an American physician, coined the term 'time-sickness' to describe the obsessive belief that 'time is getting away, that there isn't enough of it, and that you must pedal faster and faster to keep up.'" *In Praise of Slowness: Challenging the Cult of Speed* (San Francisco: HarperOne, 2004), 3.

2. See Andrew Root, *The Pastor in a Secular Age: Ministry to People Who No Longer Need a God* (Grand Rapids: Baker Academic, 2019), chap. 2. Anxiety is the subtext of that chapter, which discusses the anxiety that surrounded enchantment and even the Eucharist. People in medieval Europe were often frightened, bearing deep anxiety about their eternal destiny.

spiritual torque it could rip their mortal, sinful souls to pieces, destining them for hell. Those were anxious times, Taylor says. Yet for the most part our secular age has freed us from these anxieties. We no longer assume that an external or supernatural force threatens us. The source of our threats is no longer from without but from within. In modernity, the call of impending crisis is coming from within the house.

Modernity itself, and the societies we've built from its pursuits, threatens us. Even in my relatively short lifetime there have been multiple existential threats to the West and modernity itself. To name just a few, I have been told to worry about, maybe even to expect modernity to be threatened by, nuclear holocaust, Y2K, financial collapse, Islamic terrorism, global warming, fake news, and a global pandemic.[3] These are only the major crises. News shows report hundreds, even thousands more crises, many able to be filed under the above. We have a child-obsessed crisis, a debt crisis, a bee crisis, an opioid crisis, a financial crisis, an antibiotic resistance crisis, an internet security crisis, and many more crises to concern us. Modernity is never absent pending doom. And all these crises come not from outside but from within modernity. The quickened pace, the waning of institutions, and the shifting and disappearing of meaning in modern society means it takes very little for us to entertain all sorts of threats. Even our entertainment envisions the dissolving of modernity itself—next season of *The Handmaid's Tale* coming soon!

Mobilized Wills at the Speed of Paul Revere

When the *ancien regime*—the premodern world of kings and queens—was overcome by what Taylor calls the age of mobilization—think of America or France after their revolutions—our societies were no longer connected directly to heaven.[4] There is no longer even a sense that the created realm participates directly in a heavenly one. Eternity is shut out of time, and now time is free to rev its engines and speed up. The kingdoms of the world—let's no longer call them kingdoms but republics or countries or nation-states—and the kingdom of heaven are assumed to be no longer attached, at least not directly through

3. Maybe only Islamic terrorism could be argued as coming from outside the West, though it's the conditions of the West—even its technology and banking laws—that make such a response possible. Soviet communism was similar but also quite different. It was a system that was in a death fight with Western capitalism, because it too was a system forged from within modernity. Nicolas Berdyaev has argued that communism and capitalism are both modern, atheistic systems, an interesting comment made by a Russian exile in Western Europe. See *The End of Our Time* (San Rafael, CA: Semantron, 2009), 50, 92, 190–92.

4. Taylor discusses mobilization in *A Secular Age* (Cambridge, MA: Belknap, 2007), 449–60.

societal orders. The lower realm is no longer dependent on the higher, the earthly no longer under obligation to reflect the divine.

We sever this umbilical cord for the sake of freedom and reason.[5] Speed itself is the scissors that makes the cut. The age of mobilization is such a radical change because it not only cuts us loose from heaven but also presumes something never thought of before in the West. We discover that we can change our whole order, shifting our whole fundamental way of being in the world, by our own human wills.

If we can connect wills quickly—with speed—across space, we can create a collective will that creates the new order we wish for. It's no wonder that one of the core tales of the American Revolution surrounds speed. Paul Revere's ability to move quickly, shouting, "The British are coming, the British are coming!" readied the wills of the people to fight a battle to overthrow the *ancien regime* and God's elect King George III. As Revere shows, it takes speed to mobilize wills. Speed allows the colonists to fight for the sake of a new order mobilized from the will of the people.

Speed in a new age of mobilization is assumed to be so powerful it can even unhook human orders from the divine. Thanks to speed and through speed, we the people can will to live under an order that we create. We no longer need to submit to what comes before us, assuming that its weighty tradition and thick meaning is a direct reflection of heaven itself. Rather, with our own wills we can change what was once assumed to be unchangeable. Now, only individual wills, even private lives, connect us to heaven or the divine—if that's what *we* wish. No wonder modernity has always had a problem with inflated hubris. Being able to change what was assumed to be unchangeable has a way of doing that.

In the *ancien regime*, change (particularly fundamental changes like the ordering of political and social lives) would have to come through divine revelation. Heaven itself would have to communicate such a change. Welcome to the world of the prophets. It would be the will of God, not the will of the people, that would bring any direct change. It was rare for any group of willing people seeking freedom and following reason to change anything. The king ruled his domain as God ruled his heavens. It would take a transcendent event, call it a miracle, to change anything of significance. This is why when one king conquered another, the ensuing change in the shape of the kingdom was assumed to be the very will of God. "We've been overcome by our enemies because of our own sin, because God (not us) has willed for

---

5. By "reason" I mean for the sake of controlling nature, following Michael Gillespie, *The Theological Origins of Modernity* (Chicago: University of Chicago Press, 2008).

a new king, because we had no longer reflected heaven here in the human domain." "God has saved us by the hand of this new king." "God has given us this mad king because of our own sinfulness." Not until wills can be united across space through speed can we imagine it differently.

In the ancient world and the medieval *ancien regime*, stories, songs, and architecture told the tale of miraculous change of one ruler for another, or one order for the next.[6] Connecting change to prophesies of old would be as important as any new innovations. Divine meaning and connection to history would need to be firmly tied to any change. The new was rarely welcomed without some deep sense of how it connected to the past. God, not we, could do a new thing. We would know this new thing, not through results or by it producing subjective feelings like happiness, but in its connection to what had come before. (Isaiah 43:18–19 tells us that the God of Israel—the God who frees people from slavery—is doing a new thing. This new thing is bound not in severing the heavy story of the past but in fulfilling it.)[7] Change in the *ancien regime* required a new moral horizon that was tied firmly to the past moral tradition. Not so in modernity. Modernity makes things light. And change is so fundamental (such a high good) that it comes without any necessary connection to a past story, even free of meaning other than the good of change itself.

Sacred Time

The kingdoms of the *ancien regime* weren't timeless, but nevertheless time seemed to hover over them like eternity itself. Change, newness, advancement, and innovation were far from obsessions. Silicon Valley and Avignon couldn't be more different,[8] and not just because one has microprocessors and electric scooters, and the other transubstantiation and the bones of saints. Rather, in places like Avignon in the fourteenth century, all time was ordered

6. For more on this historically, see Ernst H. Kantorowicz's classic *The King's Two Bodies: A Study in Medieval Theology* (Princeton: Princeton University Press, 1997), 170–74. Kantorowicz helpfully, for our purposes, discusses the king and time: "Concerning Time the king was a *gemina persona*; he was time-bound in some respects, and was above or beyond time in others" (172).

7. See Boris Groys, *On the New* (London: Verso, 2014), 22–23, for a discussion on how the new was looked down on in times before modernity.

8. I use Avignon as a placeholder for a society in which sacred time hangs over all things. Or better, a time when the church was the timekeeper. This is not necessarily a historical statement about Avignon but a conceptual sense of time being held as sacred, and the church keeping this time for the whole of society. I suppose I could have used Rome or the Vatican or Christendom as a similar conceptual placeholder. I chose Avignon because I often return, following Taylor, to the medieval *ancien regime*, and Avignon's popes rest squarely in this time.

under sacred time.[9] This sacred time was the baseline. It was the speed limit of society.[10] The *ancien regime* had many times: the time of work, the time of war, and the time of harvest. But ultimately, all these times were ordered under sacred time.

Sacred time was the time that mattered, the time you set your being to.[11] You did so because sacred time was a full and gathered time, not an accelerating time. Modernity has exchanged a gathered time heavy with meaning and divine consequence for an accelerating time (busyness is a fullness in the logic of acceleration). To get time to speed up, it had to have its meaning hollowed out, unhooked from divine consequence.

In Avignon, the church and its priest kept time for the rest of society, literally ringing bells to signal time, but more importantly, informing others of when it was time to enter directly into sacred time through the liturgy of Mass.[12] In Islamic societies today, sacred time has not completely been eclipsed. Over speakers, imams tell those working at the speed of labor, commerce, and even cyberspeed to stop, turn east, and submit their being to sacred time. Such an act is mostly lost to us in the Western world, but in Avignon of the *ancien regime*, it would have been clear. The laborer and warrior lived at the speed

9. For a historical take on Avignon, see Jaroslav Pelikan, *The Christian Tradition: A History of the Development of Doctrine*, vol. 4, *Reformation of Church and Dogma (1300-1700)* (Chicago: University of Chicago Press, 1984), 70–75. Justo González tells the story of Avignon in *The Story of Christianity*, vol. 1, *The Early Church to the Dawn of the Reformation* (San Francisco: HarperOne, 2010), 398–407, showing how these were dark days for the church but nevertheless influential from a political and cultural perspective. It couples with my point that the church was keeping time. That's as far as I mean to push with my use of "Avignon." However, the best full-length text on the Avignon popes is Joelle Rollo-Koster, *Avignon and Its Papacy, 1309–1417* (Lanham, MD: Rowman & Littlefield, 2015), whose thesis seeks to dull some of the critiques of those like González.

10. Taylor discusses this at length in *A Secular Age* (Cambridge, MA: Belknap, 2007), 61–63. Nicholas H. Smith, in "Taylor and the Hermeneutic Tradition," in *Charles Taylor*, ed. Ruth Abbey (London: Cambridge University Press, 2004), 43–48, discusses the importance of time for Taylor's conception of identity and therefore the secular. Carolyn Chau provides a nice overview of Taylor's view of time in solidarity with the world: "In the Middle Ages, participation in higher time, which lent a kind of texture to time, involved a dialectic between order and disorder, through oscillation between ordinary time and carnivals and 'feasts of misrule.' Societies were ordered to and reflected an eternal order; with the move to providential deism, such feasts diminished in prominence." Chau, *Solidarity with the World: Charles Taylor and Hans Urs von Balthasar on Faith, Modernity, and Catholic Mission* (Eugene, OR: Cascade, 2016), 67.

11. Hartmut Rosa discusses sacred time in *Social Acceleration: A New Theory of Modernity* (New York: Columbia University Press, 2015), 10–12.

12. Rosa explains, "With the help of sacred time, everyday time, the time of life and the time of the world are bound together in a meaningful whole that orients culture and action, one in which cultural patterns and structural necessities, systemic requirements and actor perspectives are made congruent." *Social Acceleration*, 11.

of work and warfare. The priest, monk, and nun lived at the speed of sacred time. Not everyone could live always set to sacred time. It was assumed by everyone to be the ultimate time, but the times of harvest and war called for attention. While these lower times beckoned, the priests, monks, and nuns kept sacred time in and through the rhythms of their own bodies and lives. The monasteries—their bells and the praying monks—were the clock of society. The gears and numbers of this clock were bound in the bodies of those in practice, praying, fasting, and attending to divine things as a way to correlate the time on earth with eternity itself.

It was the job of the priest, the monk, and the nun to keep this time, and they did it (at its best) as a service to the people. The worker and the warrior knew they could reset themselves, connecting again to sacred time, even after a long harvest or a bloody war, by joining the practice of the priest, by praying with the monk and the nun. Even if only for a while, they could reset their being to sacred time. The praying class was the timekeeping class. The time they kept was sacred from beginning to (no) end. The objective was to join the fullness of gathered time. Not to speed up time.

Time and the Church

Regardless of the era in human history, we need someone to keep time. We need a collective sense of time. Especially within the age of authenticity, we imagine that we can individualize anything. But time is a construct of existence, which can never be individualized. We are not so self-determined and self-efficient that we can live inside a time of our own making. We might, for instance, ask our kids on winter break, "What are you going to do with your time?" But they only have such time because we collectively agree that there is a time when all schools stop teaching.

To be a creature, begotten and made, is to be the kind of being not able to live outside a social construct of time. A person who "lives by his own clock" is always late and seems unbothered by what this does to other people, but this only proves that he is far from having *his own* clock. His own use of time affects others. To be creatures who are finite, having our being in and through attachments with others, is to be bound to a shared sense of time.

To be true God of true God is to be truly free to be in time.[13] The Creator's own being is not contingent on some social construct of time—as it is for all

13. Here I'm tipping my hat to Robert W. Jenson, who believes that God chooses to be fully in time. Because God can be known through only the narrative-drama of God's act, God chooses to have time. See Chris Green, *The End Is Music: A Companion to Robert W. Jenson's*

created things. It is a profound articulation of the Nicene Creed to say that
Jesus is true God of true God, begotten, not made. It claims that Jesus is true
God because he is not made and therefore stands outside the contingencies
of time—he is even present as the Logos at creation, eternal with the Father
(John 1).

But though Jesus is not made, he is begotten (an interesting paradox).
Though he is the Creator, he is creature, sharing in a time-bound reality true
for all creatures. All creatures are ontologically bound to time because they
are begotten, born at a time and place, by the union of others. Others acted
in time to bring them into time. To be born is to be swaddled in time even
more than in a warm blanket. To be born is to have time intrinsically fused to
your being. Therefore, this true God of true God, who is not bound by time,
fully enters into time. He does so to remake time, by bending time's penchant
for death and sin into participation in the eternal being of God. The Nicene
Creed is breaking profound ground.

Yet, to return to us time-bound creatures, we can remember that Martin
Heidegger has taught us that we are *Dasein* (literally, "being there"). We are
beings in time (hence the title of his famous book *Sein und Zeit—Being and
Time*). We are beings that are *here*, at a particular time. Our use of language,
which Heidegger calls "the house of being," is necessarily connected with
tenses and locations. We speak in past, present, or future tense.[14]

What all this means is that someone has to keep time. Some collective has
to order time for us. We can individually decide what to do with our time,
but there is always a collective imaginary of how time works and in what
ways it is good and morally right to use and even think about time (as in our
discussion of guilt above).

The church, at least in the West, has always been a timekeeping community. Even in its pre-Constantine days (the days of the early church) it
kept time. Maybe not for the whole of the empire, like it would after the
Edict of Milan in 313. But even in a pagan world, which in its own way was
soaked in the sacred time of gods and temples, the early church kept time.
That's what made this band of weirdos so disconcerting to the powerful.
The church enacted the narrative of Jesus's final days each week, correlat-
ing their own being to Jesus's own time. They gathered for worship and the

---

Theology (Eugene, OR: Cascade, 2018), 52–58; and Antje Jackelén, *Time and Eternity: The
Question of Time in Church, Science, and Theology* (Philadelphia: Templeton Foundation
Press, 2005), 195–200.

14. Until the heptapod aliens arrive! I discussed the history of Israel next to the movie *Arrival* in *The Pastor in a Secular Age*, chap. 10. The heptapods have no tenses in their language,
and therefore they have a very different relationship with time.

meal on the first day of the week, the day of his resurrection, which was the giving of a new time.

The church knew that this new time was radically aimed at something. Time was so full and gathered, the early Christians claimed, that the time the little church was keeping would birth an apocalyptic reality that would shake the Roman Empire to rubble. In time, Jesus would return. This little band of households was now preparing for this eschatological time, recasting pagan sacred time as the time of the death, resurrection, and return of this once-dead but now-alive Jesus. The little church claimed that the time of one kingdom was coming to an end in order to bring forth the next (we can see how this period connects to the *ancien regime*).

This timekeeping (the claim of a distinct sacred time through the resurrected body of Jesus) made Roman power brokers worry. These household gatherings claimed that they lived in the time of the Spirit, unthreatened even by death. The time they shared in and anticipated was so full that even death, time's great dark promise, had no claim on them, for even while they were in time, they nevertheless partook in eternity.

When Secular Time Replaced Sacred Time

Today we live in a secular age because sacred time has evaporated, even for devoted believers. For even the pietistic, Jesus is in our hearts, communicating with and affecting our individual wills while we live within the speed of modernity and its thirst for continued acceleration. We live in a secular age because time itself has been emptied of the sacred. This makes the church, and its keeping of and attending to the fullness of gathered time, unnecessary. And this unnecessariness unmoors the church, leading us to wonder what the church is for at all.

This stripping of sacred time gives us further insight into why trying to change the church can lead the congregation into depression (*la fatigue d'être eglise*). The church is constituted, from the beginning, to keep sacred time in one way or another. But when time is emptied for the sake of speed, the church loses a fundamental purpose. To say that the church must change is to assert that in the vacuum of sacred time, the church must no longer make a claim about time but instead concede to cultural time.[15] It must change and catch up.

15. This is most acute in Protestantism. Taylor has taught us that the devotion of the Reformers created the conditions for this unbelief, this ending of sacred time. Protestantism secularizes time, not by limiting the church's power, but by trying to make all time sacred, even that of the workers and warriors. The worker and warrior are to be priests even in times of harvest and war. The ability

Catch up to what? Stripped of any sense of the sacred, and simply seeking more speed, it's hard to say. Merely to catch up, to go fast, is the plea, so that the church can be perceived as relevant. In a secular age, where time is hollowed and sacred time is only a memory (frozen in tourist sites like Chartres or Durham Cathedral), change is a high good in itself (it is made good by the new keepers of time). But thus conceptualized, time has no real end or aim. Change for change's sake is the goal. We are reaching for change after change, always wanting something new, usually by disregarding or forgetting the past. It's no wonder my friend felt stale. We are now aerodynamic enough to go fast for the sake of always chasing something new, and changing again for something even newer.

Instead of keeping time, now the church is always behind time, feeling the constant pinch to speed up and change. This change is not necessarily for the sake of anything. Or, if there is something, it is often for the sake of the congregation's own existence. Conceding to the secular age, we claim that the church must change, running faster for the sake of outracing decline—to avoid a crisis that is produced and perpetuated by modernity itself. We are very far from a sense of sacred time when we contend that the church's own speed will determine the shape and existence of Jesus's very body on earth.

It is no longer the church that, in keeping time, tells all other cultural institutions vying for ultimacy that they are on the clock, that a time is coming when they will be no more, that indeed Jesus's return is coming in time, bringing the ultimate fullness and gathering of time.

Such days are over, though thinkers such as Walter Brueggemann have reminded us that they shouldn't be.[16] Things have flipped, and now the church must listen as bankers, tech innovators, woke young adults, and all sorts of entrepreneurs tell the church it had better hurry. It had better speed up—not to the fullness of sacred time but to an accelerating time. If the church doesn't, if it is unable to change, the assumption is that it will be no more.

The apologetic has turned 180 degrees. Now the church, not the empire, worries that its own time-based prophesies might not be true. The early church said to the empire, "Bow to the sacred time of the once-dead and now-alive Jesus Christ! Attend to the time of the Spirit!" Even in the early church's feeble weakness, it said, "Repent or be lost in eschatological time." Today the hedge fund managers and Silicon Valley executives say to the church, "Run and change, or be lost in the wave of disruptive newness that is coming!" Looking

of all time to be sacred creates the conditions—when met by other changes—for a world in which Silicon Valley becomes the new timekeeper of human existence.

16. See, e.g., Brueggemann, *Mandate to Difference: An Invitation to the Contemporary Church* (Louisville: Westminster John Knox, 2007).

up from their phones, they say, "Innovate or die!" "Speed up or disappear" is their immanent-frame-bound prophesy.

Too many congregational and denominational leaders concede to this significant switch without any pushback. They do so because we need *some* entity to keep time. In our secular age, Silicon Valley is the new Avignon. Those keeping time are no longer priests and monks, but hedge fund managers and tech executives. Their timekeeping is hyperaccelerated, where the highest good is disruption that eliminates and forgets the past for the sole good of something new.[17] Facebook's internal motto is "hack," meaning disrupt for the sake of the new.[18] "Hack" is itself a moral horizon that concedes that time is only for speeding up. The timekeeping of Silicon Valley is fused with material technology, but it seeks more. Its technology affects our social lives, reforming our ways of living and the very pace of our lives. Silicon Valley is the Vatican of an accelerated modernity. It keeps time for every entity that wants to survive and thrive. It makes us cringe to think about how the church, in the *ancien regime*, shouted, "Convert or die!" But we nod and fall in line when Silicon Valley shouts, "Innovate, change, or die!"

Modernity does something to time. Time is made into something different. I learned this in the other class all freshmen had to take: Creativity in the Fine Arts. I learned it in an art class by overhearing a passive-aggressive argument.

17. For this very argument, see Robert Pogue Harrison, *Juvenescence: A Cultural History of Our Age* (Chicago: University of Chicago Press, 2014). See also his insightful review of the HBO show *Silicon Valley*: "The Children of Silicon Valley," *New York Review of Books*, July 17, 2014, https://www.nybooks.com/daily/2014/07/17/children-silicon-valley.

18. Zuckerberg began as a hacker, and Facebook's street address is 1 Hacker Way. Facebook's original motto was "Move Fast and Break Things," though its current iteration is "Move Fast and Please Please Please Don't Break Anything." "Facebook's New Motto: 'Move Fast And Please Please Please Don't Break Anything,'" *Halting Problem* (blog), May 21, 2017, https://medium.com/halting-problem/facebooks-new-motto-move-fast-and-please-please-please-don-t-break-anything-8aefdd405d15.

PART 2

examining
congregational
despondency;
our issue is time

5

when time isn't what it used to be

what's speeding up time?

Creativity in the Fine Arts (CIFA) was taught by professors from the theater, art, and music departments. A requirement for all first-year students, it was painful for reasons other than the heavy reading load. Looking back on it twenty-five years later, I think I'd actually enjoy this course now. But at the time it was a major snoozefest. We all hated it, and most of us slept through it, hiding in the corners of the auditorium lecture hall to snooze through the dark slides of fine art. I can remember literally nothing from the course content—zero! Which makes those monthly student loan payments sting even more.

But one thing I can remember. It had come back to me while talking to my friend in Kansas City. One morning, I somehow arrived early to this 8:00 a.m. class. While sitting quietly in the front row and trying to stay awake, I overheard a conversation between the two lecturing professors that day, one from the music department and one from the art department.

"I have no time," the disheveled art professor said.

The music professor only nodded absently. It was clear this was going to be a one-sided conversation.

"This feels different," continued the art professor, annoyed that his colleague wouldn't entertain his musings. "I've been at this for thirty-five years and this is the fastest semester of them all. Each semester seems to go faster, but now it feels like we hit light speed."

He paused, and then he was ready to go fully philosophical. "What do you think? Do you think there is something happening in the universe to speed us all up? Because I really think that time is going faster—like objectively. I don't think it's just *my* perception. It's going faster. Maybe with quantum clocks we could discover that we're caught in a spiral where time is quickening. Maybe this happens as the universe expands?"

The music professor was not one for such thoughts. He responded as if talking to an eight-year-old. "I don't know. I don't think things work like that. I think that's just your perception. It's just the end of the semester talking."

Just before class started, the art professor responded, determined to get the last word. "I don't think so! I think we're entering a crisis. I think our planet or galaxy is speeding up and will be knocked off-kilter soon. Then all this crap won't matter, but go ahead and tell us about Mozart."

What Speeds Up Time?

One of Germany's oldest universities (Friedrich-Schiller University of Jena, founded in 1558) is home to one of the world's top social theorists, Hartmut Rosa. Rosa is a star in the German-speaking world. (Less so in the English-speaking world, but this might change soon.) Rosa's work on time and acceleration has determined much of what I've said in the earlier chapters. While Rosa is officially a sociologist, his interests have taken him onto larger philosophical ground. As Rosa began thinking about time, speed, and modernity, Charles Taylor became central to his thought. Rosa wrote his first book on Taylor in 1998, called *Individual Identity and Cultural Praxis: The Political Philosophy of Charles Taylor.*[1] Since those early days, Rosa has seen his task as answering and developing the challenges that Taylor raises.

Rosa articulates the acceleration of modernity. Individual identity and culture itself have been formed and molded to deal with the acceleration of time. Rosa shows how speeding up molds our cultural realities by affecting our sense of identity, even shifting our sense of the good life. This leads Rosa to see three interlaced, interconnected, and mutually penetrating dimensions that are the source of our speed-up: technological acceleration, acceleration of social life, and acceleration of the pace of life (we'll explore each of these in the next few chapters).

If the art professor had made his claim about time to Rosa, I imagine that Rosa would have responded, "Well, yes, indeed, I do think time is accelerating.

1. The German title is *Individuelle Identität und kulturelle Praxis: Politische Philosophie nach Charles Taylor.*

For whole societies, things are going faster, and we can feel that acutely in our own lives. But I don't think this has anything to do with the universe. There are some things, like the orbit of planets, that we can't speed up, so I don't think it's particles or the three dimensions of space that are speeding up. Rather, the dimensions that are speeding up our world are technology, social change, and the pace of life. All three of these dimensions are connected, which is why you can actually feel the quickening, and know it is a much faster pace than it was thirty-five years ago. It's not just that you personally are busier, and moving faster, though undoubtedly you are. Rather, it's our whole societal and cultural lives that are accelerating!"

If technology, social change, and the pace of life are the cause of our speeding up, then the church cannot get stuck in just imagining change in one of those three modes, assuming it doesn't affect the others. Neither can we fail to see how each of these three are interlaced. What opens the church to despondency is that it is always trying to catch up, and we envision catching up as taking place inside or alongside technological change. Yet technological change is never disconnected from social change—and the timekeepers of Silicon Valley know this, which is what gives them such hubris, believing that a new app can change the world.

The church seeking the speed of technological change will open itself up to an acceleration of social change and the pace of life, because they are inextricably linked. As we've seen in chapters 2 and 3, calling congregations to do the work of catching up will affect the pace of life of the pastoral staff and lay members. When one dimension speeds up, the others must follow, even if dragged in a wake of acceleration. When the pace of life cannot match technology and social change, fatigue produces a personal or congregational depression. There'd be no risk of *la fatigue d'être eglise* if the technological changes in the church's models and programs didn't tax the pace of life and open us up to new social transitions. This fatigue in the pace of life is what my friend felt, making everything stale. The chase of the new made the life of ministry feel flat.

Ultimately, few church leaders, consultants, or denominational officials have seen that calling the church to catch up to technological acceleration will have a deeper impact than just making the church more culturally relevant. Accelerating in the technological dimension will result in shifting the moral norms (social change) and the speed of our daily lives (pace of life), offering new conceptions of fullness. If we're not careful, this fullness will be busyness.

When consultants and young pastors speak of the church needing to change—to catch up—they often justify this by pointing to technology. Or at the least they use the technological speed-up as evidence for why the church needs to propel itself to a new speed and seek change. It's assumed that in a social media world birthed from new technologies, the church needs innovative and fresh forms.[2] They may be right; the congregation may need new forms. But these new forms will be fundamentally flawed, perpetuating the false fullness of busyness and further ostracizing sacred time, if we don't examine more closely the three dimensions of speed increase, seeing their interconnection. We need to ask, *What is innovation and freshness inside the acceleration of modernity itself?*

Following Rosa, we'll try to do what the music professor wouldn't: explore the dimensions of our speeding up and how these dimensions are interconnected and interdependent. Doing so will help us understand the staleness that my friend experienced and the congregation-wide depression the pastor in North Dakota articulated.

———

As we move into this first dimension of acceleration—technological acceleration—we have to face a crisis: technology fries your brain!

2. Many authors have pointed this out. Examples would be Clint Schnekloth, *Mediating Faith: Faith Formation in a Trans-Media Era* (Minneapolis: Fortress, 2014); Keith Anderson and Elizabeth Drescher, *The Digital Cathedral: Network Ministry in a Wireless World* (Harrisburg, PA: Morehouse, 2015); and Pete Ward, *Liquid Church* (Eugene, OR: Wipf & Stock, 2013). Ward's ecclesiology is much deeper than just claiming that technology changes things. It is robust theologically and culturally. However, it is the distributed nature of late modernity, thanks mainly to its technology, that ignites his imagination. See also Ward, *Liquid Ecclesiology: The Gospel and the Church* (Leiden: Brill, 2017); and Ward, *Participation and Mediation: A Practical Theology for the Liquid Church* (London: SCM, 2008).

Even large institutions have supported this kind of catching up, for example the Lilly Endowment (innovation) and the Church of England (with Fresh Expressions). Andrew Dunlop provides a brief overview of Fresh Expressions: "The Fresh Expressions organization defines fresh expressions as: 'new forms of church that emerge within contemporary culture and engage primarily with those who don't 'go to church.'" Dunlop, *Out of Nothing: A Cross-Shaped Approach to Fresh Expression* (London: SCM, 2018), 8.

6

when brains explode

Fried brains is a ubiquitous crisis in modernity. In the first years of the new millennium, amid spiking cell phone use, stories of brain tumors ballooned. It became a legitimate fear that holding this technological breakthrough to your ear for hours at a time would fry your brain. That crisis, it turns out, didn't have staying power. The invention of the iPhone in 2007 by Apple—one of the reigning timekeepers—moved our phones away from our heads. Fewer people were holding phones to their ears for long periods, but everyone was carrying one in their pocket. It became much better (faster) to text, keeping multiple conversations going, while multitasking and doing other things, like posting videos to a social media site to reach hundreds or thousands in a split second. But the fear of fried brains remains. Now we worry that too much screen time will turn our children's brains to mush. It seems that fried brains is a modern crisis rerun.

Though sacred time is not inherently local (it is, after all, the meeting of eternity in time), time is more easily seen as eternal and sacred when it is local. Times of labor and war were bound tightly in a certain locale. In the age of mobilization, Paul Revere is a hero because he raced across these different locales to put all the New England villages on the same clock of readying for battle. But even in Thomas Jefferson's post-revolution America, what

63

mattered was the time of the local village and farm. Time was not based on the sacred but on the laws of gravity. When the sun was at its highest, it was noon. While the sacred was evacuated from colonial village time, the village itself remained sealed in its own time. It's hard for us to imagine, but there was simply no reason to coordinate clocks across space even with towns as close as fifty or a hundred miles apart.

It took too long to cross this space to be concerned about the coordination of time. Carl Honoré provides some concrete data: "In the early 1880s, for instance, New Orleans was twenty-three minutes behind Baton Rouge, eighty miles to the west. When no one could travel faster than a horse, such absurdities hardly mattered." Who cared if it was 10:45 in Minneapolis, 10:55 in Duluth, and 11:05 in Madison? There was no direct and immediate way to talk to those in Duluth and Madison anyway. Because we moved much slower, timekeeping was far from precise.[1]

The coordination of clocks became necessary only when time was able to be accelerated and distance was able to be traversed at a rapid pace. It wasn't until 1883 that America standardized its clocks, producing the five time zones. That's less than 140 years ago! It wasn't until the technological breakthrough of the railroad that this even became necessary.[2] The railroad made it possible to cross 130 miles at a pace that made it necessary for Minneapolis and Duluth to be on the same clock.[3] Technology changed the pace of life, which in turn shifted our social lives and the very way we understood ourselves in the world. But this is where we get back to fried brains.[4]

As the railroad arrived and sped up our lives, it became a major fear, mirroring the cell phone, that our brains were in danger. There was serious thought that the human brain couldn't handle speeds above twenty-five miles

1. Honoré, *In Praise of Slowness: Challenging the Cult of Speed* (San Francisco: HarperOne, 2004), 26.
2. James Gleick explains further: "Railroads demanded punctuality—they forced people to be 'on the clocker' or even 'on time.' Until they could ride on trains, few people traveled fast enough to notice clocks set differently at their destination. It took telegraphs and telephones to synchronize clocks separated by hundreds of miles. In a networked world, time as a universal, ticking away everywhere in unison, seems normal, but to the nineteenth century, railroad time came as a shock—an unwelcome side effect of technology. . . . With the century ending, some towns and cities resisted the onslaught of precise and standardized railroad time. It was not until the end of World War I that the United States codified standard time in the law." Gleick, *Faster: The Acceleration of Just About Everything* (New York: Pantheon Books, 1999), 44.
3. The telegraph also made commerce possible across space, making it even more imperative that clocks be standardized.
4. For a stirring philosophical history of the railroad, see Albert Borgmann, *Crossing the Postmodern Divide* (Chicago: University of Chicago Press, 1992), chap. 2.

per hour.[5] It appears that when technology produces the increase in speed that modernity longs for, though we welcome the speed-up, we worry it will fry our brains. We worry that the technology we desire will destroy us. This is because the increase in speed affects more than just our technology.

The art professor in the previous chapter worried that time was speeding up at the cosmological level, as if the universe were running hotter and faster. This might be an interesting sci-fi movie, but it is more likely that the art professor was experiencing a different kind of speeding up. He was right that something is happening. Time is speeding up. It's more than just his perception. This speeding up is a fundamental social reality. It is as objective as it is subjective, as Hartmut Rosa will show us. Yet the art professor was wrong on what exactly is speeding up. Worries over fried brains show us where this speeding up is occurring. We fear for our brains because the speed-up is happening at the technological level. We fear for our brains because this technological speed-up affects much more than the material functions of our lives. It has a broader impact on us.

Technological Acceleration

Rosa defines technological acceleration as "the intentional speeding up of the *goal-directed* processes of transport, communication, and production."[6] We worry that our brains can be fried when our bodies are thrust through time and space by the acceleration of technology. It's the hidden technological power to communicate across massive space at such rapid speed, with no cords or power lines, that makes it plausible that brain tumors are coming.

Technological breakthroughs and modernity go together. If modernity is speed, then technology is one of the dimensions that produces that speed. Our direct experience with technology—through communication, transportation, and production—speeds up our lives. The art professor sensed that something had changed and he was going faster. He was, and it was because of his interactions with communication, transportation, and production. It's not just that he was getting older, both in body and in technological savvy, making it feel as though the world were passing him by. It's also that the components (transportation, communication, and production) of technology have fundamentally increased their speed.

5. Gleick, *Faster*, 44.
6. Hartmut Rosa, *Alienation and Acceleration: Towards a Critical Theory of Late-Modern Temporality* (Malmö, Sweden: NSU Press, 2014), 16 (emphasis original).

These three components that make up technological acceleration have been empirically accelerating. And not just by degree but exponentially. James Gleick, discussing the frantic race of the computer hardware business, points to Moore's law. "The semiconductor pioneer Gordon Moore predicted in 1965 that chip density—and thus all kinds of computing power—would double every eighteen months or so. This has been correct. Moore's law codified our lightning speed-up in the pace of technological change."[7] Rosa discusses "an example from the history of innovation diffusion: the period from the invention of the radio at the end of the nineteenth century to its distribution to 50 million listeners lasted 38 years; the television, introduced a quarter of a century later, needed only 13 years to achieve this, while the Internet went from the first to the 50-millionth connection in barely 4 [years]."[8] This is an objective speed-up! The acceleration of technology creates a wake that pulls us all into it. The accelerating speed of technology had multiplied over the art professor's thirty years of teaching. The innovations, particularly in communication, speed things up radically.

It would be hard for us to think of technological innovation—or any innovation—as not tied to speed. To be innovative is to produce a breakthrough into something new, and this new thing is often tied to increasing speed in transportation, communication, and production.[9] To be innovative is to welcome a moral conception that honors the new over the old. I'll unpack this further below, but for now it's important to see that if we're not careful, innovation can even denigrate the past (and the slow, substantive moral traditions that nurtured it).

Silicon Valley is the timekeeper of society, and its clock is not the sacred time of past traditions and slow moral formation but the heightened race

7. Gleick, *Faster*, 77.
8. Rosa, *Social Acceleration: A New Theory of Modernity* (New York: Columbia University Press, 2015), 75.
9. It's hard for us to see innovation as even existing before modernity. It's not that people didn't do or create new things. They did, but they did so outside the moral horizon of innovation and the idea of the new as a fundamental good. People stumbled onto the new, even welcomed it, but there was no drive for the new as a good. It was better to trust the past tradition than to aim for the new. And no one had a conception that the old was worse—less good—than the new. The popular dimension of technology was not in place until the seventeenth century, when the moral sense of the new came to be. Of course, technology existed before then. But this desire for advance, like the pointed arch in architecture, was for a different moral horizon than just a drive for the new—it sought to build a space where time and eternity could cohabitate. The point of these buildings, such as Durham Cathedral, wasn't to create something innovative and new but to house something holy, in this case Cuthbert's saintly bones. The old had power. The new needed to protect the old. When technology becomes a core dimension of accelerated modernity, innovation and the new take on a different moral horizon.

to innovate something new and disrupt what has been. Innovation is Silicon Valley's hypergood, as Charles Taylor would call it. The new has its own value, not only in being unique or original but also in being first (*Shark Tank* and *Dragons' Den* are proof that many products rely on their ability to go fast and blitz the market). Therefore, if innovation is about the new, then we must see that the new makes moral claims, asserting that being first is a high good. Competition and speed go together: the modern economy is built on the technology of acceleration.[10]

A Convenience That Produces Guilt

Innovation doesn't always feel like competition, even if this is the underlying code in the technological dimension of an accelerated modernity. For instance, we seek technological breakthroughs for the sake of convenience. A meditation app, for instance, at first blush seems to be an innovation for the sake of slowing down and taking a break from rushed competition. This supposed purpose even gives the creators of the app some moral ground for producing the innovation. The creator of the app plays the game of accelerated production but feels morally superior because it's for meditation, not consumption. But this falls apart. Push deeper and we see something very different.

The point of the app was to make meditation convenient, able to happen anywhere, with fewer slowing frictions such as carrying a book, or seeking a guru, or finding a community. This convenient new app allows meditation to happen quickly, not costing too much in time. You can now meditate at work amid the stressful rush to produce. The innovation of a meditation app allows for the quick convenience of dealing with acceleration itself. It doesn't, however, promise to shift people away from the need for speed and the potential staleness that speed produces. It doesn't oppose acceleration, but it does provide a way to quickly cope with the rushing pace of modernity.

A meditation app can be a convenient way to cope with *Zeitkrankheit* (the German word for "time sickness"). Using the app is like a dose of medicine, like a few aspirin to get us back to speed, maybe even go faster. That's why tech companies such as Google and Yahoo! have meditation rooms on-site. Their employees particularly need convenient ways to deal with *Zeitkrankheit*

---

10. Richard Sennett explains how speed got into the economy. He tells a powerful story about how military forms shaped business in the late nineteenth century. This was coupled with a shift to shareholders, who wanted short-term returns, as opposed to long-term results. This had the effect of compressing the present, which will become a major theme for us. See *The Culture of the New Capitalism* (New Haven: Yale University Press, 2006), 20–27, 38–42.

because they're keeping time for the whole of society. They're the hare on the stick that sets the race pace—the very experience of time—for us all.[11]

Even if you're not one of these Silicon Valley technological timekeepers, they've produced a convenient app for you to cope with the time sickness of technology. And so we take our medicine, conceding that a *new* dose of technology will be the best medicine for our time sickness induced in the first place by technological acceleration (the vicious circle again). Accelerating time through technology is both our burden and yet somehow our savior, or so we imagine.

It is no wonder that our deepest nightmares are linked to technological acceleration. All recent dystopias and even superhero movies have their plot tensions and plausibility structures in technology. Black Panther receives his power not from a supernatural force but from the deposit of vibranium found in Wakanda. Vibranium is a raw material that produces amazing technological breakthroughs, but if this technology gets into the wrong hands, then a dystopia will dawn, and so Wakanda must remain hidden. Like Iron Man's, Black Panther's power is technology.

Inside this circle of technology being both the cause of our sickness and our best medicine, it's no wonder we assume technology is both our prime hope and our most direct threat. The encompassing frame of immanence (living in the immanent frame) is made plausible by technology itself. Technology so fully frames our lives that we can only assume both our greatest evil and our highest hope inside its movements.[12] Technology replaces transcendence as the source of hope, evil, and harmony.[13]

Technology's continued acceleration keeps us from revolting against the reductions of the immanent frame. It feels exciting, almost spiritual, to get something technologically new and advanced. Apple even created a breakthrough

11. Hubert Dreyfus and Sean Kelly discuss this conundrum of technology in *All Things Shining: Reading the Western Classics to Find Meaning in a Secular Age* (New York: Free Press, 2011), 214–16.

12. Taylor discusses the impact of technology on Western society, drawing out its legacy from the Enlightenment and its opposition to the romantic urge to embrace nature instead of possessing it. Taylor, *Hegel and Modern Society* (London: Cambridge University Press, 1979), 68–72. In light of Taylor's comments, it is interesting how Silicon Valley fuses the rationalist technological pursuit to control nature with a romantic assertion about interconnection, doing no evil, and giving us outlets to tell our stories and be our unique selves. Silicon Valley is so powerful because of its ability to romanticize (in a technical philosophical sense) while affirming the Enlightenment rationalist desires for production and mastery of nature. Silicon Valley is a rigid rationalist in a romantic hoodie. It moves back and forth between seeking to dominate nature and somehow being pro-nature.

13. See Rosa, *Social Acceleration*, 146–48, for more on how technological acceleration is connected to moral vision.

in the 1980s, and then again in the 2000s, by combining technology with Buddhist-inspired simple design. Apple was the first to recognize that the pure power of computing is not as impactful as combining the moral pull of technology's need for speed with art. Apple invites the artist and teacher to shift off of the past moral traditions, which are slow and take time, and embrace the benefits of technological speed. This feels exciting because it produces a conversion in our ways of being in the world. We feel a fullness because we're moving fast. Yet the conversion is not to the grace of sacred time or the slow pedagogies of moral visions but to acceleration itself, to a fullness of busyness with more connections, more reach, more access.

When we can't keep up with technological acceleration, we feel something we shouldn't. We sense something that is supposed to be old and foreign, unable to haunt us. We feel something that shouldn't be there: guilt. Speed can create guilt in many forms, but technological acceleration creates a unique flavor of guilt. Technology promises us a free zone where only speed and convenience are important. Technology seeks innovation beyond older moral traditions and structures, throwing them off for the sake of acceleration. But what we didn't expect, the fatal error in the whole system—like the thermal exhaust port in the Death Star[14]—is that the fullness of technological busyness cannot relieve this creeping, heavy guilt.

The more we speed up, the more we feel like we can't do it right, can't take advantage of all the convenience and opportunities, can't find the benefits of all these connections and avenues to curate and broadcast a truly unique identity. There is so much more available, yet not enough time for it all, though we are taking every step to speed up. We feel particularly guilty because others—those elite timekeepers with their flashy phones, witty Twitter accounts, and techno fashion—appear to be doing better, going faster, and flourishing inside the technology acceleration.

This same phenomenon, of technology being both the problem and the solution, occurs in our ecological crisis. The birth of modernity, with the arrival of the machine, led us to release poisonous fumes into the atmosphere. But when we think of what will save us from the polluting machines of technological acceleration, our horizons of hope take us back to technology itself (electric cars, solar panels, and so on). Technology is both the reason for our crisis and the only hope to solve it (the vicious circle again).

Both those who resist and those who support environmental restrictions have embraced the acceleration of technology. Those against the restrictions claim they will bottleneck the acceleration of production. It's bad for the

14. Yep, that's a Star Wars reference.

economy because it does something immoral within technological acceleration: it forces slowdown and undercuts growth. For such people, slowdown is fundamentally opposed to the good of acceleration. They even imagine slowdown as evil—the very enemy of the good of acceleration. They'd rather choke to death on hot fumes than slow down. In their mind it is better (good-er) to die than slow down production. (Rosa is right: you can never escape the explicit or hidden moral conceptions in our views of modernity.)

Those on the other side, who believe environmental restrictions are necessary, are not free from the speeding up of technology. Technology got us into this wicked problem, and yet they believe technology will save us. Our only hope is to speed up to the innovation of electric cars, solar panels, and solar paint. For the most part, both sides live out of a similar logic of acceleration, never doubting that we should technologically speed up.

But all of us wonder if speeding up will fry our brains, or burn up what makes us human.

7

minding the time

why the church feels socially behind

Back in Kansas City, I woke up the next morning (after dinner with my old college friend) ready to present to a group of denominational pastors. I arrived early at the church, set up my computer, and chatted with dozens of pastors who had come for this day of training. Before my presentation, a man from the organizing committee came on stage to pitch the next gathering in two months.

"We as congregations need to do better. We're losing so much—members, young adults, money, but ultimately people's time," he says.

My eyes widen when I hear "time."

He continues, "We can feel bad about this. Or we can innovate. This could be an exciting time because we can make our church—even this gathering!—a hub of innovation. That's good news to me! In two months we'll have a great presentation to address this. It's called 'New Strategies for Assessing and Accelerating the Impact of Your Congregation.'[1] It's going to help us innovate, folks!"

1. This presentation title was used by an international speaker at the Presbytery of the Twin Cities Area in 2018.

I almost spit out my water when he says "accelerating." I look around the room, wondering if this is a prank. Maybe Hartmut Rosa is here to punk me.

"At our next gathering we'll also be talking about young adults. We need to realize that so much is changing so fast in the social lives of young adults. If the church doesn't change with it, then those young adults won't come. They care about social issues. We need to innovate, and that means socially too. Honestly, if the church doesn't change I think we're just being hypocrites."

Looking out at the pastors in the room, I see that a few are nodding excitedly in anticipation, but most look tired, as if Ambien just got vaporized and pumped through the air-conditioning ducts. It sure looks like *Zeitkrankheit*, the time sickness caused by acceleration. I'm not confident that this advertised presentation will help. Sure, it offers a new technological acceleration that promises to escalate production and impact. But for most of these pastors, just the thought of it produces a depressing guilt, a call to master another strategy they probably can't. It will leave them in the dark shadow of supposedly knowing what will accelerate their congregation's impact (innovation) but lacking the energy or skill (or luck) to pull it off.

Acceleration of Social Life

To engage in society is to live with some corporate sense of shared time. Our sense of time is a social construction indelibly fused with our social lives.[2] Our social lives fundamentally shape our sense of time. Our sense of time is always shared and therefore constructed in and through social practices.

A form of time exists outside even our shared human minds.[3] The universe has existed, and therefore has been in time, for almost 14 billion years. The big bang theory claims that the universe is not timeless, unlike what Aristotle thought. Having a distinct bang into existence means that the universe has some relation to time. And all but 200,000 years of this huge sea of time has been without human consciousness. Only in the last 12,000 to 15,000 years have there been societies that produce thick and stretching constructs of time, doing things like having festivals, marking the passing of moons, creating calendars,

2. I'm affirming a weak social construction. See Christian Smith, *What Is a Person?* (Chicago: University of Chicago Press, 2010), 122.

3. Following critical realism, I'm asserting that time is an ontological structure that is more than any human epistemological category. Humans do not create time; nevertheless, any sense of time, and how it affects our shared lives, is socially constructed. For more, see Margaret Archer, Andrew Collier, and Douglas Porpora, *Transcendence: Critical Realism and God* (London: Routledge, 2004); and Margaret Archer, *Being Human: The Problem of Agency* (London: Cambridge University Press, 2000).

inventing clocks, organizing time zones, and creating flight schedules. It's only in these last 15,000 years that the universe has had the kind of creatures who could count the years that the planet and its universe have been in existence.[4]

Though time is outside of human minds (it's not a complete invention of human consciousness), it is nevertheless only human beings who count years. In other words, when we say that the universe is 14 billion years old, we mean that, from within the human constructs of time, the human capacities for knowing and reasoning mark that the universe is 14 billion earth years old.

It's important to say it this way, because Einstein taught us that cosmological time is relative. Time can act differently at different places in the universe. But we can describe this only from within the shared constructs of time we've built from within our own human experience of time. For instance, we assert that a year is the time it takes for the earth to orbit the sun. The earth would orbit the sun with or without human minds to count its circling.[5] Therefore, in a sense, time would exist without human minds. But there would be no one to call this a "year," no one to find meaning in counting the number of orbits they have been in love or without a loved one.

It is only human minds that connect the orbit with making meaning and counting time—and most importantly, using time to shape and order our social lives. Inside time we create norms and ways of life. We always concede that some structure, institution, or collective keeps time for our social lives, because we can only have time through rituals and practices, giving meaning to the feeling of one, or ten, or a lifetime of orbits. The art professor couldn't accept the music professor's explanation that this sense of speeding up was just his perception. He knew it was more. He felt the whole of his social life shifting to a higher gear.

When Technology and Our Social Lives Meet

When the innovation of technological acceleration meets our social lives (e.g., in trains and cell phones), we begin to worry. There is no way to embrace the innovative goods of technological acceleration and not have it torque the shape of our social lives. If technological acceleration speeds up communication, transportation, and production, it will in turn affect our shared sense of our social lives, indelibly shifting the practices and norms by which we

4. Assuming there is not conscious—advanced—life on other planets, which there might be. For more on the universe becoming conscious of itself, see John Polkinghorne, *Quarks, Chaos, and Christianity: Questions to Science and Religion* (London: Crossroad, 2005), 44.

5. Johannes Kepler taught us long ago that the earth doesn't *circle* the sun but rather that earth's orbit is more of an *oval*. Circling just sounds better.

live. This is why the announcement from the front of the stage, shared at the beginning of this chapter, intuitively connected accelerating a congregation's impact with the need to reach young adults by accelerating social change.[6]

This connection between technological acceleration and the acceleration of social life happens because these three components (communication, transportation, and production) of technological acceleration are inextricable from social life. We cannot have a social life without communication, transportation, and even production.

Human beings are fundamentally social. We are unable to extract ourselves from communities, clans, and societies (though we can try). Inside these collectives we can only have our humanity as we communicate, move in and out of each other's lives, and produce at least enough food and shelter to make it through the winter. But to be truly human is not simply to participate in these components but to give them symbolic meaning. We receive our very identities (both collectively and individually) through the narrative meaning of our stories, journeys, and creations.

When our social lives shift, acute pressure is put on the church. Like time, the church is more than a social construction, but nevertheless it is indelibly bound in the practices, imaginaries, and rituals of our social lives.

The pastors and theologians who point to technological acceleration as the raison d'être for the church to seek innovative change are not wrong. But for the congregation to change, it *cannot* just move from technological acceleration to new practices, forms, and functions. To think it can is to miss a larger issue. What should never be overlooked is that because technological acceleration affects the acceleration of social life, it has moral purchase. In order to speed up and innovate, the church not only must change its forms and functions: it must shift its moral horizon, recalibrate its goods.

Without direct awareness that the holders and perpetuators of these innovative goods are the timekeepers of Silicon Valley, we potentially adopt practices and norms that trap more than free the church to be ministers of the living God in the world. Let's see how.

The Moral Ground

Within social acceleration, those who are thriving in innovation (particularly elites) look back and make negative moral valuations of Avignon and its priests (the world built around sacred time). Of course, some (even much) of this is justified. But often Avignon receives negative moral evaluation because its legacy

---

6. Rosa discusses how social acceleration is affected by technological acceleration in *Social Acceleration: A New Theory of Modernity* (New York: Columbia University Press, 2015), 153–60.

faintly remains today—but only faintly (dimly enough to be misunderstood). We can still sense its pull ever so slightly. Some find this faint pull repulsive, seeing its faintness as a warning that it could reappear if not castigated as immoral and too slow to support the freedom of identity construction. Some degrade the *ancien* age, asserting that those priests imposed on our social lives, telling us how and with whom to have sex and telling us the meaning of our work.[7] The overseers of sacred time (it's assumed) restricted our identities. In the shadow of the ethic of authenticity, the old world is cursed or icky.

But the truth is whoever keeps time does so by imposing on our social lives and therefore directs our identities, even in an age of authenticity. We cannot see it, and so we often don't question it. Many of those who lived in Avignon also did not question the priest directing their social lives into sacred time. The openness to transcendence made the priest's mold of the social life more than acceptable. It made great sense to pray, fast, and go to Mass. It was obvious that the human soul was weak and that demons were on the hunt. We find Avignon deeply chafing now only because our moral horizon has shifted in the wake of our changing social lives.

The new timekeepers too are imposing on our social lives.[8] We don't see it because its muzzle fits our moral horizon. For instance, some of Silicon Valley's high goods are the freedom to claim whatever identity you want, to have sex with whomever you wish, and to untether your work from the stiff institutional structures in order to more conveniently pursue production and innovation. This seems like anything but a muzzle! It feels like freedom, allowing us to run loose in the field of openness and tolerance. Never mind that it can only get to this good by constantly and consistently speeding up our lives.

This sense of openness allows Silicon Valley as the timekeeper to fool us (and itself) into thinking that it imposes no moral strictures, other than freedom and openness, on anyone. But that's not possible. To form time, as we've seen, is to shape our social lives, and to shape our social lives is to offer a direct assertion about the moral structure of our lives. It must entail holding up some goods over and against others. Silicon Valley may assert that it

7. It's only less dramatic because of how the age of authenticity is connected to the sexual revolution. Taylor discusses this in *A Secular Age* (Cambridge, MA: Belknap, 2007), 493–500. How we work and what our work means should have more direct impact on us. But the romantic revolution of sexual expression has instead done the most work of clearing the ground for authenticity. Therefore it becomes moralized. Any force that tells you with whom and how to have sex is a tyrant, for our authentic freedom is interconnected to who we want to sleep with, our identities most directly formed through our desire for how and with whom to have sex.

8. It's usually only those who have a very different sense of the good who can recognize that Silicon Valley and others too are imposing a way of life that is just as direct as Avignon but in a much different style.

doesn't impose any moral trajectory except openness to the new. But openness to the new is itself a heavy moral commitment. The freedom to be whomever you wish must follow the moral shape of accelerating innovative newness.[9]

Thus, looking back at *older* moral traditions for your own identity is questionable at best and often completely opposed by the new timekeepers. Freedom for innovation and newness are core moral norms Silicon Valley holds as the timekeeper of society. It opposes all other timekeepers who may find this freedom disorienting in its openness or ultimately flat in its individual, immanent pursuits.

The congregation seeking change through innovation risks opening our social lives to a moral horizon that may deliver a false sense of fullness, a warped conception of humanity, and a flat notion of the yearning of the human spirit. Sacred time was upended and the timekeepers of society shifted away from the church because technological acceleration can never be cordoned off from our social lives. For church leaders to adopt innovation as the frame for birthing the congregation's future, using innovative practices to update the church to meet the accelerating speed of modernity, is to (knowingly or not) shift the shape of our social lives onto a constant accelerating path.

For a stark satirical example of Silicon Valley's moral commitments, watch episode 4 of season 5 of HBO's show *Silicon Valley*. This show has received high critical praise, with many insiders saying it perfectly catches the ethos of Silicon Valley. In this episode, the startup company Pied Piper is discussing whether it should allow a Christian dating app on its network. One of the characters says about life in Silicon Valley, "You can be openly polyamorous and people here will call you brave. You can put microdoses of LSD in your cereal, and people will call you a pioneer. But the one thing you cannot be is a Christian." Being a Christian is a way of life that is too susceptible to looking back and slowing down. Its moral tradition is assumed to be too restricting. Christian faith has a very different conception of communication, transportation, and production than the constant pursuit of new innovation.

9. For a stark example of how this obsession for newness functions in Silicon Valley, allowing for moral shortcoming, see the HBO documentary *The Inventor: Out for Blood in Silicon Valley*. This is the story of Theranos, which was led by Elizabeth Holmes. She so deeply believed that innovation was a good, and newness was worth seeking, that she convinced dozens of venture capitalists to give her hundreds of millions of dollars. And she convinced some of the top politicians, lawyers, and leaders in the US to come on her board, though she had no concrete way of meeting the objectives she sought. Yet the new—innovation and disruption—was such a high good that these powerful people were willing to put "faith" in her. They were acting as stupidly as anyone buying a relic or an indulgence in medieval Europe (there was no seeing to their believing). They were actually the same! They took action in relation to goods that the timekeeper set, seeing their unwise actions as plausible and in accordance with the good the timekeeper pursued. What is faithful is determined by the societal timekeeper's good.

Or it doesn't. Some pastors and Christian leaders seek to get the church up to speed by adopting the moral conceptions of the new timekeepers, affirming that, for instance, sex should be fast and open and that church life should be innovative and seek the new. It's hard to know if this call to match the moral horizon of the new timekeepers will make the church appear more relevant or even more out of place in the acceleration of modernity. But it's no surprise to hear about a pastors conference that champions acceleration and social change.

Nice, Soft Norms

Silicon Valley's direct impact on our social lives makes it our crowned timekeeper, and therefore gives it a sense of power. If Avignon and its priests had their power in our social lives needing to match—at least a few times a year—the pace of sacred time, Silicon Valley can do something similar. They are able to shift and shape our social lives by demanding we match, in one degree or another, the accelerating speed of innovation. They are the ones who create our delight in racing for the new, and this becomes the desire that animates our social lives.

This happens at both the consumer level (racing to get something new) and the identity level ("I'm always seeking to innovate my sense of myself"). The announcement for the upcoming pastors conferences correlated with both of these levels of desire.

Silicon Valley is the powerful timekeeper, not because it nobly refuses to impose on our social lives, but rather because we desire this imposition. Its timekeeping is substantiated, and so powerfully formative, because it matches our pursuits of a good life. Accepting the imminent framing of our lives, we (tacitly) believe that innovation and its craving for the new give our lives meaning and an overall feeling of goodness.[10] Just as the Avignon timekeepers asserted that the Eucharist would save, so the Silicon Valley timekeepers assert, with almost the same strict normativity, that innovation will do the same. Yet Silicon Valley is crowned the new timekeeper not by a transcendent force, or even by the will of a democratic collective,[11] but by its ability to use technology, and its three components, to directly and extensively shape our social lives for what we concede is good. We laud

10. Against this backdrop the Catholic *nouvelle theologie* of France in the middle of the twentieth century (through theologians like Yves Congar [Charles Taylor's favorite], Henri de Lubac, and Hans Urs von Balthasar) sought a return to the sources.

11. Rather, with Facebook we're seeing that its impact on our social practices can destroy democracy, speeding this up to not allow for the kind of deliberation and perspective-taking on which Jeffersonian democracy is dependent.

them by saying, "They are so innovative!" which means that they affect our social lives so deeply that they reorder our forms of communication, transportation, and production.

Silicon Valley has given us the good of making our lives more convenient in all three of these areas. But it has done so by accelerating life to a pace even modernity has never seen. It has given us these goods by speeding up our social lives. Its ability to wield accelerating technologies—which directly affect how we communicate (Facebook, Instagram, Skype, Zoom), move (Uber, Lyft),[12] and produce (the information age of data rather than skilled or unskilled factory production)—quickens the decay rate of social norms.[13]

In speeding up communication, transportation, and production—making them go so fast that the lines between them blur—the norms of our shared social life change quickly. Besides the hypergood of speeding up for new innovation, Silicon Valley has no other real normative structures to offer our social lives. Silicon Valley endorses all forms of social innovation, all ways of seeking freedom and authenticity. The more that norms shift, the more people are open to the new, willing to make innovation a state of their own being. Inside the technological acceleration, any firm norms of social life are softened, allowing them to break down and decay quickly inside the technological acceleration (more on decay rates in the next chapter).

More than likely, most in Silicon Valley aren't concerned, or even reflective, about which norms to uphold and which to downgrade, though they all contend that technological acceleration will disrupt our social lives. They find this exciting. Technological acceleration is never value-neutral, because it interpenetrates social acceleration. And Silicon Valley knows it.

The excitement of being in the tech industry might be the chips, wiring, and algorithms, but for most, it's the ability to affect our social lives, "to change the world," as they say. (Think of Steve Jobs asking John Sculley, then president of Pepsi, in 1983, "Do you want to sell sugar water for the rest of your life, or do you want to come with me and change the world?"[14]) Sure, coding is part of the business, but the real telos, the real pursuit, is to hack our social lives by accelerating our communication, transportation, and production. Facebook would agree. Silicon Valley elites like Apple's Tim Cook and others make

12. Or are these last two better filed under communication? This is part of what the hyperacceleration means. Silicon Valley is so quickly speeding up our social lives that even the boundaries between communication, transportation, and production are blurred.

13. In the parentheticals I'm pointing to only the most obvious ways that it has affected us in these three areas. It is more pronounced if one scratches deeper.

14. For a discussion of this, see Walter Isaacson's biography of Jobs, *Steve Jobs* (New York: Simon & Schuster, 2011). See also Leslie Berlin, *Troublemakers: Silicon Valley's Coming of Age* (New York: Simon & Schuster, 2017).

claims about freedom for authenticity. And yet it appears that authenticity and the drive to disrupt our social lives is not free from corruption and is even evil. Uber was harshly opposed because of sexual harassment allegations against its executives. And Mark Zuckerberg seemed overwhelmingly oblivious to how his own drive for the acceleration of communication could undercut, and even suffocate, other goods necessary for democracy.[15]

We are actually seeing norms in conflict here. Democracy requires communication to slow down to be healthy, but this will be very difficult for Silicon Valley to affirm. Any slowdown is outside its own moral pursuit of always pushing faster into disruptive innovation. To slow down, even for the good of democracy, is to stand in opposition to the accelerated time that Silicon Valley keeps. While the timekeepers of Silicon Valley have a deep sense of how the good of innovation will disrupt our social lives, there is less reflection on how our social norms in turn will be shifted.[16]

The pursuit of newness through innovation is made easier by the norms of our social lives also being in constant flux. We are more receptive to all innovation when our social norms are fluid. When letting go of older social norms, particularly those formed by looking backward (as with Avignon), we are told we're more authentic because we're faster. But as we've seen in the last few years, and any social networking site will reveal, this has not led us to a utopian space free of conflict. Rather, conflict is rife because there are no outside social norms of decorum, humility, and mercy. Those are norms and virtues that are just too slow for a curated self in the world of social acceleration.

The timekeepers of Avignon established firm social strictures based on what was believed to be the eternal law of the transcendent being of God (for Neoplatonists these social forms were so strong that they were earthly forms of eternity itself).[17] By stark contrast, Silicon Valley's norms are soft and porous, and they quickly decay next to the technological acceleration of communication, transportation, and production.

Which brings us to *The Office*. Remember that show? Of course you do. You're probably streaming it right now.

15. In many ways the crisis of the 2016 election shows legitimate issues with how technological acceleration holds a moral place and can be used to smother other goods that democracy needs. It reveals the utopia of Silicon Valley to be a lie. The 2016 election is to Silicon Valley what the Borgia pope is to Rome.

16. And if there is, the fact that they'll change is a good high enough to support it.

17. It is a long argument that I don't have time to rehearse here but nevertheless connects to this point. Michael Gillespie argues that the shift into nominalism around the fourteenth and sixteenth centuries cleared ground for the secular age that Taylor articulates. This move to nominalism does start to soften the rock-hard ground I'm discussing in the above sentence. See Gillespie, *The Theological Origins of Modernity* (Chicago: University of Chicago Press, 2008), 14–45.

8

why *The Office* can't be rebooted

the decay rate of social change

dimension two: acceleration of social life (part two)

I closed my morning session at the denominational continuing education event with a clip of Michael Scott doing something crazy at the corporate office. It connected to a point I was making about what we expect from relationships. But apparently, for at least one pastor in the audience, it got him thinking about the lost world of *The Office*. This pastor approached me afterward with nostalgia written all over his face.

"I miss that show because it comes from a time when you could screw up, say something stupid, and not be completely destroyed on social media. I'm pushing hard for my denomination to change, but sometimes even I feel like it's too fast. Like the jokes that were allowed last week aren't allowed this week. The callout trigger is warp speed. And to be honest, it's hard to keep up. But Michael Scott never had to sweat the constant callout."

I was slightly confused and didn't know how to respond. His words had none of the feel of the guy who peaked in high school and just wanted to return to his letter-jacket days. I can't remember how I responded, but this conversation stuck with me for a while.

To get a handle on why he feels like this and how this contributes to a depressed congregation that risks staleness within its fullness as busyness, we need to look at what Hartmut Rosa calls *decay rates*.

A decay rate, say of organic material like a banana or a corpse, can be measured against the environmental conditions. To figure out a decay rate, we ask, How quickly will a dead mouse decay in the wall if it's hot or cold? Is the rate different if it's stuck in insulation or in earth? But most often, decay rate refers to radioactive material. It's a measurement of how long it takes for the material to lose half its potency, or its half-life. A decay rate, then, is the amount of time it takes something to dissolve in relation to the environmental conditions, to move from being present to being part of the past. It's a way of marking time, a natural clock like the orbit of the earth around the sun.

A decay rate is about time. Applying this concept to our social lives, we can ask, How long is the decay rate of technology and our social norms? How long does it take for what is of the present to be considered of the past (and therefore old)?

Welcome to a Compressed Present

Rosa uses decay rate to explore the acceleration of our social lives in relation to technological and social acceleration. Decay rates of both technology and the norms of our social lives were once much slower. This is because the present is not what it used to be. Our present has been compressed. For instance, the decay rate of a computer compared to a typewriter is much faster. A typewriter took close to a decade to decay from a present—new—device to something old or past. In contrast, it takes a computer only three years max to no longer be new and therefore no longer bound in the present (an iPad is probably half this time).[1] After three short years the computer has decayed and is now a piece of the past.

People sense this intuitively. If someone drops a computer at a coffee shop, they might say, "That was a new computer! It's less than two years old." Or someone might say, "That's embarrassing, but oh well, it's an old computer. It's four years old." This response often has little to do with its operation. The four-year-old computer might work just as well as the two-year-old computer, even if it lacks some new features. But the evaluative measure is not necessarily function but newness, or being *of* the present. Rarely does someone say, when a computer falls at a coffee shop, "Bummer, that was a well-working

---

1. This sense of becoming old, of course, relates to the cost. A computer takes three years to be old because it takes more resources to replace it.

computer." Instead we use the categories of new and old, showing that the new and old distinction has deeper moral significance.

These categories have this moral significance because the new is the now. It's not of the past, nor has the future dawned enough to make it slide into the past. This process of moving from the past to the present into the future is not something we can speed up at a cosmological level. We can't make the sun come up later, keep the future from dawning, or extend the present (though we try with daylight saving time).[2] But this is exactly what happens at the level of technology and social life. In speeding up these two dimensions, the present itself has been compressed. In an accelerated modernity the present is not as long as it used to be, and it's pushing to be ever shorter. No wonder we feel like *The Office* ran a lifetime ago. The art professor at the beginning of chapter 5 is right. Something is indeed speeding up. The present is not what it was at the beginning of his career. He can feel its compression.

Rosa's point is that our technology and social norms have a much faster decay rate because there has been a contraction of the present.[3] We can see how this contraction exists and is always pushing for further compression of the present: just consider the life span of computers, video game systems, and cell phones, which have an even shorter decay rate.

Decay Rate of Technology

Try picking up the first version of the iPhone, released in 2007. I literally own multiple sweatshirts twice its age. But it feels like an artifact in your hand, even though *The Office* was into its third season when it appeared. The 2007 iPhone feels so old, like something from a past age, because in a real sense it is. The iPhone from 2007 has long decayed, replaced by more than a dozen newer versions. Inside the compression of the present, the first iPhone is indeed a relic, bound in the past, taken far away from our regular social lives.

Recently I found my old Sega in a box. The decay rate of game systems and other communication technologies is so quick that it feels much older

2. An interesting exhibit at the German Historical Museum (*Deutsches Historisches Museum*) in Berlin shows some of the first mechanical clocks. The recorded guided tour explains that it wasn't until the invention of mechanical counting and timekeeping machines that people understood that an hour was always an hour. Before, Europeans figured hours were shorter in the winter and became longer in summer—the warm air expanding hours like wood. This shows that an hour is always an hour whether we know it or not, and at the same time that our social imagination affects our sense of time.

3. Rosa is drawing from philosopher Hermann Lübbe in "The Contraction of the Present," in *High-Speed Society: Social Acceleration, Power and Modernity*, ed. Hartmut Rosa and William E. Scheuerman (Happy Valley: Pennsylvania State University Press, 2009), 159–78.

than those sweatshirts from college. The game system feels like an artifact, while the sweatshirts don't, because the former is more central to the pursuit of innovation. Phones and game systems decay much more quickly than sweatshirts in an accelerated modernity where Silicon Valley is the timekeeper.

Of course, the sweatshirt too comes under the evaluative judgment of innovation. We call this fashion. But unlike technological acceleration, fashion can circle back, making my old college hoodie cool again, even in the present. Alas, the game system cannot experience the same fate. It can become cool in a retro kind of way, perhaps at a bar that has all the old game systems. But though it might take on a retro sense of cool, the game system can never again be part of the present. It will be cool because it offers a fun experience with an artifact.

This compression of the present gives Silicon Valley its right to keep time. When our ancestors lived in a world much different than ours (framed by immanence), they had a deep sense that eternity broke into time. Avignon needed to keep time for the present, allowing the divine or the demonic to break through into the long present. Sacred time spilled into present time, delivering meaning. The decay rate of the present was very slow (painfully and even abusively slow at times). It took decades or even centuries for something to be considered old. The moral category of old versus new was actually flipped from what it is in our modern age. Unlike how it is today, the old was trusted because it set the terms for the social lives of the people.

In our world, the present is compressed—and always contracting—but is nevertheless thick in the sense that it allows no divine reality or sense of eternity to break through. This thick immanence is compensated for by the shifting present, always confronted by the new. We can concede to the immanent frame, and the lack of transcendence, because the present has been compressed, making it short. We're distracted in the present from the flatness of our lives, without transcendence, by the fact that our social lives are so accelerated. Though we feel this flat, stale, meaninglessness in the present, it can be avoided by the shortness of the present. This gives us a way to deal with immanence: throw off the decaying present by seeking novelty. We can concede to the immanent frame because modernity has compressed the present, and it keeps us moving so that the burden of meaninglessness is walked off as we enter something shiny and new.

Here, then, is another warning for church leaders seeking innovation as the way for the church to catch up. Innovation is the hypergood of the new, and seeking the new through innovation has the ramification of compressing the present. Compressing the present shortens its life span by upping the decay rate. This means that we always need to be ready to make more innovative changes, never stopping the process of seeking the new. Innovation makes the present too short for us to rest. This is the first hint for why these two dimensions of acceleration (technological and social) affect the pace of our lives and can produce an idolatrous sense of fullness as busyness.

Decay Rate of Social Norms

Computers and game systems are only material examples of the decay rate, touching just on technological acceleration. No doubt technological acceleration can quickly make some of us feel old, as if we're not keeping up with the present.[4] Yet the acceleration of communication, transportation, and production does more than provide new phones, computers, and game systems. By compressing the present in relation to our social lives, it accelerates the decay rate of our social norms.

Particularly over the last few years, as millions of people have accelerated their lives to the speed of social media, we have witnessed a radical shift in what is allowed and what is policed. This is what the pastor who approached me after my session experienced. Try it for yourself: rewatch *The Office*. Its first episode was in 2005, its last in 2013. *This is not that long ago!* Yet the decay rate of social norms is so rapid that the show just couldn't be launched today. Its humor violates too many new social norms. Michael's sexual innuendos, and much of the comedy, are no longer allowed. It has decayed and become part of the past. It's still allowed to be viewed on Netflix, but only because, like many other artifacts, it has a veneer of being old, from a time not yet woke. Steve Carrell himself, when asked about a potential reboot, has admitted that the social norms from a decade ago have so fully decayed that the show simply couldn't work in the accelerated social life of today. The outrage, and therefore the callout, would be too much.[5]

More powerful than the compression of technology, particularly for the congregation, is the decay rate of social norms.[6] As the present becomes more

---

4. I've personally experienced this when watching how my own children use YouTube. YouTube stars and personalities make no sense to me. I use YouTube mainly as a library for DIY jobs, finding just what I need (how to fix the toilet, or maybe an interview with Jason Bateman on the making of *Ozark*). But my children just allow the algorithm to take them where it will, from the room of one personality to the next.

5. See Chris Harnick, "Steve Carell Says *The Office* Revival Won't Work Because Its Humor Is 'Completely Wrong-Minded' Today," E! News, October 11, 2018, https://www.eonline.com /news/976059/steve-carell-says-the-office-revival-won-t-work-because-its-humor-is-complete ly-wrong-minded-today.

6. Jean Twenge shows that the coming generation conceives of the church as old and unable to be in the present when it comes to moral norms. They are going to be the most secular

compressed by the acceleration of modernity, the church seems not only antiquated but immoral in its slow practices of prayer, reading Scripture, and
humble service, as well as in its moral sources in sacred texts and traditions.
The church's use of the slow wisdom of the past seems completely out of place
in the compression of the present and the moral pursuit of identity innovation.

For the church to seek change through innovation, then, is to inseparably
take on certain new moral conceptions that are sanctioned by the timekeepers
of Silicon Valley. It's to enter into the same logic that accelerates the decay
rate of social norms, which often still have some connection to the Christian
tradition. To call the church to innovate without considering the consequences
is a big problem, because when social norms rapidly decay, many people are
inevitably left behind. Our social lives are accelerating to such a degree that
some are left feeling socially and therefore morally *old*, considered a pejora-
tive term by the timekeepers of Silicon Valley. Old means that which is past,
left behind, even morally slow (*slow* being even worse than *old*).[7] Against
the hypergood of innovative newness, what is old needs to be left behind and
forgotten for moral reasons.

There are some who feel like they once had a good sense of the norms and
the shape of social life. But these norms have decayed, and too quickly for
many to keep up. Those falling behind can't even seem to talk right, and are
told their language is no longer appropriate, because the norms they assume
have decayed and are now old. These people are "put on blast" by much
younger people for violating the present social norms by wrongly assuming
that the old, decaying norms are operative.

Moral norms decay and shift at such a rate that once you catch up to one
moral language game, it seems to decay and be replaced by another. You are
always susceptible to being called out (a kind of public shaming done almost
exclusively on social media).[8] Not able to keep up, those who fall behind are
excoriated by much younger people for using old words. They are judged
for possessing an old moral conception that is no longer legitimate in the

---

generation in American history, but this secularization has the moral weight of assuming that
the church needs to be left behind inside the new moral conceptions. See Twenge, *iGen: Why
Today's Super-Connected Kids Are Growing Up Less Rebellious, More Tolerant, Less Happy—
and Completely Unprepared for Adulthood* (New York: Atria Books, 2017), chap. 5.

7. The work of John Swinton (and others) on disability and theology is so important here.
See, particularly, Swinton, *Becoming Friends of Time: Disability, Timefullness, and Gentle
Discipleship* (Waco: Baylor University Press, 2017); Swinton, *Resurrecting the Person: Friend-
ship and the Care of People with Mental Health Problems* (Nashville: Abingdon, 2000); and
Benjamin Conner, *Disabling Mission, Enabling Witness: Exploring Missiology Through the
Lens of Disability Studies* (Downers Grove, IL: IVP, 2018).

8. See Jon Ronson, *So You've Been Publicly Shamed* (New York: Riverhead Books, 2015).

compressed present of acceleration and the quest for identity innovation. For those falling behind, this can feel like an aggressive push out of the present, making some deeply resentful and leading to a culture of contempt.[9] To understand why this happens, we need to step back and look more broadly at how the present is compressed in relation to our social lives.

How Is Our Present Compressed?

Rosa explains that to have a sense of the present, especially at the social level, there must be coherence between experience and expectations. To be in the present is to have some sense that the experiences I possess are reliable for norming my social life. To feel yourself in the present is to have "the horizon of experience and expectation coincide."[10] Or to say it the other way around, when my experience can no longer be expected to deliver me into socially affirmed norms, I'm struck with a sense that I'm old. I'm of the past because my experience no longer helps me anticipate how to be in the world.[11]

This can be disorienting for a forty-two-year-old mother of three. Inside the callout culture that sets the terms for our social norms, she is old, not of the present. Her experience and expectations of social norms are no longer congruent, even by degree. She doesn't *feel* old. She isn't ready to concede that her experience pushes her out of the present. Nevertheless, she is told that she is disconnected from the new social norms. This can be acutely painful, because in an accelerated modernity inside a culture of youthfulness, to be of the past is to not be revered for your wisdom and the perspective of your experience.[12] Rather, her experience is as antiquated and irrelevant as the iPod Nano.

To feel solidly in the present, I have to believe that the experiences that form me help me anticipate and participate in social life. This coherence between experience and expectation produces in me a sense of reliability. I have a sense that I'm squarely in the present only when I feel like my social

9. For a discussion on this, see Arthur Brooks, *Love Your Enemies: How Decent People Can Save America from the Culture of Contempt* (New York: Broadside Books, 2019).

10. Hartmut Rosa, *Alienation and Acceleration: Towards a Critical Theory of Late-Modern Temporality* (Malmö, Sweden: NSU Press, 2014), 18.

11. This can lead to an identity crisis. We can see how identity is connected to our sense of the moral as it's played out in social relationships of discourse. Charles Taylor discusses this in *Human Agency and Language: Philosophical Papers 1* (London: Cambridge University Press, 1999), 34–35.

12. See Stephan Bertman, *Hyperculture: The Human Cost of Speed* (Westport, CT: Praeger, 1998), for more on the compression of the present and the fetish for youthfulness (and the overall lack of wisdom).

life is reliable.[13] I feel congruently part of a social life only if I can know what to expect from it, even anticipate it.

I'm struck with culture shock when I travel to China, because all my present experiences of social norms are of no assistance. I don't know what to expect, even in simple acts like ordering food or catching a train. My experience of social norms in the West is little help in Asia. There is a divide between my experience of social life and my expectation of social life in this new place. What makes this culture shock so uncomfortable is that I keep bumping up against social norms that are moral.

All social norms are always moral. We keep norms because we have some explicit or hidden sense of the good. That's why being called out on social media for holding on to decaying norms is so deeply painful and damaging, even scary, to a pastor who is fighting for innovations of identity. The callout always occurs because someone needs to be exposed for being immoral.[14] The one doing the calling out states that the victimizer is incongruent with the good. They say they did the calling out because X just isn't a good person (never mind that mercilessly exposing others for being *not* good may also make *you* not good).[15]

Back to China: Not only do I feel overwhelmed because I sense a division in the link between my experience and my expectations, but I also experience an inner sense of shock because to violate the norms is to make a moral misstep. Being a visitor usually causes such missteps to be easily forgiven, but this doesn't change my shock. I feel out of place and exposed, painfully aware that my experience and my expectations are not correlated, and therefore I don't have a reliable social world. I'm deeply aware that I'm from another place.

---

13. This could be read as a statement of privilege, but it need not be. Even those pushed out of privileged spaces live with a sense that their experience and expectation are connected. Even in difficult situations they have a sense that their social environment is reliable. Elijah Anderson has touched on this, articulating the moral codes of young African Americans living on Germantown Avenue of Philadelphia. See *The Code of the Street* (New York: Norton, 1999). We can hear such statements even on the street, like "These young bucks play the game differently."

14. Norms in the compressed present don't seem to hold the exposer responsible for doing this exposing for their own pleasure of receiving attention and recognition, and ultimately having no sense of how this exposure will lead to reconciliation and return to the humanity of the one exposed. Rather, the objective is to receive pleasure and fame for righteously exposing the moral violations through the new social norm of calling out and putting someone on blast. It fortifies your own identity, keeping it in the present, assuring you that you're not being passed over, because look at how many people are paying attention to you for speaking up for what's "right"!

15. For stark examples of this logic, see Greg Lukianoff and Jonathan Haidt, *The Coddling of the American Mind: How Good Intentions and Bad Ideas Are Setting Up a Generation for Failure* (New York: Penguin, 2018), esp. chaps. 4 and 5.

9

when sex and work are in a fast present

the church and the decay rate of our social structures

When the pastor in North Dakota said his church was struck with a case of depression, *la fatigue d'être eglise* (the fatigue of being the church), I knew exactly what he meant, because I had lived through *la fatigue d'être séminaire* (the fatigue of being a seminary). Our seminary found itself in a financial crisis in 2012. The faculty was told to speed up: the only way to save the school was to accelerate and innovate. From my perception, rather than generate creative energy, this only caused *Zeitkrankheit*, a time sickness that hovered over us for years. Though we tried new things, we felt like we were falling behind. We were too grieved by what had been, too disoriented from being shoved into this new, compressing future.

The seminary assumed that outside voices were the best medicine for our *Zeitkrankheit*, the most poignant treatment for our *la fatigue d'être séminaire*. Of course, bringing in outside voices created more meetings, and nothing (I mean nothing!) causes *Zeitkrankheit* more than meetings!

I vividly remember sitting in one of those meetings. Demographers from the denomination presented some hard numbers on what was facing the denomination. The idea was that with a better sense of the numbers, we'd be

89

more equipped to create an innovative curriculum. Yet, for most of us, it just increased our *Zeitkrankheit*. The demographers themselves had little hope: the changing—let's call it accelerating—dynamics of production (how we work and fuel our society) and reproduction (how we bring newborn people into our society and into families through sex) had turned against mainline denominations. And they didn't know why, but the statistics were clear. Decline and disappearing resources were our destiny. The demographers could only muster one response: "These are the numbers. We're not sure why, but we're getting demographically hammered. We need to do better."

We probably could do better, I admit. But these frightening demographics didn't seem to be what initially pushed our seminary into *la fatigue d'être séminaire* or any congregation into *la fatigue d'être eglise*. It's not just the loss of numbers; it's how the loss of numbers decreases resources. Yet, as I thought about Hartmut Rosa, I wondered whether *la fatigue d'être* was caused by losses at all. Perhaps *la fatigue* was caused by imagining that the only response to the loss is to accelerate, making up for the loss. After all, it was speeding up, not the loss itself, that led to our seminary-wide *la fatigue*. An accelerated modernity makes growth its high (maybe the highest) good. Growth is the only answer.

Innovation is a willful disposition toward accelerating to meet growth and ward off decline. But innovation itself has a hidden problem, a genetic flaw. Innovation seeks growth and newness as a hypergood. It calls, like a siren, for acceleration.

But the demographers also seemed to be right about the transitions in production and reproduction. Our most basic social institutions (including the denomination and its congregations) had radically shifted. What shifted them was our reevaluation of ways of working and making money (production), as well as our ways of having sex, raising children, and thinking about family (reproduction). More interesting than the numbers was how the goods that rested inside these evolving realities of production and reproduction had shifted, and how the congregation was made to be in deficit because of these transitions. I wondered, What is the sense of the good life in regard to production and reproduction that drives these numbers? And what does this mean for the church?

The Accelerated Decay Rates in Our Social Institutions

In the previous chapter, we saw how mobile phones decay faster than computers, and computers much faster than typewriters. We also saw how the decay rate of social norms compresses the present. This compression causes sudden shifts in our moral horizon, creating deep cultural fissures of conflict about which norms are good and about the overall shape of a good life.

These decay rates of technology and social norms directly affect our societal structures. The acceleration of these social structures radically compresses the present. Rosa believes we can empirically see the contraction of the present by looking at the "institutions that organize the processes of production and reproduction."[1] In other words, changes in work (production) and family/sex (reproduction) reveal that the present has become very short. The demographers in our faculty meeting hoped to show *how* these structures have changed, but they couldn't explain *why*—nor could they say what this does to our sense of the present.

With Rosa and Charles Taylor's help, I'll seek to do just that. But to answer the why—particularly with Taylor's help—we must first look to how production and reproduction (work and family/sex) have evolved. Telling this story will also allow us to see how Silicon Valley becomes our new timekeeper.

Work, Family, and Sex in the Early Church

Throughout human history, our social lives have been framed around work and family. It's hard to imagine human life without these two institutions. Though in late modernity individual freedom and expression has challenged the importance and shape of these structures, modernity has nevertheless been unable to bury them entirely. Thus work and family have remained central, even though humans have lived with many other structures as well. These two have been the most stable, or constant, structures from early agrarian societies to our own day. They've been shifted and reshaped in radically different ways across the millennia, but nevertheless production and reproduction have fundamentally structured our social lives.

Silicon Valley is allowed to be the timekeeper because its moral pursuit of the new fits with our own conceptions of freedom in production and reproduction (work and sex).[2] Avignon's timekeeping seems old and therefore

1. Rosa, *Alienation and Acceleration: Towards a Critical Theory of Late-Modern Temporality* (Malmö, Sweden: NSU Press, 2014), 19.
2. Family endures in our time, but sex has replaced family in some respects. Obsessing over sex reshapes the family for late modernity's moral pursuit of radical freedom. Late modernity wants to separate sex, family, and even reproduction, saying that sex (and even family) has nothing to do with reproduction but with pleasure and identity. Even being married should not assume children—that's for you and your partner to decide. And marriage (or the lack thereof) shouldn't keep you from the freedom of having children. These all *might* be gains, but they are

immoral against the backdrop of innovation because its views of work and sex are very different. Whoever keeps time will determine the moral shape—and the decay rate—of production and reproduction.

For example, in the ancient world, the early church made distinct claims about production and reproduction, which put these tiny households in conflict with the empire. The church claimed, for instance, that a leader should be the spouse of one husband or wife (1 Tim. 3) and that fathers should not abandon their children and should respect their wives (Eph. 5:22–6:9). Household codes were not unusual in the ancient world.[3] But the church's household code prepared families for the coming eschatological advent.

The early church molded the structures of work and family around its eschatological view of time. Some of these New Testament household codes appear in the disputed Pauline epistles. Certain scholars hold that these epistles blunt some of the earlier—genuinely Pauline—eschatological immediacy. Presumably, these household codes were a way of structuring church life now that it appeared that the *parousia* was not coming in that first generation.

Yet this structuring, even of ordinary time, does not upend the church's continued anticipation of Christ's coming. The church keeps time by anticipating the return of Jesus. Unlike in our epoch, this anticipation does not *compress* but *lengthens* the present. Those who are dead are not absent but present in the continued memory of the church community through practices and proclamation.[4] The church community, with the dead, anticipates the coming of Jesus.[5] The dead are still (in the) present because they too are waiting, just like the living and the worshiping.

---

innovations connected deeply to the ethic of authenticity and late modernity's desire for radical freedom. They play a part in compressing the present.

3. Stephen Barton discusses these codes in *The Family in Theological Perspective* (Edinburgh: T&T Clark, 2000), 52–57.

4. Jürgen Moltmann says, "The community of Christ is a community not only of the living but of the dead as well. It is not just a community of 'brothers and sisters'; it is a community of mothers and daughters, and of fathers and sons—or of mothers and sons, and fathers and daughters. . . . So the community of Christ is in him a community of the living with the dead, and of the dead with the living. . . . In this community with Christ the dead are not 'dead' in the modern sense; they 'have a presence.'" Moltmann, *In the End— The Beginning: The Life of Hope* (Minneapolis: Fortress, 2004), 135. Christos Yannaras says something similar, speaking of the Eucharist: "The Eucharist dissolves the past and the future in the immediacy of presence." Yannaras, *Person and Eros* (Brookline, MA: Holy Cross Orthodox Press, 2007), 153; see also 127, 137. Graham Ward, *Cities of God* (London: Routledge, 2000), 170–71, also discusses this.

5. The veneration of saints is the lengthening of the present, anticipating the return of Jesus and keeping those saints in memory. Those who are dead are not absent, because they too await the return of Christ. In waiting together, we can still remember their practices as we practice our faith, bending our lives toward the time of eschatological fulfillment.

For Swiss theologian Karl Barth, the present itself is constituted by grace. Grace as the encounter with God in time extends the present. The past, for instance, doesn't determine God—God's act in Jesus Christ determines the past. This leads Barth to discuss the possibility of Judas being offered reconciliation and forgiveness after his death, for even death cannot determine God's grace.[6]

The household codes have helped the church continue, even for multiple generations, to live in the time of anticipation.[7] The church is the household of multiple generations, dead and alive, living in Christ and waiting for Christ's return. It is an intergenerational community: children and adults partaking in each other's lives, and those who are dead waiting with the living for the return of Jesus. The dead even continue to teach the living how to live in anticipation of Christ's return—and how to be "in Christ" within this anticipation. The present is everything that occurs in the eon before Jesus returns.[8]

The Dead and Intergenerational Ministry

In our contemporary setting, the church must embrace intergenerational community more fundamentally than just through programs and functions. Over the last handful of years, intergenerational programming has been lauded as the core to faith formation, as a way of breaking the siloing of children and youth ministry. Some have even claimed that an intergenerational focus is the best way to upend decline.[9] This has been more than commendable! I personally have advocated for this kind of intergenerational attention.

6. This brief reference to Barth and time is, of course, much more complicated. My point is to reference this interesting discussion of Judas, which shows how the present is extended by grace and the economy of reconciliation. See Barth, *Church Dogmatics* II/2 (Edinburgh: T&T Clark, 1957), 492–506. But Barth's conception of time is much richer and complicated. For a longer and more helpful discussion on Barth and time, see Daniel M. Griswold, *Triune Eternality: God's Relationship to Time in the Theology of Karl Barth* (Minneapolis: Fortress, 2015). For a book-length discussion of this Judas passage, see Ray Anderson, *The Gospel according to Judas* (Colorado Springs: NavPress, 1991).

7. The time of anticipation is different from the time of innovation. The time of anticipation reaches for a future (an advent). Unlike the innovation of the new, it awaits a complete rupturing of the present with an eschatological future. Innovative time compresses the present. Anticipatory eschatological time lengthens it, as generations wait and as history itself is embraced (not forgotten) for its place in the coming reign of God.

8. And to follow Moltmann, the eschatological advent breaks into this present, bringing moments of healing and many foretastes of the culmination. See *Theology of Hope* (Minneapolis: Fortress, 1993).

9. See Kara Powell, Jake Mulder, and Brad Griffin, *Growing Young: Essential Strategies to Help Young People Discover and Love Your Church* (Grand Rapids: Baker Books, 2016).

But this narrow view of intergenerational community is an unintended concession to modernity and its compressed present. We forfeit the true inter-generational character of the church if we simply gather different age groups to do programs together. If we step back and observe the intergenerational character of the church outside the acceleration of modernity, we notice some-thing much deeper. The church is fundamentally intergenerational because of its very conception of time (not programming!). Transcendence occurs when the present is extended, the living and the dead awaiting consumma-tion.[10] It's no surprise that in our secular age transcendence is opaque, even in our churches. Our concept of the intergenerational has been conceived inside a compressed present. Our imagination cannot think beyond simply the eight-year-old and the eighty-eight-year-old doing programs together. We have forgotten the twenty centuries of others awaiting Jesus's return.

With this narrow understanding of the intergenerational, the church loses the resounding voices of those who prayed and worshiped before us in this same eon of anticipation. We are their children, living the faith they taught us.[11] We lose the mystical connection to the saints.[12] We lose the sense that these saints are still part of the present, still waiting with us, still teaching us, and still helping us discern the good and follow the living Christ. Faith is formed in and through anticipation of the consummation, awaiting and anticipating the return of Jesus. Our own worship and prayer become flat-tened by the immanent frame, locked in a compressed time that wants not the mystery of a lengthy anticipatory present but the sensation of something immanent and new. We want innovation more than revelation.

The acceleration of late modernity has little patience for such an expansive view of the present (and the practices and disciplines it demands) because it has little time. Like straightening roads in the eighteenth century, compressing

10. For a stark example of this in pastoral ministry, see Friedrich Zuendel, *The Awakening: One Man's Battle with Darkness* (Rifton, NY: Plough Publishing House, 2000), which tells the story of nineteenth-century pastor Johann Christoph Blumhardt, who engaged with the dead in his congregation. Blumhardt, along with his son Christoph, would influence Karl Barth, causing him in his own way to think about how revelation breaks into time. This recovery of a long present with the living and dead caused Barth's imagination to seek for a way of not conceding theology to the immanent frame.

11. Bonhoeffer claims that the eschatological form of humanity is to be a child. See *Act and Being* (Minneapolis: Fortress, 1996), 157–61.

12. Taylor examines how Protestantism creates such conditions for acceleration by chang-ing the sense of the Eucharist, Mary, and the place of the saints. Protestantism was correct that these realities had been abused and theologically misguided in the times of the Reforma-tion. But the space it opened up allowed for market capitalism to fill this void. And time, too, could be compressed through the individual sense of pietistic responsibility. See Regina Mara Schwartz, *Sacramental Poetics at the Dawn of Secularism* (Stanford, CA: Stanford University Press, 2008), esp. chaps. 1–3.

the present makes for faster movement into the new.[13] Ultimately, an accelerated modernity has little interest in anything intergenerational.

In a compressed present with accelerating decay rates, the intergenerational is meaningless. The decay rates prevent older generations from possibly offering any wisdom. The dead are silent in the present, and the living assume that the dead have no wisdom.[14] Even those who are not yet deceased, but who are slow to adopt new technology and social norms, are harshly pushed out of the present. They bear the marks of the decay; they are as if dead. Though not yet in the grave, they are rendered meaningless. An accelerated modernity says *not* "though they are dead, they live" but instead "though they live, they are dead." (No wonder we're obsessed with zombies.)

Work, Family, and Sex: From the Medieval to the Modern

More than a thousand years after setting down the household codes, the church still waits. In Avignon, when land and family were fused, the present was expansive enough to encompass and affect multiple generations. Marriage was not for the will of the couple but for the linking of multiple generations of the living and dead.[15] As in the early church, the decay rate of production and reproduction was set at the dial of intergenerational.

We can see this in how work was fused to sacred time. Of course, not all work directly attended to or managed sacred time. But all kinds of work played

13. The "new" is clearly a motif in Paul—the new humanity, the new Adam (Eph. 2:11–16; Rom. 5; 1 Cor. 15). However, Paul's *new* is not bound to the compressed present, in which there is no need to justify the new in relation to the past and in which the new itself is its own moral universe. For late modernity, wanting the new is the only justification necessary. This is not how Paul understands the new. The new for Paul is always justified or even imagined within the history of Israel and the words and works of the prophets. Jesus fulfills this history. The new is in discourse with the past. Jesus's own statement about wine in new wineskins (Matt. 9:14–17) can be seen similarly. The Christian tradition anticipates the future and therefore has a relation to the new. But this newness is not a fetish or even an idol. It is a promise. The promise creates an extended present that not only orders our sense of what is to come but also interprets what has already been. For an interesting cultural analysis on this theological point, and a discussion on Paul, see Robert Pogue Harrison, *Juvenescence: A Cultural History of Our Age* (Chicago: University of Chicago Press, 2014), 83–89.

14. Call this *tradition*. See Hans-Georg Gadamer, *Truth and Method* (New York: Continuum, 2002) for what I mean and for much more on tradition—and its overall necessity for interpretation.

15. For a history of marriage in the West, see Stephanie Coontz, *Marriage, a History: From Obedience to Intimacy or How Love Conquered Marriage* (New York: Viking Press, 2005); Nancy Cott, *Public Vows: A History of Marriage and the Nation* (Cambridge, MA: Harvard University Press, 2000); and Hendrik Hartog, *Man and Wife in America: A History* (Cambridge, MA: Harvard University Press, 2000).

an important part in the ecosystem of sacred time. Those working the fields or defending the realm did so in order to allow others—like nuns, monks, and priests—to pray and keep sacred time for all. Production, even for the king's opulent throne room, was for the sake of the sacred. King Louis's golden throne room existed for a much different purpose (and moral aim) than Donald Trump's golden penthouse at Trump Tower. Trump's gold unabashedly points to himself and what he has made with his own time. In the best of circumstances, Louis's gold pointed to the glory of God and reminded all that the king played an essential role in connecting them with sacred time. Because the king was God's representative on earth, the king's courtrooms needed to reflect the heavenly realm of sacred time. The rooms needed to be a faint glimpse of heaven itself.

Sacred time not only directed work. It was glued firmly to marriage. Production and reproduction were nearly one thing. In the medieval Europe of Avignon and its serfdom system, the church served as the notary for the union of families. Though also legal, marriage was foremost sacramental. Marriage, as a sacrament, ushered the couple into sacred time. These sacred unions, administered by the church, shaped the work of the realm. When Avignon was a timekeeper, production (work) and reproduction (sex) were fused within sacred time itself. The lord oversaw the land as his God-given right, but the lord needed an heir for the production of the land to continue uninterrupted. If this heir was from a rival family, peace could be achieved, even peace for generations past. Rival families who had battled against each other for generations were united through marriage in sacred time. Past rivalries and crimes were reconciled. Marriage was a duty to the legacy of multiple generations—not a romantic feeling. To echo *The Bachelor*, "you had to be there for the right reasons," and the right reason was legacy, not an individual desire for romance. The decay rate was firmly set at intergenerational.

Modernity boldly sought to separate production and reproduction forever. The sharp divide occurred because of the desire for freedom, expression, and reason[16]—all three imagined outside the legacy of generations. The old world could be over, replaced by something new. It would take until the nineteenth century to fully unlink production from reproduction.[17] The technological acceleration of full-blown industrialization caused wealth to become untethered

16. Here and elsewhere I'm leaning heavily on Taylor's *Hegel and Modern Society* (London: Cambridge University Press, 1979), in which he lucidly describes how modernity is fundamentally about radical freedom and expression, as the Enlightenment and the romantics (the Counter-Enlightenment) shaped modern sensibility. Reason, too, plays its part.

17. In this separation of public and private, we move into what Taylor calls *secular 1*. This divide creates the secular world where transcendence is eclipsed. See *A Secular Age* (Cambridge, MA: Belknap, 2007), 3–10.

from land, and reproduction from legacy. This untying, particularly of reproduction from historical legacy, did its part in upending the Christian sense of a lengthy extended present, in which the dead continue to wait with us for the return of Christ. Protestantism even rendered marriage no longer a sacrament, separating it from sacred time.[18]

Before modernization, the church community remembered the dead, not only because they were buried in the churchyard but because our practices linked us with these generations of dead but still waiting. The church was necessarily multigenerational, or intergenerational. But after the Reformation, marriage was released from an intergenerational reality of sacred time. And work, too, found itself without a part in the sacred time ecosystem. Making capital replaced the sacred telos of work. According to Max Weber, making capital took on its own spiritual force, outside an expansive present of generations.[19] With these radical changes, the dial on the decay rate was turned up.

To show this further, think about the nineteenth-century Victorian age. It compressed the present by dividing production from reproduction, creating separate spheres for the public and the private.[20] Work was filed under public, separated from family, because commerce and money markets made it possible for you to make your own capital. Being a rich industrial bachelor was now a possibility. Some multigenerational guilds remained, but for all classes of people, production was conceived as your job. Your job was no longer connected to a long legacy of generations: it was something you did in your own lifetime, in your own cordoned-off generation. The decay rate of production empirically moved from *intergenerational* to *generational*.

Something very similar happened with reproduction. In the private sphere, marriage, sex, and child-rearing became the sole business of the couple. Reproduction became private not only from the outside world but from the legacy of other generations. Inside the separate sphere, the institution of marriage and its norms moved from multigenerational to generational as well. Beginning in

18. This wasn't to lower the bar of marriage but actually to infuse it with a deeper piety. By heightening the affirmation of ordinary life, attention to marriage and parenting was even more important. However, connecting this with the story Taylor is telling, once marriage and child-rearing were placed outside sacred time, and lodged in ordinary time, the possibility was open that ordinary time could eventually be fully secularized. See *Sources of the Self: The Making of Modern Identity* (Cambridge, MA: Harvard University Press, 1989), 14–23, 206–27.

19. Taylor reminds us that both these moves—to release marriage from a sacramental reality, and to free work from sacred time—were done for deeply pietistic reasons: to move devotion deeper into the heart of the individual. It was about raising the bar. But in the centuries moving into modernity, the bar was allowed to drop, lowering us into a secular age, in which people are free from any consideration of sacred time at all. For Taylor's articulation of the Reformation, see part 1 of *Secular Age*.

20. This is only one of many changes that bring about this radical change.

the nineteenth century, marriage was entered into through subjective feelings of love, not the duty of legacy.

Shifting reproduction from legacy to romantic love compresses the present. Romantic love is bound within the history of my own generation. It lasts as long as my lifetime, because this kind of love is inseparable from my own subjective feelings.[21] Love is bound in the couple alone, not in and through the duty of generations.[22] Marriage is for *my* life, not the continuation of the name and reach of my long-dead great-great-grandfather. This shift quickened the decay rate and therefore compressed the present. The new decay rate, brought about by this shift, was turned up and distributed to the whole of Western cultures, in large part thanks to the romantic ethos of the nineteenth century, coming in novels and poetry. Jane Austen[23] convinced many that love, not land, was the true source of marriage and happiness.[24]

Yet it's important to balance these statements and not be too nostalgic. It'd be wrong to interpret the move from intergenerational to generational as nothing but bad. There are great gains with this transition, like the rise of the compassionate marriage and family.[25] The love-based marriage has

21. Love too here is struck with immanence in a sense, at least a kind of immanence that is bound in the individual. Yet in some ways this kind of electric feeling of love also becomes a way of coping with the immanent frame and the loss of meaning in modernity. Love is a way to return to the ecstatic without direct experiences of communion with transcendence. So love becomes immanent only because it becomes locked in the individual, but this actually allows its intensity to be turned up, feeling like an exciting way to live inside the reductions of the immanent frame.

22. It's only with this shift that no-fault divorce could be. For a history of divorce, see Norma Basch, *Framing American Divorce: From the Revolutionary Generation to the Victorians* (Berkeley: University of California Press, 1999).

23. Austen wrote in the early nineteenth century, but her impact on the changing modern culture of the mid-nineteenth century can't be overlooked.

24. Of course, just when we think this divide between work and family/sex is complete, we see lingering connections between the two (we're never as modern as we think we are). For instance, consumer sex appeal is almost always coupled with status symbols like cars and clothes. Rich people are almost universally considered sexier. Rich men particularly seem to be able to date much younger women. For example, sixty-five-year-old Bill Belichick, the oldest coach to ever win a Super Bowl, was photographed walking off the field after winning Super Bowl LIII hand in hand with his much younger girlfriend. Social scientific research shows that money makes people more sexually attractive. See Vinita Mehta, "Are Women Shallow? A Woman's Desire for a Wealthy Man May Have an Evolutionary Basis," *Psychology Today*, July 19, 2012, https://www.psychologytoday.com/us/blog/head-games/201207/are-women -shallow. Even the most modern of rituals like dating cannot completely separate production and reproduction, the romantic dreams of Jane Austen never fully coming to fruition. Nevertheless this effort to separate work and sex can radically shift each of these structure's core. For example, what makes hoodie-wearing Bill Belichick attractive is not really production itself but the money it gives him.

25. Taylor beautifully discusses how this transition into a compassionate marriage and family does its part in creating the modern self. See *Sources of the Self*, 227–91.

biblical and theological justification in Song of Songs—and the place of Eros in the tradition is very important, as we'll see in later chapters. There are gains in production as well—for instance, a growing middle class. But with these gains comes acceleration and a compressed present, as our attention is directed toward the innovation of the new instead of the legacy of a long present. The new technology of production through industry speeds up our social lives. The present is no longer multigenerational or intergenerational, but a single generation. Marriage is now for *your* lifetime.

Today the thought of a *whole* lifetime makes dating couples sweat, giving them a feeling of heavy—even restricting—responsibility. When asked about marriage, young couples are likely to evade. "I don't know. A lifetime is a *loooong* time." Perhaps they might even say, "I'm not even sure human beings are supposed to love just one person their whole lives. I mean, so few other animals do."

Such statements would make our ancient ancestors laugh (if they weren't overcome with confusion and a spiritual unease, or just completely mesmerized by our iPhones). It would be like a world-class marathon runner overhearing a group complaining about a 2K run, saying, "That's so long, is that even normal? Are human beings meant to run that far?" Our ancient ancestors might respond, "If you think the weight of a lifetime is long and heavy, try ten generations, try eternity." The young couple's anxiety about a lifetime being a very long time further shows us that the present has been compressed, the decay rates quickening. But we have more work to do, particularly as this relates to the church, before we speak of the decay rate in our own time.

Here Comes a New Timekeeper

In the nineteenth and into the twentieth century, the present shifted from the eon between Jesus's ascension and return (or the legacy of intergenerations) to the short length of one's life span.[26] This began to shift our consciousness of time. Religion, filed in the private sphere, having little to do with production and having little to say about my own subjective feelings of love, was no longer keeping time. The mid- and late nineteenth century completely stripped Avignon, or anything like it, from being our primary timekeeper. When religion is filed away in the private sphere and the decay rate runs at

26. Those living in the nineteenth and early twentieth century certainly possessed a sense of the old or ancient. But the wisdom of those earlier generations, bleeding into the now, was no longer forming one's actions, setting the terms for identity, or determining the moral good. I stretch this point (perhaps more than can be justified) only to show how modernity compresses the present and how the church accepts a conception of time born from modernity.

the level of a generation, the timekeeper is the modern nation-state (e.g., the country). Though later on it would become Silicon Valley, in the nineteenth and early twentieth centuries it was the state. Party politics and the democratic voting process encourage—and even shape—this sense of the present. It moves much faster than the *ancien regime*, functioning at the pace of a generation, asking you to willfully enact your life as, for instance, an American. You're encouraged to form your own life, with no obligation to correlate with past ways of life. But you are asked to give loyalty and some level of commitment to the nation throughout your lifetime.

Benedict Anderson, in *Imagined Communities*, demonstrates that we always imagine ourselves inside a community.[27] From the early church to modernity, this imagined community was intergenerational. Your imagined community included the living and the dead. Anderson makes the point that the nation acquires its power by leading us to imagine it as a community. And to connect Anderson with Rosa, this community is no longer intergenerational but generational. The imagined community of the nation compresses the present into a generation, shifting our imaginations in more immanent directions than mystical or transcendent.

The imagined community becomes so powerful that, above anything else, I think of myself as an American, even above smaller collectives that might more directly relate to my life.[28] Though I'll never come close to interacting with even 1 percent of this community (at least not face-to-face), technological advances like the newspaper, radio, and television play a major role in substantiating this imagined community.[29]

Inside this imagined community I live out my own distinct lifetime. And because I imagine myself in this community, the nation can ask for my loyalty.

27. Anderson, *Imagined Communities: Reflections on the Origin and Spread of Nationalism* (London: Verso, 2016). This book is lauded by many scholars, particularly Charles Taylor, who uses some of Anderson's thought in developing his own understanding of social imaginaries (see *Modern Social Imaginaries* [Durham, NC: Duke University Press, 2007]). Graham Ward provides a rich discussion of Anderson's and Taylor's sense of imaginaries in *Cultural Transformations and Religious Practice* (London: University of Cambridge Press, 2005), part 3.

28. My own imagined community, for instance, isn't even found within a community of faith that stretches back to Luther and Calvin. They are alive to me through their ideas, but it is hard for me—even as a theologian writing this book—to imagine them as part of my community, still forming and directing my life. But this is exactly what people once thought about the saints and those gone before.

29. Radio and television cannot produce community, but they can create a substantive sense of an imagined community. They give users a shared experience with others. The radio and TV give narrative to the imagined community that knits together this sense of being in an imagined community. The internet, I think, does something different. It, too, functions within imagined communities, but it tends to fragment things to such a level that it heightens the cultural wars. For a discussion on television, see Pierre Bourdieu, *On Television* (New York: New Press, 1996).

John F. Kennedy, in his inauguration speech on January 20, 1961, uttered the famous line, "Ask not what your country can do for you, ask what you can do for your country." For this line to send shivers down my back, to inspire me to action, I need to imagine myself inside a collective called "country." I have to imagine myself as an American. I have to assume that there is some obligation that this collective owes me or I owe it. But, most relevant to our argument, this imagined community, revealed in this famous line, assumes a present that is but a lifetime. My imaginative interaction with my nation is assumed to bear the time of my life. Kennedy is essentially saying, "Ask not what your country can do for you *in your lifetime*, ask what you can do for your country *in your lifetime*."

This is an assumed lifetime cut off from the past, because this imagined community itself is enacted not through the past but through the willful loyalty of this generation. Of course, I assume there was a past founding of America, but with my freedom to do what I want with my own lifetime, I must willfully enact my life as a citizen of this nation. Kennedy is reminding the people that they must willfully enact being this imaginative community. He wants people to imagine themselves as a community, as a great country. The speech lives in glorious remembrance, not because we can point to all sorts of concrete results it produced but rather because inside a new, sped-up modernity, the speech and this line *moved* (emotionally/subjectively) so many to reimagine themselves in this imaginary community called America. That line has the power to do this even today.[30]

But to be clear, *imaginary* does not equal *impotent*, as Anderson points out. Rather, this reenacting of an imaginary community would ready the nation to accelerate their lives at the technological dimension, picking up the challenge of winning the space race and landing on the moon. In a speech in 1962, Kennedy would say, "We choose to go to the moon." Who is this "we"? Not strictly the government or NASA, but the same "we" that the Declaration of Independence refers to: "we the people," we the imagined community will *will* this.[31]

30. This isn't all bad. As we'll see in chapter 14, the answer to acceleration is resonance, and resonance needs emotion and affection. This speech is powerful because it creates resonance. The point here is that it has a hidden conception of time (time at the rate of a generation) embedded in it.

31. Mark Lilla points to the way time and politics work and to how the Kennedy sense of time has sped up to something very different. "There is no again in politics, just the future. . . . JFK's challenge, What can I do for my country?—which had inspired the early sixties generation—became unintelligible. The only meaningful question became a deeply personal one: what does my country owe me by virtue of my identity?" Lilla, *The Once and Future Liberal: After Identity Politics* (New York: Harper, 2017), 16, 65.

Because the nation is created by the will of the people, it can exist only as long as this generation imagines itself in this community. Institutions and other cultural realties—like sports, holidays, and names of bridges—give the nation-state some constancy over time. But even so, the idea, as Kennedy's inaugural speech shows, is that we in our generation must enact this, as an imaginative community. The timekeeper of the country must function with a present that is as long as a generation. The present must be compressed into a lifetime to encourage people to imagine themselves in a community called a country and therefore be loyal to its democratic and nation-building pursuits.

In exchange for your loyalty, and to make your lifetime meaningful, the nation-state will oversee and attend to your work and family. But this won't happen by giving sacred significance to production and reproduction.[32] Even before World War II, countries like the US, Canada, France, and Britain imposed no direct meaning on work or family—particularly none that stretched beyond your own will and lifetime. The structure of production and reproduction had decayed to a generation. Therefore, the nation promised you the opportunity to work and legal protection in your lifetime.[33] It would offer workers' compensation (or Roosevelt's New Deal) and marriage licenses. In turn, it would use unemployment rates, tax cuts, and abortion laws to win the loyalty of your lifetime.

In that 1962 speech, Kennedy repeats his line just a few moments later, "We choose to go to the moon *in this decade.*" The imaginative community will feel as connected as ever when Apollo 11 lands and Neil Armstrong walks on the moon, the TV knitting together the nation into one imagined community.

Kennedy's point in 1962 was *not* that we choose the moon as some far-off goal or task. We choose it now, within this decade. We will accelerate to reach it. It must happen soon, in this lifetime, or it has no real political value. The speech will have no power, no existential significance, unless it names a reality in this generation. What matters is what happens in this lifetime (no wonder we have a hard time getting people to care about climate change when it's assumed to be a crisis coming in another lifetime).

32. It might have been this way, but this perspective was defeated in World War II. National Socialism made production and reproduction a sacred act, done not unto God but the Führer. The TV series *The Man in the High Castle* gives us a frightening thought experiment of what life might have been like if the Nazis had won and America had become part of the Third Reich.

33. To this day our political system is divided between economic and social issues. Sometimes the easiest way to win an election is to protect jobs. And sometimes it's to protect social norms around marriage and reproduction. The American political system has been stuck between tax cuts and abortion for decades, and we see why above.

The Church Becomes the Denomination, and the Denomination Is in Trouble

When this shift to compress the present to a generation occurs, the church falls behind. What do you do when you're no longer the timekeeper? You go private and complementary, just what the new timekeeper wants. The new timekeeper, particularly in America, found a way to include the church. Civic religion, not timekeeping, would be the church's new task.[34] This complementary role is all the church would be allowed, the private enactment of religion. However, this private religion seemed adequate, particularly for mainline Protestantism, because so many people willfully chose to participate in religion as part of their private lives, filling church buildings. The buildings were so full that many church leaders didn't notice or care that they were no longer keeping time.

The nation, though displacing the church, asserted that the church had an important function to play. The new timekeeper depended on people willfully living certain kinds of lives, and the church could play its part in encouraging people to be religious. Combining patriotism with religion would move loyalty to the nation deep into the private lives of the people, supporting their lifelong enactment of the nation's vision of the good life.[35]

When the decay rate of production and reproduction is set at a generation, and the nation is the timekeeper, the church becomes equated with the denomination. By denomination I don't necessarily mean differences in tradition and polity between, say, the Eastern and Western church. Rather, I mean a form of religious organization that arises out of the public/private split. The modern denomination is the creation of a world where religion becomes a private matter. Denominationalism is a form of religion that accommodates to this sense that religion is a private choice. The denomination is the form the church takes when the present is compressed to a lifetime. The denomination is religion for a lifetime.[36] The denomination, particularly in America, is a free association. Like the nation, it's an imagined community.

34. This was mainly the task of Protestantism in America. For more on American civic religion, see Robert Bellah's work, especially the classic *Habits of the Heart: Individualism and Commitment in American Life* (New York: Harper & Row, 1985).

35. One could interpret Stanley Hauerwas's theology as a response to this reality, claiming something much different for the church in relation to the new timekeeper. But he nevertheless contends that this new timekeeper is setting the terms for the culture. See Hauerwas, *A Community of Character* (South Bend, IN: University of Notre Dame Press, 1991); and Hauerwas and William Willimon, *Resident Aliens* (Nashville: Abingdon, 1989).

36. Taylor discusses religion and denominations in *Dilemmas and Connections: Selected Essays* (Cambridge, MA: Belknap, 2011), 162–78.

Yet for most people in Roosevelt's, Eisenhower's, or Kennedy's America, the congregation (in contradistinction to the denomination) was more than imagined, because it was local: it was also their neighbor's congregation, for instance. But the denomination itself, like the nation, was entirely an imagined community. I may have been on the council at my local Lutheran church, but the congregation was associated with a larger body like the American Lutheran Church (ALC), for instance. This congregation was part of a denomination.

And while this denomination set the trajectory for the congregation, overseeing the education of the pastor and determining who was equipped to be ordained, it remained imaginary. The denomination had millions of members in thousands of congregations. I was told that together we were the ALC, but I never interacted with even 1 percent of those people. Magazines and youth gatherings would produce mediums for this imagined community to feel concrete. But what kept me in the denomination was my own volition. The denomination became *the* religious form when the church was no longer timekeeper. The present compressed into a lifetime, and the decay rate was set at generational.

Of course, some members of the denomination may have had a slight hint of historical memory. Your grandfather, for instance, may have been a pastor in the denomination, or your parents were longtime members of that church. Or even you yourself were confirmed in that church, and you wanted the same experience for your children. But this historical memory bore the weight of a single lifetime, not the weight of legacy and an intergenerational present. The denomination was good enough for the lifetime of your father, so you figure it's good enough for you.

The denomination often takes on no more weight than what it means for a particular lifetime. As mainly a bureaucratic imagined community, the denomination only has its weight through the will, making it only for a generation. The denomination would make no sense if the present were conceived as longer than a lifetime, and the decay rate intergenerational. Your lifetime would be too embedded in legacy, land, and sacred time for you to assume you could gather others and willfully start a new group, finding an acronym of your own making.

The denomination could be birthed only when modernity compressed the present into a lifetime. But what happens when late modernity accelerates things even faster and the present is compressed into a mode even shorter than a lifetime? What happens when the decay rate is faster than a generation? What happens when the nation-state is no longer keeping time?

The denomination moves us far beyond an embeddedness in legacy and land, responding to how production and reproduction were located in a lifetime.

But it depends on different embedded cultural realities that move at the pace of a generation. It needs the lifetime speed of production and reproduction. The denomination works when most people live in one place, often even one neighborhood, for their whole lives. The denomination is stable when people marry early and remain married for sixty years. The denomination can exist when these structures are dynamic enough to be but a generation, but also firm and static enough not to decay quicker than a lifetime.

Yet, when production and reproduction speed up, the denomination is quickly undercut. The generational structures it depended on are no longer there. And yet these structures *seem* to still function. People seem to still hold jobs, marry, and have children—the same structures as during Eisenhower's and Kennedy's America. We know things have changed, but it still seems logical that denominations could thrive because a silhouette of the structures of production and reproduction can still be seen. We're led to assume these structures still function. And they do. But the present is not what it used to be: the decay rate has been turned up. Now production and reproduction are no longer for a lifetime. When this occurs, the denomination is put in crisis.

Work, Family, and Sex in Late Modernity

It isn't until the late 1960s, when the nation's moral vision was exposed as corrupt, that a transition in timekeepers could occur. Morality has central importance to humanity. Those who keep time do so by making claims about what is good and what it means to live a good life. When the 1960s counterculture exposed the nation as corrupt, and the civil rights movement, the Vietnam War, and then the Watergate scandal confirmed this opinion, a new timekeeper, with a different moral vision, was needed.

The countercultural movement created a coup d'état in timekeepers. It sought revolution, switching the moral horizon from loyalty to the nation and its pursuits of power and nation building to a radical freedom of expression—to free love (love that was free of the responsibility of a lifetime).[37] The nation-state had taken over timekeeping from Avignon as modernity separated production from reproduction, using the desire for freedom and expression as a means to pry them apart. The counterculture movement would do the same. The nation-state, ironically, was considered immoral because it restricted freedom and expression, though these were the same motivations the nation had for overthrowing the *ancien regime*.

37. Enter an age of authenticity. See Taylor, *Secular Age*, 407–504. See also his *The Ethics of Authenticity* (Cambridge, MA: Harvard University Press, 1991).

Hence, it wasn't that the nation opposed freedom and expression as much as the nation had fallen behind the pace of freedom and expression. Freedom and expression were accelerating and being redefined through a deeper (or *faster*) romantic bohemianism.[38] Loyalty to the nation's pursuit of freedom and expression was for a past time. The nation was unable to keep up.

The nation had asserted in the eighteenth and nineteenth centuries that Avignon and its sacred time was too slow. A good life could not be embraced through Avignon's long present with intergenerational decay rates. Now the nation was stabbed with the same knife it had used to take power. The counter-cultural revolution of the late 1960s asserted that the nation was too slow and therefore too immoral to produce the freedom and expression it promised. The decay rate of a lifetime, a generation, seemed far too restrictive and slow. The nation's quest for true freedom and expression was getting snagged in its nets of loyalty and willful—lifetime—commitment.[39] As the revolution took off, a repeated mantra was, "Never trust anyone over thirty." Those over thirty had a much different sense of the present. They were socialized by different social norms, bound in a different rate of decay.

Starting in the late 1960s, it was assumed that a lifetime was too long. One job and one lover for a lifetime!?! The suburban life of one early marriage and one long career at one job behind one desk seemed like anything but freedom. The nascent consumer culture of the mass society in the 1950s was teaching a cohort of young people to be aware of—and uneasy with—boredom.[40] Boredom was a direct sign that you were imprisoned, kept from the good. And nothing was more boring than waiting. Staying still. Nothing was more boring than an overall conception that the present was long, not allowing for the constant birthing of the new. The thought of an unchanging (never new) job or sexual partner for a lifetime began to feel like a threat to freedom.

The revolution began as much against the vision of the suburban good life as against Washington. I would contend that the frontal attack was on the lifetime-pace of the suburban good life. But to overthrow this suburban sense of the good life, you needed to discredit the timekeepers themselves. So march on Washington they did. They shouted that the timekeepers of the present, who required a lifetime of loyalty and commitment, were restricting.

38. For more on this, see my *Faith Formation in a Secular Age: Responding to the Church's Obsession with Youthfulness* (Grand Rapids: Baker Academic, 2017).

39. It justified its need to lie in order to keep the loyalty. McNamara even cooked the books on kill rates in Vietnam.

40. In 1951 social scientist Martha Wolfenstein coined the phrase "fun morality." She argues that fun was overtaking—even back in 1951—other moral goods. Wolfenstein, "The Emergence of Fun Morality," *Journal of Social Issues* 7, no. 4 (Fall 1951): 15–25, https://spssi.onlinelibrary.wiley.com/doi/abs/10.1111/j.1540-4560.1951.tb02249.x.

The revolutionaries called the leaders of these institutions "fascist pigs" who were against freedom. This made no sense to those leaders, many of whom fought for freedom, even freeing the world from tyranny in World War II and working in Kennedy's administration. In actuality it wasn't really a fight *for* freedom but a fight for *the speed of* freedom. It was a struggle for who would set the pace of freedom and therefore shape its constituting goods. The young counterculture revolutionaries screamed that the nation's call for a lifetime commitment was wrong. And their accusations landed with moral weight because the timekeepers who called for this loyalty were shown to be liars. How could you commit to a lifetime of production and reproduction if the whole system of loyalty was corrupt?

The late 1960s was indeed a revolution because it compressed the present, making the generational decay rate too slow to produce a good life. The generation gap was expansive: parents and their children were living with two very different senses of the present. For parents, social norms and participation in production and reproduction were at the rate of a lifetime. You were free to do what you wanted with your lifetime, but you needed to be loyal to the commitments you made for this lifetime. To be of the present was to maintain continuity in your commitments inside of production and reproduction.

This was not so for their children, causing a disorienting gap between the two. Children of the late 1960s threw off this sense that the present was as long as a lifetime. They imagined the good life in a much different way than their parents. They turned up the dial on the decay rate, setting it to *intra*generational. The decay rate of the practices and perspectives of production and reproduction clicked forward, moving from a rate of intergenerational to generational to intragenerational—that is, from multiple generations, to one lifetime, to the ability to live multiple lives in one lifetime.[41]

Seeking New Sex and New Work

The late-1960s revolutionaries shifted us onto different ground, seeking the new as a high good. Seeking the *new* became the measure of the good life. The consumerism of the mass society taught suburban revolutionaries to seek the new in all things. The present became compressed for the sake of the continued experience of the new. Production itself became linked with the creation of new products and the constant new version of those products. Eventually, however, as the decades passed and a new timekeeper took over,

41. For a longer discussion on these decay rates and movements from intergenerational to intragenerational, see Harmut Rosa, *Social Acceleration: A New Theory of Modernity* (New York: Columbia University Press, 2015), 111–55, 147–59.

a divide was instituted even between work and production. By the late 1980s and 1990s we had a whole economy that didn't produce anything tangible. Rather, its growth was built on the fast-paced movement of information and data. Reproduction also aimed for the new. You could use technology to separate sex from the risk of reproduction. This upended the logic of sex as a lifelong commitment.

Modernity had already divided core social realities, starting with a split between production and reproduction. Yet, once split, these structures showed more fissures, allowing for further separation. In late modernity, production split from work and reproduction split from sex. Of course, there had always been some who found ways to disconnect sex from reproduction, but as a larger social imaginary, sex and reproduction had always been necessarily fused. That is, until the pill arrived and now everyone—not just bohemian artists—could participate in sex without any risk of reproduction.

Sex no longer said anything that bore the consequence of a lifetime. Sex existed for now, for these years, for these months, for this night. Transitions in the economy of production opened up the workforce to women, giving financial autonomy for women and rendering marriage unnecessary for financial security. Marriage became expendable, no longer for a lifetime. The escalating divorce rate that started to spike in the 1970s illustrates that the decay rates of production and reproduction were set at intragenerational.

Eventually, just as sex no longer needed reproduction, reproduction no longer needed sex. Around the time that the economy separated work from production, the sex-to-reproduction equation was reversed. You could have sex without any concern for a lifetime commitment of reproduction, and you could have reproduction without sex. Fertility innovations gave the freedom of choice, separating sex even further from marriage.[42] Whether with artificial insemination or birth control, you could choose to have children when you were ready, when you decided it was time to live that kind of life. But only when you were ready. Having children remained in the future, in another lifetime that you'd eventually get to. But not now.

42. Arlie Russell Hochschild provides some insights on this multiple lifetime speed: "[The] high divorce rate has paradoxically elevated the importance of the wedding ceremony itself. In a sense, the wedding has become a symbolic stand-in for what marriage was once believed to be. There, at the ceremony, one can imagine lasting happiness. One is surrounded by joyous well-wishers at an event that affirms a reassuring permanence that marriage in America can no longer promise. A certain market logic may underlie this displacement: 'If we put this much money down,' a couple may believe, 'we've invested in something solid; we're going to last.' ('In the men's bathroom,' Chloe commented wryly, 'there's always some guy who says, "they're sure spending a lot of dough on this wedding; I hope they last long enough to pay it off."')." *The Outsourced Self: Intimate Life in Market Times* (New York: Metropolitan Books, 2012), 52.

Once modernity split reproduction from production, we were allowed to even split sex from child-rearing, and reproduction from marriage. These splits are most often held as goods. They have the appearance of freeing people from the restrictions of lifelong commitment, and they allow us to accelerate our lives. They set us up to live at the speed of multiple individual lives in one lifetime. This radically compresses the feel of the present.

Living Multiple Lifetimes

The present was now less than a lifetime. You could actually live—if you went fast enough—multiple lifetimes. Even as the Age of Aquarius never came and the bohemian spirit of the revolution was replaced by what David Brooks calls Boboism[43] (a merging of bohemian and bourgeois social practices, which combines authenticity with consumption), this sense of the present as less than a lifetime held on, even escalating. Today people get stuck all the time, fearing they've settled for a job or a marriage. People are frightened of being trapped, stuck in living just one life. We have all sorts of contemporary cultural texts like *Jerry Maguire*, *American Beauty*, *The Land of Steady Habits*, *Little Children*, and *Undone* that explore this anxiety.

In these texts the protagonists are stuck, imprisoned in living one lifetime—the suburbs have gotten them! The protagonists take a heroic, often youthful, step toward freedom to live another life. They always abruptly quit a job or find a new sexual partner who opens their eyes to imagine another life. It's often not even the new sexual partner and relationship that matter. It's the sexual encounter itself that creates an ecstatic experience with the new. It wakes up the protagonist to a new lifetime. In these movies and TV shows the protagonist makes love not really with the other person but to newness itself. The sexual partner is just a transport vessel to the new, giving the protagonist the vision to seek another new life.[44]

These so-called transformations[45] into a new life almost never happen through being formed by a spiritual or ethical tradition that comes from outside

43. See David Brooks, *Bobos in Paradise: The New Upper Class and How They Got There* (New York: Simon & Schuster, 2000).
44. The story that leads Nadia Bolz-Weber to write her book perfectly fits this narrative. Sex opens her up to the excitement of living a new life. She paints this spiritually. Not surprisingly, the celebrity class and more secular people have found the argument of the book more convincing than churchgoing types. It fits perfectly the cultural elites' sense of the present and how sex is a doorway into the new. See *Shameless: A Sexual Revolution* (New York: Convergent, 2019).
45. I call them "so-called" transformations because I don't believe they bear the marks of true transformation. Transformation must happen from "outside the self," which is also what makes resonance transformational. Resonance has a deep sense of otherness. For a dialogue on transformation, see James Loder, *The Transforming Moment* (Colorado Springs: Helmers

the self. Rarely do these so-called transformations call for anything like sacrifice. Rather, almost always they rely on the ability of the protagonists to speed up, finding the speed to live in a compressed present of multiple lives that will truly make them happy. It supposedly makes you happy because you are free to embrace the future of chasing a new life that creates meaning, giving you authenticity. Authenticity allows you to live multiple new lives from this point on, never being trapped again, never absent the electric feeling of the new.

Of course, there is a big rub. Living at an intragenerational decay rate and going at the speed of multiple lives has some fundamental conundrums that late modernity has not solved (or cannot solve). Human beings are fundamentally historical beings. We both receive and give something in such relationships of erotic encounter (we do the same, in a different way, in the creation of art—we leave some of ourselves in its making). Somewhat even over our own will and affect, we leave behind something of our own being in such deeply personal relations.[46] We have our being in relationships because we are persons, not atomistic individuals. Acts of shared creation and sexual relationships cause us to leave something of ourselves behind. In art and sex, we leave behind an impression of our being. To reject one lifetime of production and reproduction for another is an illusion, maybe even a spiritual threat. You will always leave something behind that will call for your attention and demand your responsibility. As late modernity invites us to speed up and live many new lives, our old lives will still place demands on us.

& Howard, 1989); and Loder, *Educational Ministry in the Logic of the Spirit* (Eugene, OR: Cascade, 2018), chap. 1.

46. I'm following Christos Yannaras here in arguing that art and sex are ontological events. Yannaras often uses Van Gogh as an example of how an artist leaves behind part of their personhood in a creative work. (The ramification of his view for sex is even more profound. In chapter 17, I'll touch on these perspectives in discussing the church as an erotic community.) Regarding anthropology, it is easy to be pulled into an anthropology of individualism—a necessity for an intragenerational decay rate and a compressed present. Sex is imagined as either entirely shameful or completely free. Thus you get the shame-based anthropological logic of *True Love Waits* or its similar but reverse-image opposite Nadia Bolz-Weber's *Shameless*. These are actually just two sides of the same coin, because they both hold to the same theological anthropology of individualism. Bolz-Weber claims her position is based off Luther, but only if you allow Luther to be totally co-opted by Kant and the Enlightenment. Her argument is further proof for why a more helpful and contextual reading of Luther can be found through Tuomo Mannermaa and Finnish interpretation (see Mannermaa, *Christ Present in Faith: Luther's View of Justification* [Minneapolis: Fortress, 2005]). It is only this assumed anthropology (the assumption that people are individuals and not persons) that could lead to her statements about sex, pornography, and abortion. Her argument is as deeply invested in liberalism (the individual is the highest good and freedom is *freedom from*) as any far-right evangelical who she attacks. It's a classic example of those who forcefully oppose the right by using the very same philosophical conceptions, falling into the same pits. Nancey Murphy long ago made this convincing case: see *Beyond Liberalism and Fundamentalism: How Modern and Postmodern Philosophy Set the Theological Agenda* (Valley Forge, PA: Trinity Press, 1996).

It's quite difficult for people to simply burn one life for the next—burn after using! Some people can, though we often judge this as a moral failure. We consider it wrong to move on without attending to the commitments and people left behind. In relation to reproduction, it's even illegal. A father may choose to start a new life with a new lover, or just move somewhere warm and start over. That feels exciting, new, and liberating. But soon enough the responsibilities of the old life come racing back: the court system takes 30 percent of his paycheck for child support. If he bails and relocates to the Caribbean with a new name, we call this a moral violation, labeling him a deadbeat dad. It just so happens that living at the rate of multiple lives (chasing the new) is never as clean and freeing as it's assumed. Most often it leads to a busier and more complicated life rather than a freer one.

We are free from the obligation of a lifetime of production and reproduction, but we haven't solved yet (and never will) what to do with all the ways our being is left behind in the old life. This trace (or more) of our being demands some responsibility that causes friction in our pursuit of an accelerated life. Better to put off production and reproduction as late as possible, allowing more freedom to leave one life for another.[47] This alone doesn't solve the problem, though it *may* feel better, bearing less moral weight. So we advise young adults not to find a career or a partner, or to have children, until they're *really* ready.[48] Ready for what? "To slow down," we say. Which means you need to be in a hurry now. You need to move fast, living as many lives as you can before marriage and career cage you. No wonder we've become susceptible, even (or maybe mainly) in our twenties, to *la fatigue d'être*. Inside a compressed future of multiple lives within one lifetime, where the decay rate is set at intragenerational, the sense of living a good life accelerates to a screaming pace. Young adults hear, "Hurry, hurry, and live!"

How Silicon Valley Becomes the Timekeeper

This takes us back to the coup d'état of timekeepers in the late 1960s. For the whole imagination of the present to be compressed and for time to be shifted, universally among the whole culture, a new timekeeper would be needed to

47. Putting off production and reproduction unfortunately causes us to label the twenties as the greatest years of one's life, putting another truckload of anxiety on young adults. See Donna Freitas, *The Happiness Effect: How Social Media Is Driving a Generation to Appear Perfect at Any Cost* (London: Oxford University Press, 2017).

48. For a discussion on the impact of late careers and child-rearing on the church, see, among many others, Robert Wuthnow, *After the Baby Boomers: How Twenty- and Thirty-Somethings Are Shaping the Future of American Religion* (Princeton: Princeton University Press, 2007).

sustain the feverish pace.[49] The nation-state would continue to control political power, but the pace of the good life would be set by another timekeeper.

In the late 1960s and early 1970s, the revolutionaries were able to wound the timekeeping nation. But the counterculture was neither disciplined nor organized enough to impose its own leaders as the reigning timekeepers (you need institutional weight to take the throne of timekeeping).[50] All the counterculture could manage to create was a vacuum. And soon enough this vacuum would be filled.[51]

Instead of the new timekeeper being utopian leaders of the Age of Aquarius, it would be consumerism. Seeing a path toward the throne, the institutions and corporations of consumption fanned the flames of revolution. They placed themselves on the throne as timekeeper, setting a vision for a good life at the pace of intragenerational.[52] A compressed present, with each person living multiple lifetimes, was good for business.

The 1970s through the 1990s would be lived under a divided fiefdom of timekeepers—Hollywood, Madison Avenue, MTV, and Wall Street—all united under the banner of consumption and that "greed is good," to quote Gordon Gekko from the movie *Wall Street*.[53] These leaders agreed that it was good to go fast: production and reproduction needed to move at the pace of intragenerational, supporting the divide between work and production, sex and reproduction. They demonstrated that they were committed to countercultural ideals. Particularly in the 1980s, work was for making large amounts of money, and sex (with many partners) was for freedom. Studio 54, the famous nightclub, was as much about cocaine as it was about sex, the two nearly indivisible. Fast cars, fast sex, and fast drugs were the moral vision of the good in this new compressed present.

49. A new timekeeper would be needed to create a new imagined community, one built now on consumer goods. Eventually, in our time, this would be transferred back into Washington politics through social media, leading to culture wars wherein people pick party politics like sports teams and consumer genres.

50. Eventually they would. Bill and Hillary Clinton were essential counterculture kids. It just took them decades to get to the White House, and by that time it was too late.

51. For more on this story, see my *Faith Formation in a Secular Age: Responding to the Church's Obsession with Youthfulness* (Grand Rapids: Baker Academic, 2017), part 1.

52. This sense of the good life and time was good for business. See part 1 of my *Faith Formation in a Secular Age* for more on this. See particularly the discussion in Thomas Frank, *The Conquest of Cool: Business Culture, Counterculture, and the Rise of Hip Consumerism* (Chicago: University of Chicago Press, 1998).

53. For more on the zeitgeist of "greed is good" and a full discussion of its cultural and economic location, see Paul Roberts, *The Impulse Society: America in the Age of Instant Gratification* (New York: Bloomsbury, 2014), chap. 2, in which he also discusses Richard Sennett's point about huge economic and cultural transitions when capitalism sped up to the momentum of short-term stock price returns.

By the mid-1990s, many of the most powerful entities in the fiefdom were coked-out and hungover. With the acceleration of globalization and the innovation of the microprocessor (a technological acceleration that was as transformational to our social lives as industrialization was in its time), the time was right for the consumer timekeepers to take control.[54] By the late 1990s, after a decade or more of the decay rate increasing and the present compressing, tech corporations—Silicon Valley—took hold as our new cultural timekeeper. Apple soon had more cash on hand than the US government, selling more music and movies than any studio or consumer company.

It truly was revenge of the nerds! In the 1980s few would have imagined that computer geeks would be in control of the media and the cultural sense of the good. By the early 2000s Silicon Valley had taken over other corporations' business (not that different from the Medici taking control of Tuscany in the fifteenth century). Napster nearly bankrupted the music industry, E-Trade took over trading, YouTube became the new MTV, and Netflix was crowned the new movie industry. Soon there was no part of our individual or social lives that the microprocessor wasn't disrupting. It took a thousand years for Avignon[55] to be replaced by the modern nation-state as timekeeper. It took only a few hundred for corporations in Silicon Valley to replace the modern nation-state.[56] By the late 1990s, even the elites at Harvard and other institutions were bewitched by Silicon Valley, not Washington or even New York or Los Angeles. Cultural power rested with the nerds.

Silicon Valley could readily embrace an accelerated modernity, affirming and pushing further the intragenerational decay rate. Chat rooms, simulation

54. I'm taking much of this historical sense of Silicon Valley from Leslie Berlin's fine history. She articulates how Silicon Valley was a small player in the fiefdom of timekeepers. But by the 2000s this would be very different. "In the early 1970s, Silicon Valley startup companies were largely deemed irrelevant to the real business of the United States, which was concentrated in East Coast financial centers and cities such as Detroit, Pittsburgh, and Chicago that had manufacturing at their core. The nation's new minicomputer companies, Digital Equipment Corporation (DEC) most prominent among them, were clustered near MIT and Harvard, along Boston's Route 128. A *Forbes* editor with responsibility for the West Coast stated unequivocally that the magazine was interested only in publicly held companies with sales of $50 million or more." *Troublemakers: Silicon Valley's Coming of Age* (New York: Simon & Schuster, 2017), 74.

55. I'm using Avignon only as a placeholder for the universal sense of the church, for the church as the anchor of society in Christendom.

56. Rosa makes this same point about the nation-state no longer keeping time: "Thus, in the twenty-first century, democratic governments no longer appear to be a pace-maker of social change; rather, they have shifted to a role of 'fire extinguisher' and to a mode of 'muddling through,' at best; reacting to the pressures created elsewhere rather than shaping our shared world." Rosa, "De-Synchronization, Dynamic Stabilization, Dispositional Squeeze: The Problem of Temporal Mismatch," in *The Sociology of Speed: Digital, Organizational, and Social Temporalities*, ed. Judy Wajcman and Nigel Dodd (Oxford: Oxford University Press, 2017), 37.

games (like *Second Life*), and then social media sites were the ultimate tools to live out multiple lives. Silicon Valley delivered what the others couldn't: a sense of real participation, with concrete tools, in speeding up your life to the intragenerational pace of multiple lives.

Under the new timekeeper (into the 2000s), innovation became our highest good. Innovation maintained the sensation of the new, promising a compressed future of high decay rates that affected not only sex and media but all facets of our lives. To be innovative was now to see the good life running at the pace of multiple lifetimes in one life. The good life embraced the shortened present, so short that you should aim for only the new. "Disrupt and hack everything" was the mantra. (Today that mantra has shifted to "move fast and break things," a doubling down on the logic.) The new itself bore the weight of sex and power.

Silicon Valley shipped its production to China, redefining work as the design and movement of information and data. Work became not only postproduction but even postmaterial. An accelerated modernity needs an army of coders, not manufacturers. Google and Yahoo! shaped this army of coders to disturb work such that it wouldn't even feel like work. They sought productivity from their coders by making work feel like the freedom of play. Coders were as committed to the ideals of a compressed present as any church cardinal was to sacred time in the *ancien regime*.

And thanks to Silicon Valley, sex became fully individual, sped up further, thanks to the microprocessor. By the 2000s, porn had become commonplace in the accelerated modernity of Silicon Valley. Porn was endemic in Silicon Valley not just because you consumed it through the internet but more so because it allowed you to live different lives—having thousands, or hundreds of thousands, of sexual partners. All without the time-consuming drag of meeting and dating (though there was an app for that if you wanted it).[57] With porn, all you need is your own urge. With that urge you are free to enter a digital space and get off. Sex became so divided from reproduction that it eliminated completely the need for another person. Porn is sex for a hyperaccelerated late modernity. Late modernity has no time for conversation, connection, tenderness, and shared being. Porn is sex free of the mystery of beings in union.

57. Most of Silicon Valley's greatest breakthroughs that affect our day-to-day lives were pioneered and inspired by porn. Online pay services, video streaming, and more were inspired and perfected by the porn industry. Some have even argued that consumer internet business is the porn business. If not for the desire to live multiple lives, separating sex from reproduction and even marriage, we might not have Hulu and Amazon Prime. For a discussion on this, see Pamela Paul, *Pornified: How Pornography Is Transforming Our Lives, Our Relationships, and Our Families* (New York: Times Books, 2005); and Gail Dines, *Pornland: How Porn Has Hijacked Our Sexuality* (Boston: Beacon Press, 2010).

Without another person, sex is disconnected even from love. (Which is why women in porn are universally treated like objects. Porn is sex for only *you*. It is so private that it's for only your individual experience, for what gets *you* off.) Prostitution had caused this disconnection since time immemorial. Online pornography just allowed it to happen faster. It made it so fast that you lost much of the sensory experience, like smell and touch (but VR will take care of that soon!). It's so convenient and fast because you need only yourself and a Wi-Fi connection.[58]

The Arrival of Sexbots

It's fair to wonder whether late modernity will produce sex robots, and whether these robots will accomplish a latent goal endemic to modernity: to put a complete end to both production and reproduction. We already worry that robots could eliminate human beings from the processes of production, leading to an economic crisis. We already anticipate this with the advances in smart automation and AI. And not far behind any story about robots in production is a story about advances in sexbots. The British TV show *Humans*

---

58. Many have discussed porn as being a different genus from sex. It has very little to do with otherness and can even trap you in a self-enclosed reality. It's a form of sex that is Luther's sense of sin (*incurvatus in se*). For a deeper take on this reality, see the movie *Don Jon* starring Joseph Gordon-Levitt (as well as the scholarly books mentioned in the previous note). What ultimately makes porn a (big) problem is exactly what Joseph Gordon-Levitt's character experiences: the more one watches porn, with its ability to separate sex from personhood and thereby make the other an object, the more sex is removed from experiences of resonance. Sex bears the same fate as everything else in late modernity that cannot keep up. Porn gives you the freedom to have sex at a compressed present, producing newer and newer and newer partners; but as the science shows, it makes you unable to connect with an actual partner (see Gary Wilson, *Your Brain on Porn: Internet Pornography and the Emerging Science of Addiction* [Kent, UK: Commonwealth, 2014]). Sex is no longer a discourse, no longer a conversation of bodies. Porn renders your very spirit unable to talk with another person body-to-body, spirit-to-spirit. Porn is the perfect late-modern creation because its vicious circle promises freedom, like a drug, but deadens you while doing so. It breeds on seeking the sensation of the new as a good but never delivers anything worth living for. It can continue because it promises more innovation that will more quickly get you off. When sex is a conversation of lovers, it is a slow and spiritually resonant connection. It's about persons in union with each other's being. (This high view of sex and its beauty has led the church to encourage oaths of marriage, with sacramental liturgies, to protect both the persons and sex itself from becoming a cheap consumer good, as it is in Silicon Valley. Because union is sacred to the church—echoing the Trinity—the church has the highest view of sex, imploring us to go slow with it, which annoys the new timekeepers.) Porn can promise none of this. It is a bastardized version of sex and an attack against Eros— though those who get rich on it would tell us otherwise, claiming a quick and free way to live multiple lives. For more on speed and sex, see Parisian philosopher and architect Paul Virilio, a classic Parisian intellectual who wrote many cultural pieces on speed and modernity, in "From Sexual Perversion to Sexual Diversion," in *The Paul Virilio Reader*, ed. Steve Redhead (New York: Columbia University Press, 2004), 175–89.

even contained a plot about a near future in which a husband has an affair with his robot. The TV show *Westworld* explores this further, imagining a whole theme park built on having sex with and killing humanlike bots.

An accelerating late modernity seems to be speeding toward a complete separation, or dissolving, of the human engagement in production and re-production. If this dissolving ever comes, it will likely end the modern quest for something completely different, although no one knows what this would actually be like. Yet it's interesting that we are so embedded in modernity that we can only envision a dystopia for what comes after modernity. Our nightmares are equally divided between the loss of production and the loss of reproduction. We so fully control reproduction that we're haunted by the thought that it will no longer work when we need it most. Some of our dystopian nightmares involve ecological disasters and a world in which repro-duction is no longer possible (see, e.g., *Interstellar*, *IO*, *Children of Men*, and *The Handmaid's Tale*). Or our dystopian nightmares involve the attack of the robots. Enhanced for the sake of production, they eventually acquire the power to revolt and kill us (see, e.g., *Terminator*, *Bladerunner*, and *Westworld*).[59]

An accelerating modernity has been speeding up our lives, seeking to divide production from reproduction, and further dividing sex from childbearing, and work from production. With every divide, we're promised more freedom, more space for authentic expression. But what divides next? And do we really wish for human lives without any connection to production and reproduction? Can we be human if production and reproduction decay to nothing? We worry that *Wall-E* will become our future. A world without any human connection to production gives us only a polluted, flat meaninglessness; beauty itself would be lost. A world without human connection to reproduction delivers only an incredible loneliness.

The Dystopia of the Denomination

With these happy prophecies in our mind (that's sarcasm!), we need to turn to another kind of dystopia happening right now: the dystopia of the denomination.

The purpose of the cultural analysis above is to show that when the good life is sped up to living multiple lifetimes (intragenerational), the decay rate is short and the present is compressed—which puts the denomination in crisis. It cannot not be! The denomination is built for a speed that our cultural con-ception of the good life has surpassed, leaving us susceptible to church-wide

---

59. Of course, we do get a few monster dystopias like *The Quiet Place* and *Birdbox*.

depression. The denomination and its congregations are falling behind, and they are finding it harder to even approach the speed of the good life.

If it feels like the denomination is coming apart, that's because it is. The denomination is a vehicle not built for the speed asked of it. The denomination is still moving, though shaking viciously as bolts and pieces, maybe even a tire, fly off. Everyone along for the ride (clergy, elders, seminary presidents, faculty, council members, synod and presbytery staffs, denominational publishers) is worried about when it will abruptly break down. When it does, will it sputter to a stop or flip over violently a half-dozen times? Denominational leaders are exhausted trying to keep it together while being pushed by the pace.

The denomination was built for a generational decay rate, when people lived in a present of a single lifetime, a generation. The present was a lifetime because production and reproduction were assumed to be for a lifetime. As a structure, the denomination was always bound to other structures. When production and reproduction were at the speed of a generation, the denomination could be strong, even thrive. Its own structural life is fortified by the good life imagined within production and reproduction. Though it was never keeping time even in its heyday, the denomination nevertheless thrived inside the timekeeping of the nation-state.[60] Loyalty to an imagined community for a lifetime was part of the good life. This loyalty provided the resources the denomination needed.

The denomination was lost when the decay rate of production and re-production sped up, when we shifted to a pace of intragenerational, with people living multiple lives, and when the imagined community was neither nation nor denomination but a consumer group that affirms and recognizes an individual's authentic identity. Loyalty to such imagined communities is no longer central to a conception of a good life. People's lives are changing too quickly to put much stock in the imagined community of the denomination. The denomination's call for loyalty is considered backward, maybe even an affront to freedom.

These shifts directly affect particular congregations. It's now assumed that if a congregation no longer meets your needs, no longer gives you the sense that you're living a good life, you're free to find another. You worry little whether this new congregation is Lutheran or Methodist; the denomination has little effect on your chosen congregation. A new job or a new marriage might determine what kind of congregation you're looking for, but denominational consistency is not likely high on your list. This assumes that you're even looking for a congregation at all during this particular life you're now living.

60. Probably due to its theological corruption as Stanley Hauerwas and others have made clear. See Hauerwas and Willimon, *Resident Aliens*.

At the most direct level, you'll admit you're living different lives through the life stages of your kids. You'll go to one church when your children are toddlers (a church with a good children's ministry), another when they are adolescents (for its youth ministry), finally picking another when you're an empty nester. Or maybe you'll never get that far, divorcing when your children are young, perhaps sending them to church with your ex, and you instead living the kind of new life that doesn't even think about going to church.

If you are part of a congregation, even amid your multiple shifting lives, you'll be looking for resources or assistance in coping with the speed that is pressing in on you. You'll be looking directly for affirmation of the authentic life you're living now.[61] You'll sense that it's a cultural good to be living in a compressed present of many lifetimes. And you'll expect the congregation to affirm your present by providing you with resources to live it out.

It's little wonder that congregations that have thrown off the denominational label have seemed to do best. Megachurches that have the resources for people who are moving in and out of multiple lives seem to be the only churches able to retain people, who harvest that congregation's many resources.

The congregation's new role places the pastor in her own crisis of speed.[62] It may even lead the denomination to encourage, reward, or demand the pastor to get her church to speed, which means "make it bigger" (usually framed in the language of "self-sufficient" or "sustainable"). Fast and big resources and programs are the best way of meeting the demands of the speed of multiple lives. The pastor somehow needs to take a fifty-person church with few resources, in a denomination of depleted assets, and speed things up to create a five-thousand-member church. Her first step is to make it relevant to fast people living in a compressed present, seeking the good of multiple lifetimes. Retention with these fast-paced people is won by giving

61. As was clear after her death, and radiated beautifully across the internet, Rachel Held Evans's ministry was to people who could no longer remain in the denominational (particularly conservative) churches they grew up in. She helped them stay connected to Christianity while looking for a new home that was more authentic to their growing experience. However, her followers always had a sense of discontent because that new home seemed in some far-off galaxy. They needed Rachel all the more because they were marooned.

62. It puts the denomination in its own kind of crisis. When large congregations build large audiences through the speed of multiple lifetimes, they quickly realize that they did so without much help from the denomination. They come to realize that the denomination needs them more than they need the denomination. No one cares about the imagined community of the denomination. If the denomination takes a stance, say, on sexuality or just becomes a roadblock to the speed of innovation, the big church will leave or threaten to leave, taking its resources. When a church exceeds two thousand members, it holds more resource power than most synods or presbyteries. These big congregations even hold a higher moral good by being the innovative ones who seek newness and who are not stuck in old structures.

surpluses of resources. This is why all big churches use small groups. Small groups allow for basic human connections to flourish, but they also niche out resources for the particular life you're living now.

It's not simply about the numbers: it's what the numbers produce. The numbers fuel the church's intragenerational pace. The numbers provide the resources for the activities that keep people from leaving. This kind of massive speed-up is the only thing that can keep people from speeding themselves to another church or even dropping church for another interest.

Of course, there is a catch. Innovation always moves faster than the resources the congregation can provide. Even for the biggest of churches! When people innovate their lives and don't find the church fast enough in response to this new lifetime, they take offense. When the church isn't fast enough with resources, it feels like a lack of affirmation, even opposition to your authentic way of being. Yet sometimes it's simply that you're moving much faster than the church can respond with new resources.[63] In late modernity, resources move slower than identity transitions. This is true at least for institutions built on generational structures of production and reproduction. Maybe the congregation is recognizing you at a slower pace than you wish. For some, this is just as bad as rejection.

When the denomination or large church refuses—or is too slow to respond with—the resourced affirmation you seek, you feel a deep moral violation. Now that you're living a new identity, these so-called seeker-sensitive churches seem anything but sensitive to your own pursuit of authenticity. You resent them because they promised to respond to every kind of new lifetime, but your own most authentic identity is ignored (or worse, spoken against, often to maintain resources that will keep them at speed).[64]

It's a different phenomenon, but exists in the same logic, for mainline denominations. While the mainline affirms the speed of these multiple lifetimes (for the sake of the cultural good of tolerance), it has no structural form to retain such people. The mainline ideologically affirms an intragenerational

63. A church might worry that if it supports one lifestyle it could harm their resources and slow them down. This becomes a calculation of risk and resources more than it is theological reflection.

64. This often leads to a debate about attracting young, fast people. The mainline thinks that being LGBTQIA affirming will catch them up to the cultural goods. And some younger evangelicals, pushing back against the establishment, point to the necessity of affirming LGBTQIA folks for the sake of keeping the church relevant. I find both of these unreasoned. Affirmation of and communion with all people, LGBTQIA included, needs a deeper theological rationale than utilitarian arguments of cultural relevance and acceleration. For example, Graham Ward's rich, theological argument for affirming LGBTQIA persons in *Cultural Transformation and Religious Practice* is much more generative than the arguments I've pointed to above.

pace but has no way of existing without the pace set at generational. The mainline is graying because, though it supports the pace in our social norms (deeply committed to free authenticity in sex and work), it structurally depends on the decay rate of production and reproduction being set at one lifetime.

Mainline denominations often have progressive social statements but few young, fast-moving progressive people in their pews. This is particularly true for those young people who grew up in these denominations, few of whom stay in the mainline through their lifetime. The younger people who are present in mainline churches usually grew up in conservative denominations and congregations. Disappointed, they left these churches for Methodist and Episcopal mainline churches. The mainline became the way station church for conservative young people who are speeding up for the sake of authenticity. They spend time in the mainline before exiting altogether. Overall, the mainline is stuck between (a) wanting to be socially fast in a compressed present of many lifetimes and (b) being dependent on slower structures that move at a generational decay rate.

The Real Crisis for the Church Is Time

Denominational dystopia is an issue of resources. The denomination and its congregations are resource-depleted (it's *Interstellar*). But this is really a crisis of time, a loss of speed—*not* because the church has decreased its pace but because modernity itself has continued to accelerate. The congregation can't keep up. Even the huge ones are falling behind (they are even more at risk because of their huge campuses and high overhead).

And it won't get any easier, even if we can catch up a little bit, feeling temporarily better about our resources. The new timekeepers will push all the faster for new innovation in identity, social norms, and the structures of production and reproduction. Silicon Valley, unlike the other timekeepers, holds innovation and the very compressed present as its highest good. Even if the denomination finds a draft by doubling down on the logic of the cultural timekeeper, making the local congregation into an innovation hub and the pastor into entrepreneur (encouraging pastors and congregations to match in form and vision the timekeeper of Silicon Valley), it simply cannot keep up.[65]

The church doesn't have access to formal (markets, venture capital) or imagined (the good life as bound in sacred time and ritual) engines of acceleration. Our timekeeper is not satisfied with anything but more and more

---

65. For an example of this perspective in turning the denomination, congregation, and seminary toward "disruptive innovation," see David McAllister-Wilson, *A New Church and a New Seminary: Theological Education Is the Solution* (Nashville: Abingdon, 2018), chap. 4.

speed-up. The present is too compressed, and the good is too embedded in the newness of innovation, to ever *not* push for more and more speed-up. At its core the church isn't facing an issue of losing people, money, or other resources. The church is in a deep deficiency of time!

And speeding up time creates, and keeps us in, the secular age. It does not just keep people too busy to go to church.[66] It keeps their lives moving at such a frantic pace that all the transcendent quality of mystery, divine discourse, and openness to spiritual encounter is drowned out in acceleration.[67] Our attention is focused too fully on immanent sensations of the newness of innovation to hear the voice of God and see the beauty God beckons us to.

———————

The subject line of the email read, "You'll love this . . . the Depression Increases." It was from the pastor in North Dakota.

---

66. That's a secular 2 conception, explored in my *Faith Formation in a Secular Age.*
67. This is a secular 3 reality that Taylor tells us is our real issue.

10

why email sucks, and social media even more

reach and acceleration

The North Dakota pastor's email read:

> I don't know if you'll find this interesting, but it connects with our conversation
> from before. Two weeks ago we had a parent who got very upset with our youth
> director. She was upset with something he taught at youth group on Wednesday
> night, but she also seemed angry that the youth group wouldn't be meeting in
> January. We're not sure why this made her so mad. Her daughter's on the bas-
> ketball team and never comes in January anyhow (we decided to take a break
> because we have so many busy kids like this). Well, she got a handful of other
> parents really worked up. At first I was actually happy—though I felt bad for
> our youth director. At least they were engaged! There was some energy. Kind of
> like marriage counseling: it's better when couples are fighting than disengaged.
> To protect the youth director and embrace the engagement, I offered a parent
> meeting for anyone to talk through their concerns and air their frustrations.
> All the worked-up parents immediately responded with "Good idea," "Yes,
> this is needed," and "About time." I then sent out possible times to gather. . . .
> Well, we couldn't find a time. Not one time worked, no matter how hard we tried.
> And we tried and tried for days and weeks to find a time to gather, and nothing.

As we struggled to find a time, you could see all the energy just seep out—even in this case the negative energy. Later I checked in with a few of the parents, and they basically said, "We don't care anymore, we don't have time to care." This is what I mean: church-wide depression. I thought you might find this interesting.

I hope your semester is going well.

Over the last few chapters we've been swimming in deep waters with Hartmut Rosa. We've looked directly at the first two dimensions of an accelerated modernity: technological acceleration and the acceleration of social life. We've seen how these two dimensions are interlaced. We've explored particularly how our moral norms shift under quickening decay rates. With Rosa and Charles Taylor, I'm maintaining that our shared and contested sense of the good life is fundamental to our ways of being in the world. Therefore, I agree that technological acceleration has shifted the imagination of the church. Here I'm with other ecclesiologies that have focused on technological change in relation to new media and new digital realities.[1] Unlike these perspectives, I'm asserting that the heart of the issue is not technology but the increase in speed, the shifting in our conception of time, because of the centrality of the good life.

The church is not just technologically behind. Rather, technological acceleration challenges the church, and those in it, to shift to a higher speed. This increase in speed directly affects our social norms. The church is affected by technology's constant pursuit of acceleration, in unison with the speeding up of our social lives. This imposes escalated decay rates on our norms, shifting our moral conception of production and reproduction and making the denomination far less viable.

The acceleration of our social lives has caused the church to be left behind (and the church acutely feels left behind). This shift indeed is related to technological acceleration, but technological acceleration is fed by the acceleration of our social norms. Acceleration in these two dimensions of technology and social life shortens the present, imposes movement toward the new, and establishes innovation as our moral horizon.

It would be incorrect to say that the church and its leadership need to speed up and create "disruptive innovation," a view that the "best" change comes from radically shifting the ways we act in the world by inventing something new (like products, programs, practices). Such a claim about disruptive innovation can be made only by narrowing one's vision and not examining the effects of an accelerated modernity. Without critical engagement, disruptive

---

1. I mentioned this above in note 2 of chap. 5. I'm thinking of Pete Ward, Elizabeth Drescher, Keith Anderson, and others.

innovation falls into the same trap that many of its supporters have called the church to avoid. Those in the missional church movement, who have helpfully called the church away from Christendom, often are the biggest advocates for disruptive innovation.[2] Unfortunately, these missional advocates often fail to see that this is actually just swapping one kind of Christendom for another. Disruptive innovation pushes to mold the church's life, but it will always do so in subjection to another timekeeper (ignoring that the timekeeper forms much of the unconscious conception of the good).

Nearly all of the conversations about post-Christendom assume that the nation-state is the timekeeper. Rightly, these calls for a post-Christendom have sought to move the church away from being the lapdog of the state, conceding to a mindset of civic religion. But the nation is no longer keeping time.[3] Its politics remain an attention-getting theater, like when the religious right supports nationalism or when the left goes wild with Twitter outrage. No doubt the decisions made by politicians (decisions usually made for the sake of reelection) affect our lives. But all the drama keeps us from recognizing that the new timekeeper is actively setting the pace for our cultural good life. The call to congregations and pastors to be disruptive innovators is actually just a digital or Silicon Valley version of the same Christendom ghetto.[4] A disruptive innovator is the exact profile of a loyal subscriber to the accelerated time that Silicon Valley keeps. To call the church and its leaders to be disruptive innovators is simply to adopt Silicon Valley's vision of the good life.[5] It's simply a move from a state-bound Christendom to a digitally bound one.[6]

2. See Mark Lau Branson and Nicholas Warnes, eds., *Starting Missional Churches: Life with God in the Neighborhood* (Downers Grove, IL: IVP, 2014).

3. We no longer trust Washington to hold and protect our sense of the good. We have to pick a political tribe and be loyal to it like a brand, because we believe our political enemy is coming to destroy our sense of the good, not to deliver any good. After 1968 the good of the imagined community of America was punctured. For an explanation of how this political branding happens, see Paul Roberts, *The Impulse Society: America in the Age of Instant Gratification* (New York: Bloomsbury, 2014), chap. 8.

4. In the final part of *A Secular Age* (Cambridge, MA: Belknap, 2007), 456–60, Taylor makes strong statements against Christendom.

5. This is a much more complicated argument than I have space to develop. Of course the church has always adopted forms and practices within a culture (e.g., the Christmas tree). But this has always been done to make distinct claims about time and the good life. Andrew Walls shows us that the church always transforms its cultural context through adapting it (see *The Missionary Movement in Christian History: Studies in the Transmission of Faith* [Maryknoll, NY: Orbis Books, 2009]). His point is that the incarnation calls for an enculturation that transforms culture. My point is that disruptive innovation has not been an incarnational transformation but a Christendom concession—a new digital Christendom concession. I do think this point is debatable and I welcome the debate. But for now, it appears that something like this has occurred.

6. Of course, by definition this isn't Christendom at all (I'm just using this as a way to make the larger point that we've adopted these fundamental ways of conceiving of time

I suppose a response could be, Who cares? The church and its congregations have always had to negotiate culturally different conceptions, practices, and moral perspectives. If we can innovate in the proper way, why is this a problem? Clearly, not everything about acceleration is terrible (not even everything about innovation is bad). Speed does some good things. Fast ambulances are valuable, and innovation in cancer treatment is always welcome. The problem with acceleration as an unquestioned high moral good is not that speed is bad. As a matter of fact, I'll soon assert that the response to acceleration ought not necessarily be a slowdown at all. Following Rosa, the issue is much more complicated than claiming that speed is the problem and thus slowdown is the answer. That equation is too simplistic. For instance, abruptly slowing down a roller coaster or the economy will lead to catastrophic mayhem.

The problem with acceleration is not speed but the ways that the sought goods of acceleration create alienation. The parents who the pastor wrote about in the email feel so busy that they end up alienated from their own feelings, from having the energy to fight for what they think is good. We've already discussed how depression is the speed sickness (*Zeitkrankheit*) of identity innovation and how busyness becomes a sense of fullness that produces a deep sense of guilt. Continually increasing speed (through the logic of innovation) produces alienation. Disruptive innovation comes from a moral conception of a good life that, if we're not careful, affirms racing toward the new (in a short present), which alienates us from one another, the world, and ultimately transcendence. Disruptive innovation affirms and strengthens the immanent frame. Its view of time, the good, and the future is all bound within an immanent horizon that squeezes out sacred time.[7]

---

and the good). Silicon Valley, as we've shown, is post-Christian, even anti-Christian, which makes it all the more odd that we would seek its forms. Unlike the nation-state, Silicon Valley, with it accelerated social norms, wants nothing to do with the church. The state saw a use for the church, not so for most of Silicon Valley. It feels like it's post-Christendom, but this isn't because we've taken on significant imaginations and practices to seek and live toward a different good inside a different conception of time. Rather, more pathetically, we're willing to take on Silicon Valley's innovative good of a short present of disruption without any direct engagement.

7. Here are two very different views of disruptive innovation. The first is by a seminary president, the second by a historian. Contrasting these quotes shows the problems with disruptive innovation. More specifically it shows that the seminary president doesn't quite understand what is at stake in calling pastors to be disruptive innovators. The seminary president writes, "'Disruptive innovation' is a helpful way to think about changing institutions. It's a phrase coined by Clayton Christensen from the Harvard Business School. The research question he explores is: Why do strong, seemingly well-led companies fail to take advantage of new possibilities that are right under their noses? Why did Sears with its catalog fail to become Walmart, then Amazon?" David McAllister-Wilson, *A New Church and a New Seminary: Theological Education Is the Solution* (Nashville: Abingdon, 2018), 72.

Into Dimension Three: Acceleration of the Pace of Life

The correct response to the claims that I'm making is, How? How is it that acceleration creates alienation? We'll have to take the answer one step at a time, turning first to the third dimension of an accelerated modernity: the acceleration of the pace of life. It's the acceleration of the pace of life that the North Dakota pastor witnesses to in his email.

There's little doubt that the first two dimensions, technological acceleration and the acceleration of social life, are dizzying. But dizziness is a relative feeling, and it could be positive or negative. You can be dizzy with excitement, buzzed and feeling good. Or dizziness could be the first sign that something is terribly wrong, as with a brain aneurism. The timekeepers of Silicon Valley tell us that this dizziness is the thrilling side effect of the new. If we keep aiming for the new, forgetting the past, we can stay excitedly buzzed, never noticing, for instance, the disorienting blur this gives to transcendence and history.

This third dimension, the ratcheting up of the pace of life, reveals that the dizziness isn't just a buzzed excitement but rather a symptom that something is wrong. Without this third dimension it would be harder to see the dizziness of acceleration as symptomatic of alienation. The disruptive innovators fail to see this acceleration of the pace of life, though they feel it. They miss it because they fail to connect the feeling of a rushed pace to the other two dimensions. Not recognizing the demand of an increased pace on our lives is inextricably related to technological acceleration and the acceleration of our social lives.

All three dimensions interpenetrate one another, each wrapped around the other two. The three dimensions work together to create our accelerated modernity. But this third dimension—the continued increase in the pace of our day-to-day lives—shows most clearly that alienation is a direct effect of acceleration. At first blush, the acceleration of the pace of life seems to stand in opposition to the other two. Yet this third dimension ultimately moves the congregation, or the denomination as a whole, into a state of fatigue, which breeds church-wide depression, as the pastor in North Dakota was pointing out.

The historian writes, "Disruptive innovation as the explanation for how change happens has been subject to little serious criticism, partly because it's headlong, while critical inquiry is unhurried; partly because disrupters ridicule doubters by charging them with fogyism, as if to criticize a theory of change were identical to decrying change; and partly because, in its modern usage, innovation is the idea of progress jammed into a criticism-proof jack-in-the-box. . . . Disruptive innovation goes further, holding out the hope of salvation against the very damnation it describes: disrupt, and you will be saved." Jill Lepore, "The Disruption Machine," *New Yorker*, June 14, 2014, https://www.newyorker.com/magazine/2014/06/23/the-disruption-machine.

This third dimension of acceleration is like a sibling with blond hair in a family of brunettes. At the surface level it appears there should be a sibling rivalry between these three dimensions. For example, technological acceleration, particularly that which comes from Silicon Valley, is supposed to produce more time. It is supposed to (even promises to) slow the pace of life, producing leisure. All these innovations from Silicon Valley are supposed to be time-saving technologies. But upon closer examination they inherently do the opposite. Of course, they allow us to do more and reach further, compressing time and space, but not without also speeding up the pace of our lives.[8]

Exhibit A: Email

An example that Hartmut Rosa uses to illustrate this point is the very technological innovation that the pastor used to reach out to me: email.[9] It's safe to say that the innovation of email should cut in half the amount of time it takes to correspond. If before email you received five letters a day, it would take you about two hours of each day to draft, address, and mail your correspondence. Surely the innovation of email should at least cut that time in half, perhaps even three-fourths. With email, it should take you only fifteen to twenty minutes to respond to five correspondences. This should free up time, giving you an additional hour and a half in your life to read, relax, exercise, eat right, or play with your children. This saved hour and a half should release you from a driving pace, to contemplate your existence or breathe in the joy of being alive.

But it *never* works this way. Technological acceleration, which is supposed to produce innovations that give you more free time, does the opposite. Acceleration does not release us from speed but always seeks more speed. Gaining more time through acceleration will demand that time be filled with more actions, not fewer. Time won by acceleration wants only further acceleration.

Or we could look at it this way: innovative technologies free up space inside a unit of time. In our example, email frees up space inside the two-hour unit for correspondence. Yet the space freed by an accelerated modernity doesn't just *give* you this time; you must fill it with more actions. Technological

8. Hartmut Rosa provides a very helpful and rich articulation of the accelerating of the pace of life in *Social Acceleration: A New Theory of Modernity* (New York: Columbia University Press, 2015), 230–44. He shows vividly how practical and embedded in our day-to-day lives this acceleration is.

9. To read Rosa's discussion of email—which I'm drawing from—see *Alienation and Acceleration: Towards a Critical Theory of Late-Modern Temporality* (Malmö, Sweden: NSU Press, 2014), 24.

acceleration doesn't save time; it just allows for (infinitely) more actions inside a unit of time.

Our lives feel even more rushed because, compared to the past, we are doing exponentially more actions inside the units of time. Recalling our art professor from way back in chapter 5, he's right: things are objectively speeding up. The pace has increased. Technological acceleration doesn't give us more time for leisure, rest, and contemplation of our humanity. It gives us more access to more actions inside our units of time. This makes us feel busy! This push to get more actions inside more units of time (to do more at a quicker pace) becomes part of our social norms. This desire to get more actions done is a good, even pushing us to blur lines between distinct units of time, doing actions set for one unit in another unit to catch up or get ahead. Like brushing our teeth in the car.

We call this "multitasking," or increasing a task or action within a unit of time as a way of quickening our pace. The innovation of email ideally allows you to spend only twenty minutes on correspondence, but in reality it creates the conditions for you to receive not five but fifty-five emails a day. You now have the tools, if you push hard enough, to respond to them all. You feel frantically busy increasing the pace of actions in this unit of time. But responding to fifty-five emails also gives you a sense of being in demand. Your busyness is a sign that you're living with a kind of fullness, which seems to accelerate the pace of your life by the week, threatening you with the risk of alienation from yourself and from the world as you rush.

Soon enough you realize it's very hard to keep pace with all those emails. You decide you actually need three hours a day to do your correspondence. You'll have to take that hour from somewhere. To not fall further behind, it's best to take it from sleeping, eating, or another human-induced task that asks us to downshift. Rosa explains that we have empirical studies showing that people sleep less, eat faster, and walk more quickly than in the past (we even talk faster).[10]

One empirical measurement in the acceleration of the pace of life is the increase in multitasking. Multitasking, as we just showed, allows us to do more things inside a distinct unit of time. For instance, inside your three hours of correspondence you find a way to send emails and make phone calls at the same time. Multitasking might also be a means of finding that extra hour from other units of time. For instance, needing to find that extra hour, you send emails at your son's swim meet. This will gain you more actions, but in turn it will keep you from really being there, from sharing in this moment with him, from

10. Rosa, *Alienation and Acceleration*, 22–24.

being awake to the world around you. It will alienate you from experiencing the meet with him. You'll be present physically but absent mentally in the rush to add more (and distinct) actions to this unit of time. Your son's meet is then reduced, made flat and immanent. Inside your race to add actions to units of time, his meet is no longer allowed to be a zone of the encounter with personhood but is only a unit of time open to complete tasks within.

And let's not even mention the horror of returning from vacation to hundreds of emails. The relaxation of being away is now paid for by having to add both units of time and a faster pace of actions inside those units. You were on vacation, connecting again with your humanity, but now in the rush to catch up and keep pace, you're lost again, feeling alienated from yourself by the pace. No wonder those living at the fastest pace and highest privilege refuse to go on vacation! Or if they do, they bring their administrator with them, adding a unit of time to do the actions of email every morning before heading to the golf course or beach.

Before we can call the logic of the acceleration of the pace of life madness, we're told there is inherent good news. For instance, with email, if you forget about capitalization or other niceties, ignoring the art of letter writing of the past, you can squeeze seventy distinct email actions into the unit of three hours of time. That's an innovation! Innovation can help you catch up. (It conveniently creates and solves its own created problems. Innovation creates a pace that calls for more innovation.) The acceleration of the pace of life creates the supposed good of innovation. It demands that you find ingenious ways of getting more actions out of your units of time.

When biographers tell the stories of the people of our late accelerated modernity, they'll have gigabytes, even terabytes, of material. A person active for seventy years will send and receive about two million business emails (and probably twenty times as many text messages).[11] Could you imagine what we'd know about the life of Caesar or Churchill if we had two million of their letters? But of course it's not the same. Almost all of those emails are meaningless, giving us little sense of the person, like Harriet Beecher Stowe's letters so beautifully do. Rather, most are, "Yes, meeting switched to 2:30. BTW, printer not working." Or, "So stressed. Ugh. [Meme of a cat barely holding onto a ledge.]"

We are told that shortened sentences and omitted greetings aren't casualties of an accelerated pace of life. Rather, they are ingenious innovations to help us catch up. Innovation—while seeming to be artistic, fashionable, or even cool—is

---

11. "The Shocking Truth about How Many Emails Are Sent," Campaign Monitor, May 21, 2019, https://www.campaignmonitor.com/blog/email-marketing/2019/05/shocking-truth -about-how-many-emails-sent.

actually the only way to cope with the pace that technological innovation got us into in the first place. We should question whether innovation is really about art and style at all. Innovation is nothing more than an imperative to survive and not be crushed by the anxiety of falling behind. Innovation is made out to be hip, but it is just the necessity of not having the boulder come screaming back down the hill and crushing you. Businesses, educational institutions, and even churches have to innovate or perish. We shouldn't be surprised that fast, innovative multitaskers in our time are prone to mental ailments. Young people (very young ones now) are suffering from high levels of anxiety. They are prone to anxiety because they flirt so directly with alienation. They're often living under acute pressure to do more with less time.

Innovation and Goods Inside the Accelerating Pace of Life

Silicon Valley, in its own business functions, seeks to do more in less time, and it convinces us that this is essential to the good life itself. The most exciting way of being—of finding freedom itself—is doing more in less time. Technological acceleration is supposed to save time. And the acceleration of our social lives (at least the part that affirms the identity innovation of the ethic of authenticity) is supposed to give us the freedom to be ourselves. But technological and identity innovation never produces rest and peace. It only accelerates the pace of life, making the conditions right for alienation. The vision of the good life coded inside these pursuits toward innovation is always doing more in less time, even living more than one lifetime in the eighty-five-year unit of your existence.[12]

The pace of life increases because an accelerated modernity asks us to speed up to do more actions inside our units of time. And this becomes a high good. Fast-moving young people with their head in their phone have somehow become the measure of living an authentic good life. Do more with less time. In my mind, this is the origin of the impulse for disruptive innovation as *the* profile for the future of the congregation, pastor, seminary, and denomination. Feeling like we have less, particularly less resources, the disruptive-innovator masters get more out of less, and they do it with a style that makes them seem ingenious, unique, and authentic. We need more disruptive innovators leading our congregations and denominations because we need people who can get more from less, or so they say.

Yet we ignore that the innovator most often innovates by accelerating the pace of life. They risk alienating themselves from transcendence, and even

12. See Rosa, *Alienation and Acceleration*, 21.

from the core elements of being human, all for the sake of a high cultural good of getting more in less time. The risk in asking pastors and leaders to be disruptive innovators is that it must (it is inherent within its goods) heighten the pace of life.

Not that there shouldn't be innovation or creative impulse in ministry. There should be, and I agree we've lost a lot of creativity. But we need to be careful lest our images of what is needed become as bound in a closed spin of the immanent frame as that of any coder in Silicon Valley.

Innovation itself has to go through a dialectic of judgment and rebirth. It has to be judged for its false claims of ultimacy and reductions of the human spirit, and then it can be given back. One could argue that the Reformers were innovators, but never in the sense of trying to get more actions out of units of time. Luther's so-called innovation was to render human beings passive, unable to act to save themselves. This radically different sense of innovation (if we could even call it that) had a deep sense of retrieval to it. Augustine, Luther, and Barth all retrieve Paul's letter to the Romans as their so-called innovations. What's wrong with Silicon Valley's innovation is that its goods are opposed to retrieval.[13]

Innovation, in the Silicon Valley sense, asks a congregation of already busy people to seek a kind of good life in which they all increase their pace to get more out of the little time available. It risks depression and burnout. It hazards further alienation from transcendence. As with the disgruntled parents of the youth group in North Dakota, even trying to find a unit of time for a meeting at church can infuse despondency into congregation members.

The Reach

It would be wrong to say that acceleration and innovation are thrust upon us unwittingly by the deception of the ruling timekeeper. It's more than that. We are active, never completely passive, participants in seeking a good life.

13. Robert Pogue Harrison's critique is clear on this. See *Juvenescence: A Cultural History of Our Age* (Chicago: University of Chicago Press, 2014). More importantly, see his insightful review of the HBO show *Silicon Valley*: "The Children of Silicon Valley," *New York Review of Books*, July 17, 2014, https://www.nybooks.com/daily/2014/07/17/children-silicon-valley. Because Silicon Valley refuses some retrieval in its movement forward, it lacks wisdom. I fear that this discussion in the church of disruptive innovation overlooks the need for retrieval that *ressourcement* theologians (particularly in Catholicism) and so many others have encouraged us to remember (see Radical Orthodoxy and Alasdair MacIntyre for other examples; I'm following Taylor, who advocates a sense of retrieval without a glorification of or a disdain for the late-modern moment). Retrieval allows for the dialectic of innovation to be judged and yet remain a movement forward. It also allows for a distinct theological voice within the creative process of ministry and congregational life, which is sometimes missing from disruptive innovation thought in the church.

True, Silicon Valley uses the spin of marketing. For instance, Mike Markkula, the genius who helped form the genius of Steve Jobs in the 1980s, knew that the personal computer, and particularly Apple, had a chance of survival only with ace marketing. This core commitment has never left the company, or the valley itself. Silicon Valley uses the spin of marketing to claim that innovation is the way to avoid falling behind.[14]

But spin alone can't account for our sense that the good life is molded around innovation. Nor does it answer why we concede to the acceleration of the pace of our lives, contending that busyness is a legitimate sense of fullness. Rather, I believe there is a direct quality, beyond spin, that the technological acceleration and its innovations give to our daily lives. It's *reach*.

Returning to our email example, let's say that I grant that I now need to add an exponential amount of actions to my time unit of correspondence. I do this either because I relish reach or because I fear falling behind. I like the feeling of being able to reach fifty-five or seventy people a day. Or I fear I'll lose reach in comparison to others' reach if I don't also add actions to my units of time. Reach becomes a good that justifies the acceleration of the pace of life.

Technological acceleration has also sped up our expectations. The norms of our social lives have accelerated with technological acceleration, meaning those reaching out to me expect a response that is coordinate to the speed of their original message. Technology, in tandem with the acceleration of social norms, significantly adds to the pressure of the pace of my life. Where in the past people expected a response to a letter in weeks or months, they now expect an email response in hours.

Yet using email to talk about reach is like using bottle rockets to discuss explosives. If email is a bottle rocket to reach, social media is TNT. Through Twitter, Instagram, or Facebook, I can reach thousands in seconds. And, of course, on these sites reach is compounding. If I can reach thousands, soon

14. Some thinkers have tried to import innovation into the biblical story, giving it a theological legitimacy. I must admit I find statements like the ones below unconvincing. They become a kind of gross *tertium quid*. "Jesus is the innovator: innovating by who he is (incarnation), by what he does (ministry) and by how he dies (cross) and rises again (resurrection)." David Goodhew, Andrew Roberts, and Michael Volland, *Fresh! An Introduction to Fresh Expressions of Church and Pioneer Ministry* (London: SCM, 2012), 27. I think it's more historically accurate to consider innovation as a problem—even an insult—than seeing it as a lens into Jesus's ministry. Jaroslav Pelikan gives an example of innovation being deeply negative: "The Greek Orthodox polemist Athanasius of Paros . . . regarded the Filioque as sufficiently important to be accorded the longest chapter in his *Epitome or Collection of the Divine Dogmas of the Faith*, attacking it as an 'innovation' and going on to 'accuse the Latins of introducing this altogether novel dogma into the common teaching of the faith.'" Pelikan, *The Christian Tradition: A History of the Development of Doctrine*, vol. 5, *Christian Doctrine and Modern Culture (Since 1700)* (Chicago: University of Chicago Press, 1989), 21–22.

I'll reach tens of thousands, maybe even millions. The possibilities for reach keep compounding with social media.

Yet the nature of this reach with social media demands an open platform, not a platform of closed discourse as with email. This open platform exponentially expands reach, promising me the potential of compounding my reach again and again. But the discourse needs to remain always open, always allowing others to see it and respond to it. They must be able to have their own distinct conversations within the open system, while I have mine. It needs to be a cacophony of constant and continual (and thus accelerated) discourse.

This means I must somehow stay up to speed on the constant and multiple discourses, as well as offer my own language event—my own posts—in a way that gets all these thousands of people to notice, recognize, and interact with me. I have the possibility of reach—reach is now democratized and the markets are ready to compound it. But I have to work hard to win this reach. The pace of maintaining so many conversations gives me a metaphorical open room to thousands, even millions, of people. But they're all busy having their own multiple conversations. So I have to quicken my wit and increase my posts to actually turn my reach from potential to actual. I'll have to up my Twitter game—I'll have to give it more time, catching up to the speed of thousands of conversations—if I hope to actually cash in on this golden ticket of reach.

And there's the rub: I know that I'll have to work harder and faster to achieve this reach, but I'm seduced into doing so because social media appears to offer so much possibility. It gives me the good of reach in such a short time. With email, I can reach fifty-five people in three hours. With social media, I can reach five thousand in twenty seconds. Hypothetically, this should free time and release me from a quickened pace while giving me an incredible amount of reach. I should feel satisfied and connected.

Instead, it does the opposite. Though I can quickly post my discourse in this open, fast, and continuous conversation with thousands of people, I nevertheless have to find more time units to keep my eyes on the discussion. If I don't, I'll lose touch and decrease my reach. I'll even feel guilty when someone at work asks, "Did you see that Seth Meyers video on Facebook?" The compounding possibility of reach becomes addictive. Almost without thinking I check in with the open platform of discourse.

Innovative social media allows for an enormous amount of actions to be experienced (to reach me) inside my units of time. But there are so many—coming so fast and never stopping—that I'd better not limit my Instagram use to just one distinct unit of time (say between 2:00 and 3:30 p.m.) like I do with email. I need to be checking in all the time, reconnecting to cash in on reach—the conversations are going too fast.

The reach through these sites is constant and continual, rapidly vibrating every second of every day. So I decide, often without really deciding, to never stop multitasking, to always be checking in, to reconnect and reassure myself that I have reach. And now that multitasking becomes my default way of being in the world, the pace of my life is accelerated. I feel stretched and busy all the time, even when all I'm doing is trying to manage a family dinner. Even this family dinner feels rushed because the multitasking of social media is brought into this time unit of dinner, bringing in literally thousands of other conversations that call for my attention as they reach into my life without stop.

Reach is so intoxicating because it connects us to something legitimately good, and so I decide to never disconnect from the fast, expansive possibility of reach. Yet what's becoming self-evident is how this constant need to experience reach, and the desire for more reach (by continuously checking social media), alienates us from ourselves (and those we're supposed to be having dinner with). My head is in my phone, disconnecting me from the life in front of me, from the less rushed discourses at my dinner table. The thrill of reach keeps me rushing and refreshing my feed, accelerating the pace of my life and alienating me from the life I'm living.

The Good of Reach

Of course, reach itself isn't bad. Nor should we totally hate on social media. Reach is a legitimate good (which is why we're willing to bear the increased acceleration of the pace of our lives and can't put our phones down at dinner). As human beings there is something in us that desires, even needs, reach. We want to be reached by others, and we want the world to reach out to us. Because we are language animals who have our being in and through discourse, as Charles Taylor says, reach is always important to us.[15] All forms of language seek reach—to reach out to others, to reach out and name the world, as Adam is divinely invited to do in Genesis 2. We lose our humanity if our speaking (whether verbal or not) doesn't reach anyone.[16] In turn, we lose our humanity if others' speaking is kept from reaching us. For language

15. See Charles Taylor, *The Language Animal: The Full Shape of the Human Linguistic Capacity* (Cambridge, MA: Harvard University Press, 2016).

16. This is the horror of the asylums in the early twentieth century. They became factories that didn't allow those who could not talk to speak, locking them behind bureaucratic institutions.

animals, increasing the pace of reach seems like a deeply promising prospect that's hard to resist—as Facebook's 2.5 billion active users shows.

Yet the question becomes, Can the reach of technologies like social media go at such an accelerated pace that they can no longer house discourse? Do the algorithms of reach actually shut us into digital enclaves of only those who are saying the same things we are? Reach—though it is fast, far, and open—is ironically narrow and reductive, which in the end produces a stiff alienation.[17]

Silicon Valley would remind us, with Facebook as its example, that our reach extends so much further with technological acceleration, pushing past the constraints of the locale and rigid time units. There is some inherent good to this kind of reach. Anyone who teaches online courses experiences these goods directly. No one would doubt that communication innovations that free us from the heavy constraints of space and time *can* be helpful. These technologies can be used in good ways. In her book *The Virtual Body of Christ in a Suffering World*, religion professor Deanna Thompson explains how CaringBridge and other social media sites produced a reach in her connections that ministered directly to her as she battled cancer.[18] These are goods that shouldn't be overlooked.

Reach, as a core human need, promises escape from isolation, and social media can produce these goods in cases such as Thompson's. However, by focusing on suffering, Thompson gives a unique ethos to the accelerated technology. This explicit reaching out through suffering is a radically different experience from that of most other social media users. The attention to suffering restricts the thrust for all-out acceleration of the pace of life. It seems to bring other goods into view than just the power and sensation of reach itself. Reach for reach's sake is not a dependable and stable good. Reach points to something inherent within us, something we rightly seek. But reach alone doesn't provide us with the good. In Thompson's case, reach serves a bigger purpose. Reach is held in check by other goods, like prayer, confession, and communion. In her case, reach produces not recognition for an innovative identity[19] but an experience of shared humanity, an event of ministry. The nearness of death transforms reach. In this transformation of reach, social media is mercifully returned to its place as a tool, not an end.

17. To use Emmanuel Levinas's words, it becomes an experience not of the infinite or transcendent, not even an encounter with otherness at all, but just "the Same." See Levinas, *Totality and Infinity* (Pittsburgh: Duquesne University Press, 1969), 35–43.

18. Thompson, *The Virtual Body of Christ in a Suffering World* (Nashville: Abingdon, 2016).

19. I mean this in the sense used by Taylor in *Multiculturalism*, ed. Amy Gutmann (Princeton: Princeton University Press, 1994), 25–35.

As Marshall McLuhan, drawing from Winston Churchill, has said, "We shape our tools and thereafter they shape us."[20] Yet Thompson's case of suffering and the stark arrival of mortality unveils a more fundamental force than just tools that are making us. Death and our limited mortal time, as the impetus for reach, recasts reach. It returns reach to something much different than broadcasting identity and doing more with less time. Rather, inside the event of her cancer, the reach of social media becomes a tool for seeking the higher goods of connection and resonance. As Thompson wrestles with the suffering of her cancer, these tools are not imbued with an accelerated sense of time—a frantic push to speed up and reach more. Instead, accelerated time is replaced by a mortal time of finitude. Time becomes painfully beautiful and treasured, and the reach of social media allows others to share in this time that she bears. Next to this conception of time, reach becomes direct and deep, no longer broad and shallow.

Social media can be good when there is another need, or higher good, than just reach itself. As human beings we all need reach, but we need reach to deliver us to a higher good. Reach needs to be for the sake of encountering others, as a means to something deeper and some higher good than reach itself.

Without encountering otherness, reach is flattened. But the advantage of flattening and stripping reach so that it stands alone is that it can be accelerated. When accelerated, reach serves the innovation of doing more and reaching more people in less time. Reach becomes a resource, not an event of encounter. When reach has no higher good than more reach, the pace of our lives is accelerated and we're thrust into alienation. We rarely recognize this because the reach of accelerated technology screens us off from it as we refresh and refresh again. Thompson's experience, and therefore sense of reach, is fundamentally placed within an encounter. Because of the centrality of her suffering, in some sense she can't use social media for its desired use—to accelerate the pace of her life. But because it's an open system of discourse, her circumstance reworks social media. Reach is released from acceleration and allowed to return to serve the event of encounter. Reach can avoid alienation by hosting an event of resonance.

Thompson and others with similar experiences are the exception, not the rule. Nearly every Instagram and YouTube star (the winners who have achieved the greatest innovative reach) seeks reach itself. That's why every YouTube star, or hopeful star, is sure to say at the end of every video, "If

---

20. John Culkin, a friend of McLuhan, attributes this quote to McLuhan in "A Schoolman's Guide to Marshall McLuhan," *Saturday Review*, March 18, 1967, 51–53, 70–72, available at https://webspace.royalroads.ca/llefevre/wp-content/uploads/sites/258/2017/08/A-Schoolmans -Guide-to-Marshall-McLuhan-1.pdf.

you like this video, be sure to follow my channel." Likes and follows are the direct way to measure reach. The more likes, the more you matter. Thompson may be right: the virtual body of Christ, the *virtualis communio*, can be the *sanctorum communio*, but only when there is a good higher than reach itself.

We can make this point by comparing Thompson's experience with other researchers who tell very different stories about social media and technological acceleration. For instance, Donna Freitas has shown that young adults contend that social media is no place to express their suffering. To express suffering is to lose reach. Reach is won through echoed recognition. Your suffering conveys to the open system that you're unable to echo reach. There is no room, these young adults claim, for the time of mortality, only for innovative identity acceleration. According to Freitas's findings, these young adults contend that the point of social media is to win reach.[21] Period. And reach is won by curating a happy, successful, and fast-paced persona with shiny posts. Freitas shows through her interviews that suffering is excluded from these college students' presentations of themselves. Suffering short-circuits reach because it demands a different orientation to time than acceleration. Young adults who are suffering feel a deep sense of alienation. They lose a sense of the core human good of reach. The acceleration of reach dissuades users from sharing their suffering. In these moments of alienation, burnout, and suffering, the chorus of others' happiness sounds like a sour song of alienation.

———

The email from the pastor in North Dakota made we wonder about the session that was advertised at the denominational gathering in Kansas City. It had been a few months, and this session had now come and gone. I wondered how it went. Curiosity got the best of me, so I decided to send my own email.

---

21. Freitas, *The Happiness Effect: How Social Media Is Driving a Generation to Appear Perfect at Any Cost* (London: Oxford University Press, 2017).

11

reach and the seculars

I emailed Rhonda. She'd been the one who invited me to speak at the event in Kansas City. I'd known her for a few years, and she played host when I was in town. We had some great conversations. I wrote:

> Rhonda, I hope you're well. I'm just curious, how did the last continuing education event go? It seemed interesting.

Rhonda, who always seemed incredibly perceptive and thoughtful, responded:

> Overall, it was good. We had some good conversations. The session on "New Strategies for Assessing and Accelerating the Impact of Your Congregation" really stuck with me. It was so practical and helpful. It really pushed into examining our resources and addressing how the needs of our local communities could be reached through the resources of our congregation. I left so inspired. But it was weird because I woke up the next day and all the inspiration was gone, and in its place I only felt overwhelmed. And then that turned into apathy. I woke up and thought, *But wait, we don't really have many resources.* And then I started thinking about how many needs there were. I wish we had more resources to reach more needs to keep people at church. Then I thought about how, ever since I started in ministry, we've been talking about the church needing to do outreach. I grew up in a big evangelical church and everything

139

was about reaching out to save people. And in this denomination everything is about doing outreach to people through their needs. It was really helpful to think about, and I'll take some things with me for sure. But we've been talking like this forever and . . . I guess it just made me feel stuck.

Rhonda was right. The church has been talking about reach for a long while. The practical answer to the arrival of the secular is always to increase the church's reach. Following the timekeeper of Silicon Valley, we've conceded that growth is always the answer to our problems. Here's how the argument goes: The church faces and feels a deficit of reach. If we can expand reach, we can free ourselves from decline. Grow resources by growing users by growing reach.

But I'm not so sure it works this way. And neither does Rhonda.

The Church and Reach

Throughout the first two volumes of this series we've discussed at length Charles Taylor's view of secularity.[1] In *A Secular Age*, Taylor shows how "secular" is a multivalent reality, discussing what he calls secular 1, secular 2, and secular 3. Secular 2 and 3 are outgrowths of secular 1. Secular 1 was a divide between public and private, when religion was separated from the state (in the story I've been telling, when the church was no longer keeping time). Secular 2 arrives at different times across the West. In England it comes after World War I,[2] in Canada after World War II,[3] in the US it comes in fits and starts. Secular 2 is the loss of participation in religious institutions; it's a sense—or empirical fact—that fewer and fewer people are going to church and becoming members of congregations.

In the US the possibility for secular 2 arrives in the late 1960s. However, it never took like it did in France and Germany. Secular 2 came to the US with much less intensity and almost exclusively to the mainline denominations. It did not become a crisis in the US until the second decade of the twenty-first century.[4]

1. See particularly volume 1, *Faith Formation in a Secular Age: Responding to the Church's Obsession with Youthfulness* (Grand Rapids: Baker Academic, 2017), chap. 7, though I must admit in hindsight that this chapter misreads secular 1. It blurs the lines between what I would call secular 0—or a world without the secular—and this split between the public and the private. I wasn't as clear about this point as I am now. I believe I do a much better job articulating secular 2 and secular 3 and its challenges to faith formation.

2. Taylor discusses the situation in England after World War I in *A Secular Age* (Cambridge, MA: Belknap, 2007), 391–407.

3. Brian Clarke and Stuart Macdonald tell this complicated tale in *Leaving Christianity: Changing Allegiances in Canada since 1945* (Montreal: McGill-Queen's University Press, 2017).

4. I suppose this remains a debate, but it seems correct to look at Jean Twenge's study (see *iGen: Why Today's Super-Connected Kids Are Growing Up Less Rebellious, More Tolerant,*

There are many factors for this late US arrival into a heavy secular 2. But a core factor, particularly in relation to the acceleration of the pace of life and the desire for reach, is the innovations of American evangelicalism. Because countries like England, Germany, and the Scandinavian nations had historical memory and even remaining functions of the *ancien regime* (we could call this secular 0), their move into secular 1 was much more jagged than it was for the US.

Though the US was slow to adopt secular 2 (in comparison to the rest of the West), this was flipped in the case of secular 1. England, Germany, and France moved into secular 1 (separation between church and state, public and private) with much more tension than the US did. Secular 1 fit the American project like a glove. The separation of church and state was complete and total in the US. The crown now completely and fully evacuated from its cultural memory, America could be the most secular nation in the West. In many ways this remains true. America is more secular than all the other Western nations—but only in a secular 1 sense.

Because America is the most secular 1 of all countries, it has been much slower in experiencing the impact of secular 2. Compared to England, Canada, France, Germany, the Scandinavian nations, New Zealand, and Australia, a much higher percentage of people go to church in the US (or they lie to researchers when asked about going to church, which in itself reveals something about the firm place of religious participation in the American consciousness).

Because secular 1 did not entirely take hold in European societies, it became much more plausible and expansive across these societies to move directly into secular 2: to quit going to church altogether. As the timekeeper shifted to consumer corporations, and the doubt of the state took hold after 1918 or 1945, European societies had the "convenience" of turning their backs on both the church and the state in one swift motion.[5]

This wasn't possible in America. In Europe, the church and the state were still married, though unhappily. In America, they had been divorced for a long time: the church and the state were not linked enough to allow for one

Less Happy—and Completely Unprepared for Adulthood—and What That Means for the Rest of Us [New York: Atria, 2017], chap. 5) on the coming generation (iGen or Generation Z) as the most secular—unaffiliated with religious institutions—in American history as a sign that secular 2 has finally been established in the US, matching Europe, though still in different tone.

5. Jaroslav Pelikan explains why: "The identification of the church with the monarchy, and with the ancient regime generally, made the church one of the principal targets of the rising opposition to monarchy, aristocracy, and Christianity during the eighteenth century. The old regime had been a benefactor of the church; the church took a stand as a defender of the old regime—and almost went down with it." Pelikan, *The Riddle of Roman Catholicism* (Nashville: Abingdon, 1959), 60.

turn to be a denial of both. Because the US was the most secular 1 of places, the generation that turned its back on the timekeeper of the nation was not necessarily turning from the church and Christianity. Jesus Freaks were a legitimate element of the counterculture, and charismatic/nonmainline churches embraced much of the youths' critique of the state, even joining them in their marches.[6] The mainline bore some major blowback, and like the churches of European societies, they never recovered in a secular 2 sense. But ultimately, in America, when (young) people turned their backs on the timekeeper of the state, the church escaped this denial. The fact that America had many small denominations or nondenominational churches, especially scattered across the western states that believed themselves deeply disconnected from the elites in the east, allowed for church-based innovations to keep secular 2 from flooding America.

Even so, the new ethic of authenticity was now in place. You were invited by the new timekeeper to innovate your own identity in order to live as your most authentic self. Living beyond direct frontal critique, a congregation in America could win reach. To win this reach, the church would have to innovate, accelerating the pace of life to match the new timekeeper. These small denominational and nondenominational churches were more ready for this innovation, but they would need to match the good life that was being molded by the timekeeping of the consumer corporations.[7] It was a cultural conformity that seemed radical only because a cultural shift was taking place. But following the suit of the new corporate timekeepers, congregations needed to become fast places that gave people resources to cope with the overall increased pace of society, helping these accelerating people find purpose when the pace of life seemed to strip it away.[8] It was an innovative cultural conformity, because such churches never opposed the pace itself but conceded to this acceleration, innovating church life to match the accelerating speed and to win reach.

To achieve this reach and dam up any losses from a secular 2 conception, these churches would need to directly match the shape of the new timekeeper, taking on corporate structures, even erecting buildings patterned after the

6. See Preston Shires, *Hippies of the Religious Right* (Waco: Baylor University Press, 2007).

7. Ironically, the individualism and expressive nature matched up quite well. Many people have written about how congregations and American Christianity as a whole were pulled into consumerism. See Douglas Webster, *Selling Jesus: What's Wrong with Marketing the Church* (Eugene, OR: Wipf & Stock, 2009); Vincent Miller, *Consuming Religion: Christian Faith and Practice in a Consumer Culture* (New York: Continuum, 2003); and John Drane, *The McDonaldization of the Church: Consumer Culture and the Church's Future* (Macon, GA: Smyth & Helwys, 2001).

8. See my discussion of Rick Warren in volume 2, *The Pastor in a Secular Age: Ministry to People Who No Longer Need a God* (Grand Rapids: Baker Academic, 2019), chap. 8.

consumer ethos. They created new models to win reach, finding innovative ways to connect corporate goods of growth with a biblical centrism. Being seeker sensitive allowed for a legitimate strategy of winning reach and damming the secular 2 rivers from washing away American religion.

As the new timekeeper settled more fully into the American context, the church became locked in a secular 2 mindset, even though America was faring better in relation to secular 2 compared to the rest of the West. But it was within a secular 2 conception that American Christianity found the necessary crisis to innovate, and to continue to innovate, creating more reach. This crisis needed to continue to be heralded and obsessed over, the crisis of loss and decline, the impetus to speed up and add actions to the church's units of time. Secular 2 became the interpretation of the church's problem, producing a constant buzzing anxiety to drive pastors and congregations to an accelerated pace of life. Seeing things through a secular 2 lens made it clear that reach itself was the goal, and without reach there was only loss. This would be a loss first of people, then of purpose, meaning, and a sense of identity—not much different from an anxious YouTube star watching the stats of her followers. Pastors and leaders feared loss, or worse, the plateauing of reach.

In the logic of acceleration, standing still is falling behind. So congregations and their leaders would have to make reach their top focus (even their *summum bonum*, or highest good). They'd justify the focus on reach with language of evangelism and caring for the lost. Although, honestly, their fear was more likely induced by the alienation that the pastor and the congregation would feel without a growing sense of reach. Reach for reach's sake became a good higher than almost any other. Conferences were packed not to learn about interpreting revelation or to discuss biblical exegesis but to learn the strategies of reach—whether those were called "church growth," "purpose driven," or "church planting" (think of the Willow Creek Association).

The congregation and its leadership became about winning reach. Soon enough, the most central question for both mainline and evangelical pastors was, How can we reach more and more people? They did not ask how they could testify to God's eternity breaking into time. They asked how they could keep from losing pace up against the threat of secular 2. Churches and pastors wondered what innovations would free them from the threat of loss. Any theological sense of sharing the gospel and sharing how revelation and evangelism move in the world was eclipsed by the need for strategies to win reach.[9] Mainline congregations particularly looked enviously at large

9. Evangelism is reach, but done properly it is not solely for reach alone. Evangelism is reaching out for the sake of an encounter with the judgment and grace of God. In my mind, what has happened (as outlined above) is that, as Taylor says (in *Secular Age*, 222), grace gets

evangelical congregations and believed, naively, that it was just a matter of reach. "If only we could get the word out," these churches believed, "people would come. If only we could reach them and show them that we have something to offer. If only we could get a young pastor who could reach those kinds of people."

This is fundamentally naive, because once the issue is primarily reach, it is about resourcing acceleration. It is true that reach can solve a secular 2 issue—the American megachurch is proof. Reach can bring more people to church. But when reach is an end, which it so easily becomes in a secular 2 mindset, then it demands a constant and consistent acceleration of the pace of life. Reach for reach's sake asks the congregation to do more in less time. It is won by adding actions to units of time. And this is *the* way to win against the pressure of secular 2. We can win reach, we can make up ground against decline, but only if we go faster, only if we add more actions to our units of time, only if we do more, only if we innovate our pace of life to move faster. We'll need to add more programs to the nine o'clock education hour. We can win reach by adding more services to Sunday morning. We can win reach by adding more church plants to our network, or at least more staff to get us more reach, which of course means we'll have to accelerate our lives to oversee these new staff and fund their new positions. New staff will get us more reach, but only by accelerating all of our lives.

Reach becomes *the* solution to a secular 2 problem. Unfortunately, it adopts a set of goods that inevitably accelerates the pace of life for the leadership and congregation as a whole. Reach is the answer, but only for a secular 2 issue. We are tempted by this because it's the crisis we see. We see fewer people in church, or fewer than at the big congregation across town. This loss makes innovation appear to be the answer, because the new innovations of technological acceleration have won reach. If we can mold our lives around innovation, being disruptive like the hypercapitalist timekeeper, then we too can achieve reach and beat loss. We must ignore that this *always* means an acceleration of the pace of life and the risk of alienation and burnout.

It's no wonder that those who have successfully won reach, even in the church, using it to dam the rivers of secular 2 and build large and fast congregations, have so fully and tragically burned out. The pace of their lives becomes so

eclipsed—even in evangelical congregations—and so reaching out is no longer for the sake of the gospel (for encounters with the living God). Instead, everything gets mashed together with just winning reach for reach's sake. Evangelism becomes the building of the congregation. I've more than hinted at my position on evangelism in *Faith Formation in a Secular Age*, but a longer theology of evangelism is needed here. I'd also point to John Flett's *The Witness of God: The Trinity, Missio Dei, Karl Barth, and the Nature of Christian Community* (Grand Rapids: Eerdmans, 2010) as a theology of evangelism that keeps reach from overtaking revelation.

alienating that they violate sexual boundaries in search for some connection, or abuse power (or drugs, alcohol, etc.) to not fall behind and lose the reach they think their church, even God, needs. They leave pain, confusion, and betrayal in their accelerated wake. The innovators of reach like Bill Hybels, Mark Driscoll, and Ted Haggard (and so many others) have been tragic casualties (and perpetrators) of an accelerated pace of life and the idol of reach.

These are all examples of moral failures. But these moral failures are indivisibly linked to the accelerating pace of life and the alienation that was birthed by the pursuit of reach for reach's sake. The moral failure started by making reach alone a high good. They all took on the good of doing more with less, blurring many boundaries and passing over other goods in the race to keep pace. Each of them allowed the good of fast reach—and the power it won—to be their idol (a false good/god).

Reach invariably becomes an idol when it's the answer to a secular 2 problem. When our issue (and deepest fear) is decline, reach becomes our fetish. Locked inside a secular 2 conception, innovation becomes deeply appealing to the congregation because secular 2 is based on the logic of loss. The way to beat loss is to speed up. Speed, we assume, creates growth. In an accelerated modernity all loss is due to the inability to keep pace. What is lost is not necessarily viewed as evil or demonic but as old—that which can't keep up, can't be innovated into something new. Innovation becomes appealing to congregational leaders because it can find ways of doing more with less. And innovation always has gravitas because we've misread the heart of the problem, allowing ourselves to erroneously see our issue as only secular 2.

The Real Problem: Secular 3

Secular 2 is not the primary issue, however. Secular 2 is imagined as the loss of the church's ability to reach people, to increase members. The anxiety of this lack of reach, like all idols, screens us off from the sources that imbue reach with the good. Human beings need reach, but not just for reach's sake, which only makes us frantic, anxious, and deeply competitive—creating the conditions for all sorts of forms of alienation.

Taylor spills almost all the ink of his 770 pages in *A Secular Age* to tell us that our issue across the West isn't really secular 1 or secular 2 at all, but rather secular 3. Secular 3 is the loss of the reach of transcendence itself. To live in a secular 3 world is to inherit a sense that it's much easier *not* to believe in a God who reaches out to us. Secular 3 is an absence of belief—the nearly unthought conception—that God no longer reaches out to us. It assumes that our human acts, like prayer, confession, and worship, are feeble and therefore have no reach. Such things are a complete waste of time, or perhaps good only for ourselves. Secular 3 is an infusing of doubt (a fragility of belief) that reach can be used for anything other than the immanent and material, for winning more actions in our own units of time. Secular 3 is the contesting of all beliefs. Across the West it closes down reach from having any spiritual or transcendent end outside itself.

If Taylor is right that this is our true problem, then making reach for reach's sake and enclosing it in a secular 2 problematic only worsens the issue of secular 3. Our misdiagnosis never solves the real issue the congregation faces. We may be able to innovate congregations that can dam the rivers of decline, using reach to keep secular 2 at bay. But in so doing we'll have to accelerate the pace of both the leadership and the congregation's life, risking burnout and adding to the loss of transcendence.

At its best, the burnout will mean a slow fizzle, as the once-energetic pastor departs, too exhausted to remember why she even wanted to do ministry in the first place. At its worst, the pace will lead to an explosion of mayhem. The pastor sleeps with the administrator and bullies members to build and keep the reach that has been won. As for the congregation, it will be depressed trying to do more in less time. At its worst, the congregation will see major turnover, its own young people sensing a deep hypocrisy. The young people experience a big church with reach, but they find no real connection to a living God. Trying to shore up a secular 2 issue (that fewer people go to church) with reach only makes the living God—who reaches out to guide and speak to us—unbelievable.

Unless we're very careful, the congregation can actually add to the problem of secular 3. The accelerating pace of life draws us toward alienation. We're so busy accelerating, looking for every new innovation to help us manage acceleration, that we can't be present at dinner, the swim meet, or the prayer of confession. In almost all religious traditions, to hear God speak you have to escape the drive to accelerate. You must find freedom from the pace of your life to take on practices that offer a reach *to* something beyond acceleration itself.

Inside the accelerating pace of life, the culture is alienated from transcendence. If the church were to approach our problem as a secular 3 (loss of transcendence) and not a secular 2 (loss of church attendance) issue, we might have a much different disposition toward reach and an altered conception of a *good* congregation. The problem of secular 3 isn't that fewer people are going to our congregations but rather that many people feel alienated. Inside that alienation, divine action becomes opaque.

———

Rhonda can feel all this. The practicality and the excitement of the session turn on her because she realizes that her congregation doesn't have the resources for the kind of reach that can win growth. Ultimately, I believe she feels apathetic because even thinking within this dynamic accelerates the pace of life, alienating her and her congregation from transcendence.

In the acceleration of the pace of life, time itself becomes a resource. And when time becomes a resource, most of us find ourselves feeling like we're in a time-famine.

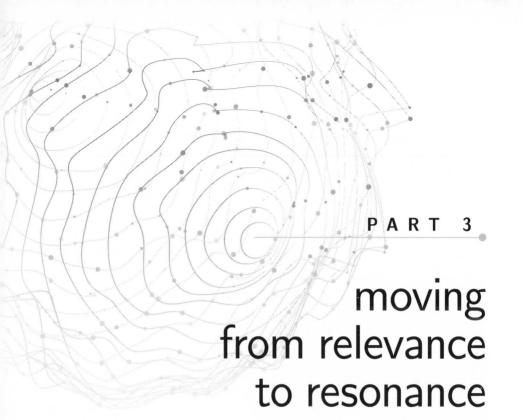

PART 3

moving
from relevance
to resonance

12

time-famine and resource obsession

another step into alienation

Rhonda and the pastor in North Dakota seem to be leading two vastly different congregations. Rhonda's church is small. Because of the church's lack of growth, she simply doesn't have the resources to meet the needs of the community. If it did, she imagines, her congregation would have meaning, purpose, and overall direction. She feels constantly rushed to find the innovation that will produce the resources she needs.

Yet this isn't completely true, and she would admit it. The problem is not that her congregation simply needs more material resources. The problem is that, because they are a small congregation that lacks the resources, they simply don't have the time to make a dent in the needs of their local community. Her little church can't win the people's attention. Being small, they *could* make a small impact. But even this small impact seems impossible to her because the congregation, being small, cannot keep people interested. In the accelerated pace of life, the church can't win people's time. Her people are giving their time (and other resources) to so many other activities and interests. They're too busy to invest in the way she wishes they would. So even when Rhonda's eyes aren't bigger than her stomach, even when she's not driven by an ambition for growth, she nevertheless feels her congregation is in the middle of a time-famine.

The pastor in North Dakota, on the other hand, has resources. His budget and staff are ten times the size that of Rhonda's. Membership is twenty times that of her little congregation. But still he too feels like his congregation is missing its impact because it lacks resources. This makes him feel a deep sense of guilt. He tells me in a follow-up email:

> I feel I'm ministering in a *Mad Max* meets *Last Man on Earth* world. I can see the resources. I have the new wing to our building staring at me every day. But I have no fuel to activate these resources. All the resources don't matter if your people don't have time for anything. Pastoring this church is like being given a lot full of BMWs without gas tanks. They have great engines, but we can't drive them. Nobody has time. I know it sounds like I'm whining, but I'd cash in that new wing for a truckload of commitment any day of the week.

They Want Our Time

The pace of our lives is always speeding up because these supposed time-saving technologies turn time into a resource. Making time into a resource is a much different conception of time than that in Avignon. In Avignon, time was a mystery, and the present was expansive. Under the technological advances of industrialization and the movements of modernization, time shifted from a transcendent reality to an immanent one. Time became natural and material, stripped of its supernatural quality.

Time-as-resource started under the timekeeper of the state. After industrialization, the earth was no longer a stage on which mystery, salvation, and frightening but holy encounters played out.[1] The earth became a controlled container of raw materials. Just as forests are no longer zones of spirits but instead collections of timber, so time itself, in relation to clocks and factory floors, is a raw material that can be expanded or depleted. Time has become consumable, like oil and coal. Benjamin Franklin, at the beginning of this period, claimed, "Time is money."

Time indeed is money, a pure resource that can be grown or lost, traded or bargained with.[2] The North Dakota pastor may have square footage and a budget surplus, but he's stuck because he has no time. The pace of people's lives makes the church time-poor.

1. This is why Jean-Jacques Rousseau and Henry David Thoreau are both such heroes in the early modern period. Rousseau believed that urban/industrialized life—society itself—corrupts the innocent spirit of humanity. The call to return to nature is a romantic response to time becoming a raw material.
2. Michel Foucault gives an interesting genealogy of how money and time are laced together. See *The Order of Things* (London: Routledge, 2002), 200–206.

Silicon Valley, seemingly a benevolent timekeeper, gave us new gadgets and innovations to *save* us time. They even supported the innovations in our individual identities. They want our money, of course. But more than that, they want our time. The revolutionary innovators of Silicon Valley embraced the bohemian countercultural disdain for industrial and corporate culture, which wanted only money. Silicon Valley shifted greed from pure dollars and cents to time itself. Allan Alcorn, Nolan Bushnell, and Ted Dabney, the founders of Atari, wanted your time, not just your cash.[3] Mike Markkula and Steve Jobs felt the same. Fast-forwarding to 2012, Facebook had the third largest IPO in US history (to that point), raising over $16 billion. Yet when going public they had little sense of how to actually make money. But they possessed a resource worth billions: they owned everyone's time. People with no time for anything nevertheless spend hours on Facebook. Globally, people spend an average of 142 minutes per day on social media.[4] For Facebook, possessing people's time was as good as gold.[5] Facebook is one of the elites of Silicon Valley because of its extraordinary amount of global time.[6]

Time-Famine

Hartmut Rosa explains this odd conundrum (another vicious circle of late modernity): the more innovation that is birthed through technology, and the more our social norms shift toward our free identities, the more we find ourselves with not a surplus but a deficit of time. Technology and the freedom to innovate our identity as we wish should give us not less but more time. But it never works this way.

Rosa shows that the more we become fertile in technological gadgets and identity options, the more we find ourselves in a time drought, or what he calls

3. This story is told in the early chapters of Leslie Berlin, *Troublemakers: Silicon Valley's Coming of Age* (New York: Simon & Schuster, 2017), 6–159.

4. Saima Salim, "How Much Time Do You Spend on Social Media? Research Says 142 Minutes Per Day," Digital Information World, January 4, 2019, https://www.digitalinformationworld .com/2019/01/how-much-time-do-people-spend-social-media-infographic.html.

5. In May 2019, Chris Hughes, former early Facebook employee and college roommate of Mark Zuckerberg, wrote an opinion piece in the *New York Times* in which he made many stirring assertions about the company and its power. But most interesting for this project are his clear statements that Facebook is a time-possessing company (there are also clear examples of accelerated modernity's need to prime—always needing growth—as well). Hughes, "It's Time to Break Up Facebook," *New York Times*, May 9, 2019, https://www.nytimes.com/2019/05/09 /opinion/sunday/chris-hughes-facebook-zuckerberg.html.

6. Of course, in possession of our time, Facebook has found ways to monetize it, essentially selling our time—our attention—directly to advertisers.

a "time-famine." "Perhaps the most pressing and astonishing facet of . . . acceleration is the spectacular and epidemic 'time-famine' of modern (western)
societies. In modernity, [people] increasingly feel that they are running out of
time, that they are short on time."[7] In both Rhonda's congregation and the
North Dakota pastor's congregation, people want to be involved, but they just
don't have the time. Though their churches are different in size and budget,
they are equally stuck in a time-famine.

An accelerated modernity creates all sorts of inequalities. Admittedly, the
growth of markets can raise the poverty level of the whole world, reducing the
risk of a food-famine. But markets, when sped up, tend to breed inequality,
which is where we find ourselves today. Markets can move so fast that they
get off-balance, shifting most of the capital to a few. The continued push for
acceleration produces not economic equality but the opposite.[8] Some speed
added to markets can lift everyone (this is why speed itself isn't the problem,
and slowdown is not the answer). But unrestricted and unregulated markets,
allowed to quicken and quicken, become risky and out of balance. Being
off-balance allows 1 percent of the global population to possess over half of
the global wealth. Often our only imagined solution is further innovation
for the sake of growth. We imagine that our only option is a higher revving
of acceleration to solve the problem that overacceleration gave us in the first
place.[9] This makes the conditions ripe for some parts of the world to fall
behind and experience famine.

Rosa's point is that when acceleration occurs, no one escapes deprivation.[10]
When modernity is accelerating (when the speed of innovation is a high good
and newness is our desire), all of us find ourselves in a time-famine. Yet this
time-famine takes unique shape across class distinctions. Rosa sees three layers of this time-famine. The top layers are elites and even the middle class
who have "completely internalized this logic of speeding up. So: saving time

7. Rosa, *Alienation and Acceleration: Towards a Critical Theory of Late-Modern Temporality* (Malmö, Sweden: NSU Press, 2014), 20.
8. A controlled—restricted—market capitalism, I believe, can bring goods to the world, helping to raise many out of poverty. But when the markets start going too fast, and are unregulated
so they can go faster, they breed mayhem and create the conditions for further inequality. When
growth is the only good, inequality will occur. Even at the economic level, the moral question
of the good is essential.
9. Some Marxists, like Nick Srnicek and Alex Williams, encourage more and more acceleration. They believe that the quickest way to bring down capitalism is to accelerate it to
such a point that it breaks down completely. See "Accelerating the New," in *The Future of the
New: Artistic Innovation in Times of Social Acceleration*, ed. Thijs Lijster (Valiz, Amsterdam:
Antennae-Arts Society, 2019), 69–82.
10. Rosa discusses the time-famine further in *Social Acceleration: A New Theory of Modernity* (New York: Columbia University Press, 2015), 309–10.

is saving money. It is the logic of competition, in particular, that they have internalized, and competition is always related to temporality: 'time is scarce, don't waste it.'"[11]

For those at the next layer, time is imposed on them. These are folks who often live in the time crunch of the service industry. Or they live paycheck to paycheck, needing time to pay the rent. "The people working [these kinds of jobs] are always short on time but usually it is someone else—the boss or the clock—who creates the pressure, and it is not so much coming from the inside."[12] They feel a time-famine that's imposed on them not by internal but by external pressure.

Those in the final layer Rosa calls the "forcefully excluded" or "forcefully decelerated."[13] These are people who are chronically unemployed, often on disability. Some are homeless. Rosa explains, "Forced or enforced deceleration is a kind of devaluation of the time you have." You're in a time-famine *not* because you feel an internal drive to speed up, or you have a boss who demands it, but because culturally your time has no value. No one in society has any time for you. Rosa continues, turning more directly to those who, for instance, are unemployed due to a work-related disability. "The time you have is without any value and the problem is that even then you feel the pressure of acceleration, because you feel like you are lagging behind more and more, that it is impossible to catch up. So, this is why I claim that acceleration is an almost totalitarian force, you feel the pressure wherever you are."[14]

Under this totalitarian force, Rhonda's sense is right. Her people don't have the resources to meet the needs of those in the community. They lack the money and the programs, but more importantly they all feel starved for time. Those who have an internalized sense of time-famine feel particularly uneasy interacting with those who find themselves in "forced deceleration." Stuck in our own internal time-famine, it becomes easy for us to blame them. We assume they have time: just get a job or use your time better than panhandling on the freeway exit. We resent, and are even morally repulsed, that they *seem* to be wasting their time, feeling none of the internal pressure that haunts us. We feel threatened by the shape of their time-famine because modernity has forced us too into a different, but nevertheless real, time-famine.

11. Rosa, "Beyond the Echo Chamber," in Lijster, *Future of the New*, 27.
12. Rosa, "Beyond the Echo Chamber," 27.
13. Rosa discusses this further in "De-Synchronization, Dynamic Stabilization, Dispositional Squeeze: The Problem of Temporal Mismatch," in *The Sociology of Speed: Digital, Organizational, and Social Temporalities*, ed. Judy Wajcman and Nigel Dodd (Oxford: Oxford University Press, 2017), 25–41.
14. Rosa, "Beyond the Echo Chamber," 28.

Resource Obsession

This expansive and multidimensional time-famine is why we become resource obsessed. It only makes sense: scarcity has a way of making everything into a resource. Because we all feel in one way or another starved for time, we accrue the resource of time. Resources become valuable because they can be used to meet future contingencies. A resource by definition is a "source or supply from which a benefit is produced and that has some utility. Resources can broadly be classified upon their availability."[15] Benefit and availability make resources valuable. A drought is turned into a famine when food resources are unavailable or when the available resources cannot meet the demand. The issue might be that it hasn't rained in fifteen months, but the depleted resources make it a famine.

When you're in the middle of the scarcity of a drought, you become obsessed with resources and find it very hard to share. If you share a resource, it will be unavailable later when you may need it. But even using it yourself, you worry that you might not mobilize it correctly and will therefore miss out. If you mobilize the resource incorrectly (such as at the wrong time), you'll waste the benefit and imperil your future.

Resources are always about time. They're held onto tightly or sought vigorously because we all feel ourselves in some kind of time-famine. Harvested resources are a way of dealing with the contingencies of the future. The congregation is obsessed with resources—pushing to innovate to get more resources, offering conferences to assess congregational resources—because it feels itself to be in the crisis of a famine brought on by a membership and relevance drought. And yet no matter the amount of resources we accrue, we still find ourselves in a deeper deficit of time. Innovating and reassessing resources often costs us more in time than it delivers in new members and relevance. At its core the congregation isn't short on membership and relevance; it's short on time.

And across the West we feel this drought of time. The resources we have to meet the drought of time cannot produce the goods we need. Innovative technology and freedom for our identities just worsens the time-famine. And here is where we become trapped. We don't give attention to the cause of the time drought (recognizing that Silicon Valley is as corrupt as Avignon ever was[16]), and therefore we take on different dispositions to time. We seek

15. "Resource," Wikipedia, accessed January 19, 2020, https://en.wikipedia.org/wiki/Resource.
16. The medieval system may have needed people to remain scared of hell to maintain its power, but if this is true then we must recognize that Silicon Valley needs us to feel always time-poor, always starving for more time, to continue with its own power.

more resources by chasing all the harder for innovation (giving more power to Silicon Valley, which helped create the time drought in the first place). We're led to believe that the only way to overcome the time-famine is to win more resources—through innovation in all three dimensions of acceleration (technology, social change, and pace of life). As we'll see, this approach only takes us further into alienation, obscuring our sense of the good and causing us to lose any sense that God speaks and acts.

Resource Obsession and the Good Life

The Western time-famine is the result of two felt forces: (1) the overall acceleration of the modern project (coming in the three dimensions discussed in the chapters above) and (2) the compression of the present brought on by this acceleration. We feel like the world is running away from us because of the three dimensions of acceleration.[17] The deficit of time caused by this acceleration becomes a time-famine, which leads us to obsess over resources, radically compressing the present. Inside this compressed present, we can barely find the time to live in the present at all. Our minds are rarely where our bodies are. This is the imposed disease of the Western time-famine (another sign that acceleration alienates).[18] Our bodies may be in the present, but our minds and our imaginations have already left the present, jumping into the future.

This has the effect for most people of making the present too short to allow for any answer on what makes for the good life. The good life cannot be lived out in the present, because our attention to the good is not in the present. Instead, we have sped into the future, riding on the well-worn road of the new. How could the good have anything to say about my present? The present is too short, decaying too rapidly to allow for it to hold our imagined or material constitutions of the good life.

Moving so quickly, we keep our imaginations always on a future we can create. We focus on what will be. Yes, people are still seeking the good life. But we are unable to find the good life in this radically compressed present.

17. This is to echo Anthony Giddens's important book *The Runaway World: How Globalization Is Reshaping Our Lives* (New York: Routledge, 2003), which articulates some of the foundational material that Rosa would draw from.

18. This is true for people in all three layers of the time-famine that Rosa discusses. It's obvious how this is true for the first layer. For them, the good life is always about the future—about 401(k)s, college tuition, and retirement. But even the second layer feels this imposed disease. Their minds are not in the present but the future, as they think about their next shift, clocking out, and their day off. Even those in the third layer, forced deceleration, move themselves into the future. "If only I could work again," they think. Or maybe some don't think that, which is what makes them so suspicious to those at the other two layers.

With little connection to the present, the good life is without content. No one can say what a good life actually is in late modernity. Somehow, this inability to express the good life in the present becomes a good itself, because it allows each individual the freedom to find his or her own future sense of the good.[19] It provides space for you to find some future good through the project of your self. The good, still important in a time-famine, is projected entirely onto the screen of the future. And because it is, the good is without content—not bound in practices, traditions, or communities. It's open, which is both exciting and disorienting.

Dreaming of the Future

Without content to the good life, the best way to prepare for a good life that is *always* before you is to harvest enough resources to achieve whatever future sense of the good life you want. You can't know or even live the good life now, but you can harvest resources that will make the future good. Having these resources, you can feel good about your present. You can even compare yourself to others by counting resources. Your future is brighter! That makes you feel good now, but its goodness is completely contingent on the resources you possess for some future undefined good life. What this shows is that you don't really feel good about the life you're living now; you feel good about the resources you have that give you the reach and scope to live some future good life. You have the resources for a future good life but never the content of the good life itself. You have no real practices, traditions, or communities that mold your sense of the good life in the present. But you do have resources to possess some undefined future good life.[20]

When the good life is cast against the future (not the present), it becomes more individualized, and it also wears the marks of a dream. The shape of the good life for the future is the ability to live your dream. Parents at that top layer of the time-famine judge their own goodness as a parent by their ability to give their child resources so that the child can . . . we're not sure, but we are sure that resources will give them every chance of living whatever dream their individual self discovers for itself.

19. Expressive individualism, in my mind, is so extensive across the West because of acceleration—because of our relation to time. Consumerism imposes this future orientation of a short present. But it all rests on time—not on consumerism alone. Consumerism feeds off our conception of time itself.
20. Newness makes this hazy unknown exciting, even giving it a sense of really living. You can't have the content of the good life because you need to be open to the sensations of the new.

Rosa says it this way: "Modern society might not have an answer to what the good life is or what it consists in, but it has a very clear-cut answer to what the *preconditions* for living a [future coming] good life are, and what to do to meet them: *Secure the resources you might need for living your dream (whatever that might be)* has become the overruling rational imperative of modernity."[21] We become resource obsessed because the shape of our good life is projected into the future, bound in the dream-state. When the good life is for the future, the present is for harvesting as many resources as you can, so that you can live your personal dream in each ever-coming future.

A more concrete example to illustrate this might help. In March 2019 the FBI uncovered a massive college-admissions scandal. Elite parents bribed, lied, and cheated the system to get their children into elite colleges. Most of us wondered why. These young people didn't need a college degree from Yale to get a good job. And they didn't need a good job to live a life of privilege. If college is for making your financial future brighter, they not only didn't need to go to USC. They didn't really need to go to college at all.

But this logic misses how the good life is completely projected into the future, making resources essential for meeting whatever dream you might have in any of the coming lifetimes you might live. The point of getting their children into Yale or USC wasn't to give them a chance to make more money but to give them another important (status) resource they could use to live out whatever dream they might want in the future.[22] Their goal wasn't to give their children the content of a good life. As good late-modern parents, their goal was to give their children the resources they would need to live whatever good life they could dream of. Rosa adds insight to this mentality: "No *matter what the future might bring, it will help if you have money, rights, friends, health, knowledge.*"[23] In light of these parents, we could add to Rosa's list a college degree from an elite university.

Though these parents had every financial advantage, they felt stuck in an absolute time-famine. They didn't have time to raise their kids' SAT scores

21. Rosa, "Two Versions of the Good Life and Two Forms of Fear: Dynamic Stabilization and the Resonance Conception of the Good Life," paper presented at the Yale Center for Faith and Culture conference on Joy, Security, and Fear, New Haven, CT, November 8–9, 2017, 7 (emphasis original). See also Rosa, "The Mindset of Growth and the Resonance Conception of the Good Life," in *The Good Life Beyond Growth*, ed. Hartmut Rosa and Christoph Henning (London: Routledge, 2019), 41.

22. Not to mention they wanted to be the kind of parents who send their children to an elite school. This motivation was wrapped up in giving their children resources for a future good, and also validating that they were good parents who had a child getting the good resource of a good degree. Although, honestly, the degree probably didn't matter as much as admittance—more on this in the paragraphs to come.

23. Rosa, "Two Versions of the Good Life," 7 (emphasis added). See also Rosa, "Mindset of Growth," 41.

or time for their children to be on the crew team. Without time, the most ef-
ficient, fastest way to be a good parent and give their children the resources
they would need to live their dream of a good life (the dream of both the
parent and the child) was to game the system.

In the end, getting into Yale wasn't for the money; it was for the resource.
Rosa says it powerfully: "The ethical imperative that guides modern subjects
is not a particular or substantive definition of the good life, but the aspiration
to acquire the resources necessary or helpful for leading one. . . . In a way, we
moderns resemble a painter who is forever concerned about improving his
materials—the colours and brushes, the air condition and lighting, the can-
vas and easel etc.—but never really starts to paint."[24] These lines from Rosa
reveal that, in this time-famine, acceleration itself produces alienation—even
alienation from the present.

When the Dream Becomes a Nightmare

With this sense of the good intrinsically projected onto the screen of the
future, taking the shape of a dream, how do you ever arrive at it? When are
the resources ever mobilized for living in the present? When do we stop seeking to accrue resources and live? Late-modern life always has a deep pinch
of discontent. But you can medicate the discontent, numbing yourself to the
pinch by staying with the dream, by never really living in the present. Just
keep adding to what you want in the future.

All this means that the resources you have are never enough! The only
response to this realization is to speed up to get more resources, projecting
your sense of the good further and further into the future, shoring up risk
and planning for contingencies. Enough is never enough because the good
that would satisfy is always out beyond you in the unattained future.

This never-ending projection into the future, to secure the dream, induces
us further into a time-famine. We are farmers who have overharvested the
land. Instead of letting it rest and living in the present, we work harder to use
infertile soil to produce the resources we believe we need for some coming
future. Most late-modern people choose the time-famine of the always-future
good over the thin emptiness of the present.

This vicious trick of a late, accelerated modernity invites us to live in a
compressed present where we are free to chase our dreams but never really

24. Rosa, "Two Versions of the Good Life," 7. This is why Rosa thinks that acceleration is able to
so deeply nestle into our lives. It actually becomes a strategy of dealing with or—better—avoiding
death. See Rosa, *Alienation and Acceleration*, 30–35, for a longer conversation on this point.

possess them. Novelist David Foster Wallace, maybe more than anyone else, saw this tragic conundrum back in the 1990s. He saw that you could never actually inhabit the good life you seek, because in the end it has no substance in the present.[25]

Like Wallace, some discover the tragic truth that they've actually achieved the core material marks of the good life they've dreamt of (a bestseller, awards, prestige, global fame). Yet their dream feels empty, nothing like the dream promised, nothing like the dream-state itself. The good of the present is no match for the good of the dream-state of the future. Achieving your dream feels deeply disappointing because the sensation of a future newness can never bear the heavy actuality of the present. The flatness of this dream happens because, in the modern age, the present is made dry and arid in order to allow the future and newness itself to become the higher good. Now that you have your dream in the present, it's no longer new, and therefore it's degraded. The present is always desolate because it is absent of the good life itself. The good is always in some future we need to speed ourselves into. The time-famine, then, isn't just due to simply not having enough time. Worse, it makes the present both short and barren.

The tragic story of Wallace is that, feeling this acutely, he ends his life. Wallace's story is hard to accept for late-modern people. Here was a talented young man who was living his dream. And yet he decided to end his life, even with his possession of stockpiled resources.[26] Like looking at the sun, it will burn our retinas if we gaze too intently at Wallace's story. Staring too long at his life story reveals that the future and its dreams never deliver the good we long for. The future dream-state can never really be a place where we can rest and live inside. Wallace tragically reveals that it's best to never arrive at your dream. It's better to just keep moving the goalposts, editing your dream to keep it always in the future. It's better to continue to chase more resources than to risk the present delivering a malaise of meaninglessness.

This is a legitimate strategy, until moving the goalposts and chasing resources for the future dream leaves you deeply fatigued. Too tired to keep reaching for the dream, you might start to despise the dream, hating it for leaving you depleted, depressed, and burned out. Your depression is heavy because you tacitly come to sense not only that the present is arid and meaningless

25. Hubert Dreyfus and Sean Dorrance Kelly provide a rich discussion of Wallace in *All Things Shining: Reading the Western Classics to Find Meaning in a Secular Age* (New York: Free Press, 2011), 40–50.

26. Wallace actually refused many of the resources, trying to get back to something real and good in the present. He moved to a nondescript town in the Midwest. But he still had his fame and reputation. And yet he found none of this could deliver a good life in the present.

but that even the future has turned on you. The dream is running away from you too fast for you to ever have the time to possess enough resources to receive the reward of its good. Wallace experienced his own unique state of *la fatigue d'être*. It is a deeply fatiguing thought to race and race, surviving the time-famine to get to your dream, only to realize it has gotten you nowhere. With the dream in your possession, its beauty fades because its beauty was bound in the new. It becomes a shock to realize that living in the time-famine of chasing resources for your dream is much better (though more fatiguing) than the meaninglessness of possessing your dream in the present.

Rhonda and the pastor in North Dakota experience *la fatigue d'être eglise* because they too sense that the only way into the good is to somehow harvest more resources. But how can you do this if you don't have the time? And how could a church like Rhonda's possibly provide, or even be a resource, for people chasing their future good? The church once helped people live the good life in the present (whether multigenerational or generational, the present was long enough for the good life to have content and be open to mystery—to have response and responsibility). Now the good life is lived in the future, not the present. Thus people want resources from the congregation. They want help coping with their own time-famines, they want assets for their children, and they want tips for obtaining their dreams. Enter megachurches and gigachurches like Rick Warren's Saddleback and Joel Osteen's Lakewood, and the thousands of less famous examples. People living in this short present ultimately want help coping with their fatigue so they can go faster and get more resources for their dreams.

A little church like Rhonda's had great importance when the good life was lived out in the present where practice, tradition, and community were important. When we were *not* in a time-famine, her little church had potency. Yet inside the time-famine, when the good life is a dream for the future and the now is about harvesting resources, her little congregation is rendered completely impotent. And her own pastoral imagination—her practical ecclesiology—is captured by the sense that she needs to innovate more resources lest the congregation perish.

Enter vocational depression. Rhonda feels depressed because the presentation "New Strategies for Assessing and Accelerating the Impact of Your Congregation" took her into her own dream-state. It inspired her to dream again of what her church could be in the future. But twenty-four hours later that dream of a good church, projected onto the future, turned on her, tasting bitter as she realized she had no resources (especially time) to actualize such a projection. The presentation captured her interest. But it made her no more ready to help her congregation live for the good or find the living God in the present. It actually did the opposite, alienating her from her own calling. Even if she could ride the wave of acceleration and give her people the resources to survive the time-famine and reach their dreams, she would only alienate them further from an imagination for a living God who encounters them with a word in the present and calls them to follow the good of Jesus's own life, death, and resurrection.

The Triple-A

Of course, most people don't take the tragic step that David Foster Wallace did (though the spiking opioid crisis and young adult depression may point to the same phenomenon).[27] Most of us have found a way to live in this arid and short present. You find meaning by seeking the resources for your dream, whatever that might be. Always seeking these resources also means, even in the midst of a time-famine, you can take on a style or disposition that gives you a sense of living a good life. It remains content-less (or allows you to infuse it with your own individual sense of what's good for you), but it nevertheless is a way of living "well" while you harvest resources and chase your dream. You can do this by taking on what Rosa calls a "Triple-A" approach to the good life. He explains, "The modern way of acting and being-in-the-world is geared toward making more and more of its qualities and quantities *available*, *accessible* and *attainable*."[28] The person (or institution) who is able to "thrive" in the short present, while always being free to chase a future dream, seeks availability, accessibility, and attainability.

To make this more concrete, let's return to the college-admissions scandal. Why break the law to get your kid admitted to Yale or USC? For those from elite families, the degree likely won't affect the child's earning potential. As a matter of fact, it might risk that earning potential. Suppose the child reads Wittgenstein in a first-year philosophy class and decides to be a philosophy major. Or worse, decides to pursue a PhD in philosophy and become an academic. This will have negative financial impact. But even this rare possibility

27. As could the rise of white supremacy. Almost all of these murderers post online that they're trying to secure a future for the white race. They sense that the future is the only place to win the good. In a deeply twisted way, they take on violence to win a future for their people. *Ressentiment* breeds in a compressed present, where the good always exists in some future dream. Enemies are spotted and must be punished when this future dream seems upended. For more on this, see Pankaj Mishra, *The Age of Anger: A History of the Present* (New York: Picador, 2017). For more on the other crises mentioned above, see Jean Twenge, "The Mental Health Crisis among America's Youth Is Real—and Staggering," Institute for Family Studies, March 18, 2019, https://ifstudies.org/blog/the-mental-health-crisis-among-americas-youth-is-realand-staggering.

28. Rosa, "Mindset of Growth," 42 (emphasis added).

is worth the cheating and illegal activity because in the end what matters is not the degree at all. The child doesn't need the degree to increase earning potential. Going to an elite university matters to these families not for the degree but for the availability, accessibility, and attainability it offers. Getting into a top school like Yale gives you availability to important people, accessibility to exclusive institutional status, and an overall attainability to whatever dream you wish.

These elite parents lie and cheat to get the Triple-A.[29] Universities can charge $60,000 a year because, as we all know, they don't offer strictly teaching and learning. Few of us would pay that sticker price for just teaching and learning (which is a shame but a reality). People are paying that exorbitant amount of money (resources) for availability, accessibility, and attainability. We might complain and even go into debt, but we are all willing to spend this huge amount of resources in exchange for these other resources of availability, accessibility, and attainability.

For people living in the first layer of Rosa's time-famine—those of us who feel the internal deficit of time—it's not an option for our children not to go to college. Yet we don't fear that they'll never read Plato or Dickens, study biology, or understand economics. What frightens us is that they'll have a future deficit of availability, accessibility, and attainability. Without these resources, we assume, they'll never be able to live their dream, never find their way into some future good life.

We ask our children and ourselves to rush, to accelerate the pace of our lives to do more in less time, so that we can achieve the resources that will give us availability, accessibility, and attainability. When it comes to teaching and learning, Minnesota State may be just as good as USC or Oxbridge. But Minnesota State is nowhere close when it comes to producing availability, accessibility, and attainability. Matriculating at one of these elite schools gives you a sense that the future promises a good life.

Acceptance to your dream college is the perfect late-modern dream. It allows for a sense of accomplishment—you're in the school you always dreamed of—but obtaining this dream is only about other future dreams. The cultural currency of college gives you the Triple-A for another dream in the future. College is a *must* because whatever lifetime you're in, whatever dream you're

29. Of course, it isn't just the elite who feel this drive for the Triple-A. Any parent who is feeling a time-famine at the internal level feels this drive to provide the Triple-A. Annette Lareau, in *Unequal Childhoods: Class, Race, and Family Life* (Berkeley: University of California Press, 2011), chap. 3, calls this "concerted cultivation." Concerted cultivation is the core parenting task of middle-class parents. It is a high-energy, high-investment means of providing children with the Triple-A.

chasing, you'll always need availability, accessibility, and attainability. This is what unconsciously goes through our heads as we write each monthly student loan check.[30]

The Style and Scope of the Triple-A

We need to explore a little deeper here. The Triple-A is important because, by delivering direct resources, it offers a style or way of being in relation to the world. This style of being allows the flat, meaningless, and even good-life-vapid present to be nevertheless inhabitable. You inhabit this short present by keeping your eyes on the goods of your future dream while seeking availability, accessibility, and attainability in the present. And you should choose to affiliate with friends and institutions that also have availability, accessibility, and attainability. They will give you more of these three resources, which further sets you up to attain your dream.

Ultimately, the Triple-A produces *scope*. In a short present, where the good is always in the future, having scope is a way to nevertheless relate to the world in the present. To have scope is to have room to act, an ability to cover a large range.[31] The good life might still be out in the future—you might still be chasing your dream and not accomplishing much of it—but if you have scope, you can have esteem. You show that you're relating to the world in a manner that promises you all the future resources to get your dream.

Rich kids need to go to Yale and USC not so they can be learned or intellectually formed but so they can have the style of scope. So they can go to a dinner party and have someone whisper, *There's Madeleine. She's so interesting! She started her own charity after visiting Mozambique. In ninth grade she launched a nail polish business. She has three hundred thousand Instagram followers, AND she went to Yale.* That's scope!

It's characters with this kind of scope that make Wes Anderson's films so interesting. The children in *Rushmore* and *The Royal Tenenbaums* have a humorous amount of scope. Their parents see it as a style necessary for a future good life. Of course, in most of Anderson's films, these children, molded for scope and with a bright future always before them, get stuck. Having little else than scope, they're tortured by an absence of any real connection to a tangible good life.

---

30. Of course now few to no one writes a check. It's faster to have it set on auto-pay, which plays its own part in keeping me from living in the present. I never have to think about what it really costs me.

31. Rosa discusses scope in "Mindset of Growth," 44–45.

Anderson's characters, or Madeleine in the example above, sense that the good is completely a projection into the future. But Madeleine relates to the world in the present through scope. And scope, to make this circular, reveals that she's the kind of talented person who can relate to the world in such a way that she can innovate, maximize, and accrue resources. Her future is bright. Her dreams will come true! (This never happens in Anderson's films.) She might not have her dreams now, but she has scope (men and women want to be with her and women want to be her), which is as good as a down payment.[32]

Misguided Scope

Like *reach*, as discussed in chapter 10, scope isn't bad in itself. Rather, because it's a way of relating to the world, it reveals something fundamental about us. Rosa explains: "The desire to increase our physical, material and social range is driven by the hope that we can find the *right* place for us, that we meet the people we *really* want to live with, the job that *actually* satisfies us, the religion . . . which is *truly ours*, the books that actually *talk to us* and the music that *speaks to us*."[33] This desire for scope isn't wrong. Rosa even adds more pointedly, "Thus, in the end, we hope, we will arrive at a form of life that turns the world into a living, breathing, speaking, responsive, 'enchanted' world."[34] And I would add: a world alive with divine action and congregations that feel alive with the love of the living God.

We hope for this kind of scope. But in late modernity, inside a time-famine, we can only imagine the good on some future plane. This makes it difficult to find a speaking, living, breathing world in the present—and difficult for people in our congregations to have the eyes to see a living God moving in their lives, speaking life to their many experiences of death and loss.

Charles Taylor has already taught us that there is a faithful way to live in a secular age. This faithful way takes on the disposition of an open searcher, embracing the scope of the present. Taylor thinks this will often demand some return (though not without reappropriation) to the sources of sacred

---

32. There is more to articulate in regard to this. I've said little about happiness. I have a very long discussion of the cultural place of happiness in the book *The End of Youth Ministry?* (Grand Rapids: Baker Academic, 2020). Rosa provides a discussion of happiness and happiness studies in *Resonance: A Sociology of Our Relationship to the World* (Medford, MA: Polity, 2019), chap. 1, sec. 2.

33. Rosa, "Mindset of Growth," 45.

34. Rosa, "Mindset of Growth," 45.

time.[35] But this return will need to guard against the temptation to live in the present by glorifying the past. That would be the opposite side of the dream-state. The present seems so short, resting on such a pitch, that some think the only way to stay in the present at all is to run like mad for the past. (Some are fundamentalists, wanting America or religion in America to be great again. But there are others who are much more sophisticated and nevertheless race for the past by attacking all forms of political liberalism, wanting a return to a medieval sense of the good.)[36] For Taylor, to stay in the present (a present that integrates both past and future), we need to see ourselves as pilgrims on a journey. He believes this is a positive way of living in the immanent frame. True discourse and storytelling with others keeps us squarely in an open present, making scope something much different from resource-accruing.

Taylor sees this as engaging the world with an open take (an openness to relate to the world as more than just a container of resources but instead as full of mystery and possibility). This, Taylor believes, keeps the immanent frame from spinning closed and violently shifting the scope from an extrinsic reality to a self-enclosed reality. Even inside our modern secular age there are ways to have a scope that reaches for transcendence.

But Rosa's point is that the time-famine alienates us from this kind of scope. We're alienated from relating to a world that is alive. We can't access the possibility that there is a living God who is speaking to us. We're cut off from the reality that there is more than our individual identity projects and the race to harvest resources for some undefined dream.

Our desire for scope shows our longing to encounter something transcendent. Yet Rosa contends that, unfortunately, we allow scope to be flattened into style. As style, scope has no referent or aim beyond itself. Scope becomes self-referential, as Wes Anderson's characters show, spinning deeper into self-actualizing projects, which enclose them deeper within the aridness of the immanent frame's present. Rosa says it this way: "Alas . . . instead of arriving [at this open-take scope], we end up turning the business of increasing our scope and our horizon of the available, attainable and accessible, and collecting resources into an end in itself, into an

35. Taylor is more direct in making this claim at the end of *The Source of the Self: The Making of Modern Identity* (Cambridge, MA: Harvard University Press, 1989), 495–515.

36. Taylor worries about this propensity in John Milbank. Taylor likes much about Milbank's analysis, but Taylor (unlike Milbank) isn't ready to simply push for a radical return to past visions of the good or ontology. See Charles Taylor, "Afterword: *Apologia pro Libro Suo*," in *Varieties of Secularism in a Secular Age*, ed. Michael Warner, Jonathan VanAntwerpen, and Craig Calhoun (Cambridge, MA: Harvard University Press, 2010), 300–324.

endless, escalatory cycle which permanently erodes its own basis and thus leads nowhere."[37]

Nowhere is exactly where the pastor in North Dakota feels his congregation is. The congregation is depressed because they feel like they're going nowhere. The pastor feels like he's pastoring them to nowhere. They've followed every consultant who reminds them that they need a defined purpose and mission, a shared story. But the more they embrace these strategies, the more the time-famine impinges and burnout returns. They lack the energy to go anywhere but nowhere. Alienated from the scope of divine encounter, the people can only ask the congregation for more resources. The resources will not be used to find the living God in the present, or even to begin to imagine how sacred time runs through their lives. Rather, they need resources to cope with the time-famine itself and to get back to getting more resources for their dream. They're going nowhere because the life of the congregation has less and less direct pull on their imagination of the good life. In their time-famine they can only ask the congregation to catch up and give them more resources. Yet the congregation only has resources when its members give, not just receive.

Squarely in the time-famine, the pastor's people have no time or energy to give. They want to take resources, but they don't have the energy to give, or they're too tired preparing for a future good life by getting resources for their and their children's dreams. Unable to give and unable to see how giving could be anything other than depleting resources, they cannot receive. And unable to receive, they can't be taken outside of themselves to relate to the living world and the speaking God. All their desire for scope is closed down, taking them nowhere but into more fatigue.

The congregation is too fatigued to enter into this movement of giving and receiving. In a secular age, when the good life is deferred to the dream-state of the future, the church loses any sense of scope. The congregation narrows and becomes a service organization of resources. It is no longer a community of practice and tradition that wears a wholly distinct orientation to time. It no longer seeks in our present for the living God to speak, to give us the crucified Christ as the seeming opposite, but nevertheless fullness, of the good. This is the deep alienation that the Protestant congregation confronts.

37. Rosa, "Availability, Accessible, Attainable: The Mindset of Growth and the Resonance Conception of the Good Life," in *The Good Life Beyond Growth*, ed. Hartmut Rosa and Christoph Henning (London: Routledge, 2019), 45.

And this alienation is tricky. The response is not just to stop or to slow down, as one might think. The time-famine cannot be solved by doing less. The North Dakota pastor has such *fatigue* because he knows, somewhere deep down, that stopping or even slowing down isn't really the answer. Slow food, slow parenting, and slow church may be a logical (and to some degree helpful) response to the time-famine.[38] But in the end, because of our need for reach and scope, it will not solve the problem. It will only be a bandage on cancer. What we long for, what seems captivatingly good, is to be connected to something full, not just slowing down. We long to find a true fullness that draws us not through time, into some future, but more deeply into time itself. We long to live so deeply in time that we hear and feel the calling of eternity.[39] We yearn to find once again the infinite in time, to find the sacred in the present, and therefore to be truly alive![40]

———

As I pondered the email from the pastor in North Dakota and considered his longing for this disposition to the good in his congregation, I thought to myself, *Wait, he does! He already has people in his congregation who rest in the present and who bathe in the mystery of time.*

38. For interesting thoughts on slow church, see Stephen Pickard, *Seeking the Church: An Introduction to Ecclesiology* (London: SCM, 2012); and C. Christopher Smith and John Pattison, *Slow Church: Cultivating Community in the Patient Way of Jesus* (Downers Grove, IL: InterVarsity, 2014).

39. This sense of time is sacramental, eternity breaking into time. This sacramental ontology, which can really connect to people's sense of a good life, will be very important for Christianity going forward. Henri de Lubac, Yves Congar, and others have articulated similar thoughts. More recently, Hans Boersma has offered many works pushing in this direction: *A Return to Mystery: Nouvelle Theologie and Sacramental Ontology* (Oxford: Oxford University Press, 2009); and *Heavenly Participation: The Weaving of the Sacramental Tapestry* (Grand Rapids: Eerdmans, 2011). Broadly I agree with him, and I hope I've shown why through this cultural analysis.

40. In my personal conversations with Hartmut Rosa it's been clear to me that he is really thinking at this level. He's a critical social theorist who, through critical social theory, philosophy, and sociology, is trying to name the ways to reclaim enchantment after having experienced disenchantment. He passionately wants a living world. After spending time with him, I thought, *He is what you get when you blend Charles Taylor, Jürgen Habermas, and Theodor Adorno, and return to the mystical.* It is a beautiful combination. He's a critical theorist seeking the spirit almost as a monk would in the Black Forest of Germany.

13

why the slow church can't work

stabilization, alienation, and the loss of the congregational will to be

I was taken back to the church gym in North Dakota. The pastor giving me a tour of their new wing. The two of us watching preschoolers playing with a parachute. We looked over the room as they finished their activity. They were running past us to retrieve their water bottles. And the little girl saying to no one in particular, "That was *great*!"

Her little being swelled with resonance. She unmistakably felt connected to the world. She was alive. She was a live wire picking up a strong current from the world. The pastor and I had looked at each other and smiled, both taking in the experience without speaking. We'd been warmed at the deepest level by her little proclamation.

She was unequivocally experiencing the good in the present. Her body was where her mind was, her connection to the world full. Her assertion, "That was *great*!" weighed heavier than a simple superlative to a sensation. It was an assertion of her experience of eternity breaking into time, of time itself becoming full of something truly good. It was *great*.

It was an experience that contained so much of the world, so much connection to it, not just so many resources. And it felt *great* to her because it lasted. Bound in time, it wore something more than time, even bearing all the movements of time. It was so full that the bleeding away, or even acceleration, of time couldn't touch it. She was at a feast, not a time-famine. She had fullness in the time of the present. The present was so full that she was able to anticipate, to expectantly ready herself for, the in-breaking of eternity itself into time.

And we too shared in it. We paused to rest in the fullness of her fullness in time. I personally felt the room change. I became aware of the sunlight filling the room, of the sun's rays hitting my body and warming it. The light felt brighter, even inviting. I could feel my body. I felt alive and grateful to be alive. Something beautiful encountered me. The rush of the moment and the anxiety of my upcoming presentations all evaporated in the beauty of the moment of being alive. I felt pulled into something real. Being aware of being alive, here in the present, brought me into mystery, into a divine encounter. Her very giving to and receiving of the world opened me up to the mystery of my existence, to the beauty and mystery of time. She became my minister.

And the half smile I shared with the pastor communicated that the child, for that moment, became his minister too. It was an event—a small one but nevertheless a true event—of eternity breaking into time. It didn't take me out of the world but placed me more deeply into it. It was an encounter of transcendence, and yet it directed me deeper into beauty, delivering a rich connection with the world.

Thinking again about that experience, I called my college friend who I had reconnected with in Kansas City, the one who left his church to spend more time with his children. It made more sense to me now why he left. He was starving. Locked in a time-famine, he was spiritually wasting away. His sabbatical, of course, gave him time, but he needed more than just indiscriminate time. This need for something more ended up pushing him to quit his job.

On the phone he said to me, "Those first two weeks of my sabbatical, I honestly thought I was going to have a mental breakdown. I even started to think that I'd spend the whole sabbatical bedridden."

He paused and continued, "I felt so depressed, even more than before my sabbatical. Here was the time I needed, and I felt sick. It didn't feel good."

In the context of the time-famine, his words made sense. Sabbaticals can maim those weary from a time-famine in the same way that overeating can kill a starving prisoner. In a time-famine, a time-starved person can't find their bearings by being given a buffet of time. Forced deceleration, either willful or not, is no response to the time-famine. We need fuller time, not just more time.

"What changed?" I asked.

"I started to really be present with my children," he said. "But I don't mean that like I would have before the sabbatical. I always prided myself on being an accessible and available parent."

My ears perked up. He almost said all of Hartmut Rosa's Triple-A.

"But being that right kind of parent just exhausted me further. It always felt like another thing that I was too busy to be better than mediocre at. When I hit the wall, something changed."

He explained that he started to need his kids to take him back into the world, to connect him to it. "Especially my little ones," he said. "They just lived; they were just present, just sought for God and beauty. I was so burnt out I felt like I couldn't live. I couldn't embrace the world, so one day I decided to let them intercede for me, that maybe through their eyes and their experience I could find a way to live again."

He started to go to the park with them. He'd always done this. But before he'd be on a bench multitasking. Returning email, texting, and watching them enough so everyone else at the park knew he was a good, involved parent. He was always running but never connected to the moment, never really in time.

"After my near breakdown, I decided they'd be my conduit, or Sherpa, or even priest—if it doesn't sound too crazy." He watched them play and played with them, engaging their engagement with the world. It revived him, connecting him to life again. It allowed him to touch something beautiful that had seemed so far away. And he wouldn't go back. He'd rather quit his job and never return to a congregation than feel that alienation from life itself again.

"That saved my life. Honestly, it saved my faith."

What Stabilizes?

These moments reveal something important that we've been pointing to throughout the last few chapters. Ironically, the response to acceleration and its imposing time-famine isn't necessarily to slow down. The little girl in the North Dakota gym could be described many ways, but *slow* would not be one of them.

Of course, in some sense we could all use a downshift. (And some of us got it in the COVID-19 pandemic.) There is something healthy and reviving to our spirituality about slowing down with silence, rest, and meditation. These practices open us to the mystery of time. They take us deeper into time, making us available to the movements of divine action breaking into time, to the very ways time is enveloped by eternity. Though being still is necessary, it creates tension, particularly for congregations in late modernity.

Congregations that take direct steps to slow down face an intrinsic and acute pressure. To defend this slowdown, they often have to boost the rhetoric of innovation. Sabbath, silent retreats, and ancient liturgies become wrapped in the language of newness or innovation to attract people. The slowdown must always be justified by the measure of relevance ("The youth and young families love these practices!").

These slowdown practices must be justified by something beyond themselves. To feel stable, the congregation that slows down needs more than the practices themselves. All institutions and ways of life need some form of stabilization. By *stabilization* I mean the process that secures an institution or way of life from failure and decline. But what is judged as a failure or decline is determined by the shape of the stabilization.

For instance, in Avignon the church was stabilized by the practices themselves. When the priest broke the bread, eternity was in time. When the community sang, prayed, and rang the church bells, the demons fled. The practices protected the realm. The potency of these practices stabilized the institution. Because the church had these enchanted practices, the church had vitality. Period. The church didn't need a new program or innovation to be stabilized. It had prayers and relics. These practices and holy things opened doorways into the divine, thus stabilizing the church. The congregation at Chartres was stabilized by its praying pilgrims and a piece of Mary's cloak.[1]

But let's not get too romantic. Stabilization through supposedly divine practices and holy relics led to corruption, like the selling of indulgences. The reforming of the church from this corruption was a major hinge of Western history, because the Reformation upended the very process of medieval institutional stabilization.

Fast-forwarding to late modernity, practices in themselves have no potency to stabilize an institution (and relics have no holy charge). Stabilization has nothing to do with divinely imposed practices or holy things. Whatever it is that stabilizes the congregation inside late modernity, it's not the divine economy of the Eucharist or the ability of the consecrated building to protect from the demonic. Stabilization has almost nothing to do with transcendence. We live in a secular age, as Charles Taylor reminds us. We live in a secular age because, even in a megachurch of ten thousand, what stabilizes the congregation is completely secular. Completely secular functions and imaginations.

Slowing Down Is Hard

A congregation trying to slow down experiences an acute tension. Because stabilization is now provided by immanent structures, functions, and imagi-

---

1. Justo González, in *The Story of Christianity*, vol. 1, *The Early Church to the Dawn of the Reformation* (San Francisco: HarperOne, 2010), 381–83, provides a very helpful overview on how the church building was seen inside the stability of the practice.

nations, slowing down as a way for the congregation to be in the world has to be justified by a different logic. In my small congregation, steps have been taken to deliberately slow down with a Saturday evening Sabbath service twice a month that invites people into a day of rest on Sunday. The congregation is already small, less than a hundred members. These Saturday services are even smaller—often, over spring break or in the summer, down to less than fifteen people (one Saturday only four people showed up). In these moments the hidden pressure of a late-modern sense of stabilization races to the surface. It's hard not to feel a stab of embarrassment, a sense that so few people indicates that I'm part of a failing congregation. I sometimes even imagine what someone new to our community will think when they walk in. I imagine they look at the sparse sanctuary and judge this congregation as unstable. This feeling of instability has a way of imposing an icky moral disdain that keeps people from returning.[2]

If I were living in medieval Avignon, it wouldn't matter how many people showed. What would matter is that such hours of prayer were kept, that such practices were echoing God's reign and goodness in the world. The pastor or priest would perform these powerful practices to bring heaven to earth whether people showed up or not. The practices were done against the horizon of sacred time. They were necessary and direct links to the divine. As long as the church had the practices and relics, it was institutionally secure.

But this is not how modernity functions. What stabilizes an institution in modernity is "systematic . . . growth, innovation and acceleration."[3] The way to keep from failure and decline is to continue increasing. Growth stabilizes. Institutions grow or die. Not all growth in nature is healthy (e.g., cancer), but in late-modern stabilization, growth is all that matters.

Therefore, if you're going to take steps to slow down, like with my little church, you'd better be able to show how it produces growth, innovation, and something new. Slowdown can only be justified by a higher good—growth. If you can't show how the slowdown produces growth, you'll always feel the hot breath of accusations of decline and coming failure.

This ultimately means that true slowdown is nearly impossible (or at least very difficult) in late modernity. What is needed is rest. But the only thing that stabilizes enough to allow rest is more growth. Another deep, vicious circle

2. This points to Jonathan Haidt's work on moral reasoning and its emotional connection. See *The Righteous Mind: Why Good People Are Divided by Politics and Religion* (New York: Vintage, 2012).

3. Hartmut Rosa, "The Mindset of Growth and the Resonance Conception of the Good Life," in *The Good Life Beyond Growth*, ed. Hartmut Rosa and Christoph Henning (London: Routledge, 2019), 45.

of late modernity. We want the freedom to rest and express ourselves, but the only way to get this freedom to rest is to grow, and then grow more. You can never rest if you want to achieve rest! Faithfulness and peace are devalued measures in late modernity's version of stabilization.

Dynamic Stabilization

This need for constant and continued growth happens, Rosa says, because what stabilizes an institution is "its structural reproduction."[4] To be stable, an institution has to produce and reproduce. He calls this *dynamic stabilization*.[5] By definition, a modern society is one in which the stabilization process is dynamic, when growth (not divine right, prayer, or obedience to a sacred book) stabilizes the society and its institutions.[6] A dynamic stabilization process asserts that the only way to keep an institution from failure is continued growth.

And this kind of growth is always a *dynamic* growth. What is grown this year must be exceeded next year. In philosophical language, dynamic stabilization becomes our hermeneutic. It becomes how we measure congregations. Dynamic stabilization justifies or judges all the congregation's actions. It's fine to slow down, start a new service, or form an initiative to feed the hungry, but all these actions will need to be evaluated through dynamic stabilization. Do they lead the institution into growth, away from decline and potential

4. Rosa, "Two Versions of the Good Life and Two Forms of Fear: Dynamic Stabilization and the Resonance Conception of the Good Life," paper presented at the Yale Center for Faith and Culture conference on Joy, Security, and Fear, New Haven, CT, November 8–9, 2017, 2.

5. Rosa is contrasting dynamic with adaptive stabilization. The following quote provides a deeper context to innovation and the new: "Of course, no social formation ever could stabilize and reproduce itself in a merely *static* way. All societies occasionally need change and development. However, in non-modern social formations, the mode of stabilization is *adaptive*: Growth, acceleration or innovations can and do occur, but they are either accidental or adaptive, i.e., they are reactions to changes in the environment (e.g., climate changes or natural disasters such as droughts, fires, earthquakes, or the appearance of new diseases or new enemies, etc.). Dynamic stabilization as I use it here, by contrast, is defined by the systematic requirement for *increase, augmentation, and acceleration* as an *internal, endogenous* requirement." Rosa, "Two Versions of the Good Life," 5 (emphasis original).

6. "The defining feature of a modern society (or, in fact, a modern institution) can be seen in the fact that it can only stabilize itself dynamically, or more precisely, that it can only reproduce its structure through an *increase* of some sort—quite regularly, through (economic) growth, (technological) acceleration, and/or higher rates of (cultural) innovation. Hence, I suggest the following definition: *A society is modern when it operates in a mode of dynamic stabilization, i.e., when it systematically requires growth, innovation and acceleration for its structural reproduction and in order to maintain its socio-economic and institutional status quo.*" Rosa, "Two Versions of the Good Life," 2 (emphasis original).

death? If not, they need to be cut (or compensated for by another initiative that produces excess growth).

The only way to keep the whole societal way of being stable is to continue to increase. Modernity cannot stabilize itself through transcendent longings, kin structures, or the wisdom of those running the polis. This is why every election since the 1970s—when the nation-state timekeeper was dethroned—has been about "the economy, stupid." Growth itself stabilizes institutions and the whole modern project. We no longer elect presidents because of their wisdom or even moral integrity; we elect them because they can grow the economy. This isn't completely about greed (of course, a lot of it is); it's also about stabilization. A strong, growing economy means a stable country, West, and world.

As I've gone through pains to show over the last dozen chapters, to get this stabilization you need to continue to ramp up the acceleration. Every year modernity must increase the speed of technology, social change, and pace of life to get the stabilization it needs. Acceleration is not a choice; it's a necessity. And it is one that all institutions must bear. Markets need to grow or they go under. If a market goes under, it takes most of the modern institutions with it. Like spinning plates, institutions are secure as long as the momentum continues to increase. When the plates lose speed they wobble, putting the plates and the plate spinner at risk. Similarly, if the momentum of dynamic stabilization doesn't continue, the institutions of the West will wobble and crash.

Inside dynamic stabilization, numbers become the clearest measure of such growth that avoids decline and the risk of failure. All we do, then, even in the church, has to be justified by dynamic stabilization.[7] Sitting in the sanctuary with seventeen people invited to slow down and pray feels like a big problem, especially when I remember twenty-five being at this service before. Sitting there, it's hard to slow down at all, because dynamic stabilization condemns me (as much as any of Avignon's priests would have scolded me for taking the Mass inappropriately), whispering that I'm in a dying church with slow people. I make this evaluation using no other measure than the fact that so few people are present. The only reading is that the slowdown service is un-wanted, and the institution itself is in peril. Dynamic stabilization screams, *Change, innovate quickly to get growth fast, or die!*

We have all been formed to judge our congregations and their practices through dynamic stabilization. The congregation needs to grow, innovate, and accelerate to have any value. If the institution does not wear these marks,

7. This is especially true in America, where the church receives no state funding and therefore cannot live outside the direct pressures of dynamic stabilization.

it's losing—it's a loser congregation. Bishops will ask if such congregations should be closed, making judgments not through sacred or consecrated means but through the logic of modernity and dynamic stabilization. They'll look at budgets, membership rolls, demographics, and projections for growth to decide if the congregation is stable enough to remain open. I know of a little congregation that has become a way station for hurting people. Its ministry is deep, but it has no way, through its part-time pastor, to sustain itself outside of funding from the synod. The bishop recently told the pastor that they would no longer throw good money after bad. What made the congregation "bad money" had nothing to do with its ministry—even its testimonies to the presence of the living Christ—but with its inability to function at the pace of dynamic stabilization. It was bad money because there was no route for this little congregation to stabilize itself dynamically. And, therefore, it was judged unsustainable for the synod. Throwing good money after bad risks the dynamic stabilization of the whole synod, the bishop reasoned.

It is right for congregations and denominations to value sustainability. But we should also recognize that what is sustainable is determined by the goods of dynamic stabilization. More work needs to be done to think about sustainability within a very different horizon: the cruciform good life. Within dynamic stabilization and the good of a short present, what is sustainable cannot be separated from what grows. Being sustainable can simply mean the peace of having what you need, but in dynamic stabilization it means putting a plan in place that promises 5 to 10 percent growth. Only growth is sustainable. Without 5 to 10 percent growth, institutions will fail. They are unsustainable. In this model, the dynamic nature of modernity and its continued pursuit of acceleration demands that to be sustainable you can never rest. No wonder congregations find themselves in *la fatigue d'être eglise*. Here's an example of this thinking entering the church: Thomas Bandy even uses the word "acceleration" when he says, "The Principle of Acceleration is the first key criterion for assessment. I sometimes call it the 'Principle of Zoom.' Every program and leader of the church should effectively grow the church. This may mean numerical or financial growth, or relational and spiritual growth. It may mean more worshipers, the multiplication of small groups, or the swell of new volunteers. Acceleration happens when churches exert themselves to learn more, try different things, welcome new people, raise the bar of accountability, increase resources, and generally get bigger and bolder."[8] The goods of community and transformation are often not in

8. Bandy, *Strategic Thinking: How to Sustain Effective Ministry* (Nashville: Abingdon, 2017), 73.

accord with a dynamic stabilization that has not come under the sign of the cross and been judged.

Inside the goods of dynamic stabilization there is little sense that the prayers and practices of my little church are necessary. The congregation proves itself unstable, because it isn't growing. The service is meaningless because it isn't increasing. It's irrelevant that life is coming out of death and persons are sharing in the person of Jesus through sharing in the life of one another. It makes no difference that we all find our humanity and the gratitude of being alive by sitting silently on a dark Saturday night in prayer. Rather, what matters inside dynamic stabilization is only growth. And as we've seen, the only way to grow in late modernity is to speed up. The slowdown practices need this kind of logic to infuse them (a true performative contradiction), because if not, the church becomes unmodern.[9]

Many congregations that have sought to missionally slow down have either abandoned the pursuit, closed, or pivoted to a more innovative imagination (those once advocating for ancient-future emerging churches are now missional innovators). They've made this shift because the institutional structures are not built with any relation to sacred time. Rather, they're justified and therefore stabilized only dynamically. To care about the church's future is not—like Luther, Calvin, de Lubac, or Barth—to turn back to the Word and Spirit of the living God who sustains his body on a cross but to get the congregation to the speed of dynamic stabilization.[10]

The Double Bind

What to do about this late-modern contradiction is tricky. It would be difficult, even unwise, to destroy dynamic stabilization. Dynamic stabilization is the structural reality our society is built upon. We must remember that our congregations are never hermetically sealed. The people who make up our congregations live within the structures and narrative of the timekeeper Silicon Valley. Therefore, no matter how much we might wish to bar dynamic

9. We can talk about *post*modern, but it really isn't *after* modernity. Postmodern is a style of thinking and being that recognizes (either in delight or horror) that the present is radically short. Therefore, no tradition or even foundation of truth (no stories from the past) can stabilize us. Often those in Protestantism who affirm postmodernity—particularly in ecclesiology—equally embrace acceleration and avoid the unmodern.

10. James K. A. Smith critiques this hyperinnovative view: "In order to foster a Christian imagination, we don't need to invent; we need to remember. We cannot hope to re-create the world if we are constantly reinventing church, because we will reinvent ourselves right out of the Story." *You Are What You Love: The Spiritual Power of Habit* (Grand Rapids: Brazos, 2016), 181.

stabilization from our congregations and even denominational structures, it's not possible. I'm not calling for an idealistic anti-sustainability or a demonizing of growth—although I am challenging us to be more reflective, even offering rich theological conceptions for such ecclesial realities. Dynamic stabilization is bred with many contradictions and perils, but it nevertheless is the system we find ourselves in. There is no way to simply opt out.

Even if it were possible, it would be a deep injustice to push the plate spinner to the ground, allowing the plates to crash, with mayhem and suffering to follow. Because the stabilization of Western modernity is built dynamically, it would be evil to simply force a slowdown that could quite easily push millions into poverty, chaos, and violence. Modernity is stable because it's a spinning top. Knock it off-kilter and war, poverty, and suffering will come with a blurring rush. Western countries have not declared war against each other for seventy-five years, for no small reason because of our trade agreements and mutual economic interest in the growth of markets. The desire for further acceleration to achieve dynamic stabilization is what has kept the West working together (this is why Brexit and Trump's spitting on our European allies are deeply worrisome).

Rosa has been clear that if acceleration is the problem, the solution isn't necessarily slowdown—not at the societal or congregational level. That would be too simple of an equation. It fails to show how much we, and our congregations, are dependent on dynamic stabilization. But this puts us on shaky ground. Though we do not wish for the demise of dynamic stabilization, its continued need for acceleration leads us to wonder how much faster modernity is built to go.

We've been increasing the speed each year for the last three hundred years. When do we hit the limit? When do we go so fast that the spinning top is no longer stable, not because it's slowed down but because it is not made for these speeds? How fast can modernity go and still be dynamic? Or we could ask it this way: Do the structures, imaginations, narratives, and psychological constitutions of modern people and their institutions have a maximum speed limit? After all, dynamic stabilization is dependent on certain structures that cannot simply be accelerated forever.

For instance, it could be argued that democracy, the economy, societal psychological well-being, and the environment are all under significant pressure, if not in crisis. And what is putting them in crisis, I believe (and have tried to show), is speed. All four are essential to the continuation of dynamic stabilization—you need psychologically stable people, democratic systems, a reliable economy, and an inhabitable environment. But dynamic stabilization has sped things up so quickly that the slower pace of democratic discourse is becoming impossible. Markets too are going so fast that inequality is becoming rampant. Social change and the pace of life are so accelerated that rates of burnout and depression are skyrocketing. And the heating of the planet for the sake of stabilization is so relentless that the earth has no time to keep the temperature from rising. We all live with dystopian nightmares, or at least stream them, because we tacitly wonder if continued dynamic stabilization is indeed stable, or if we have already crossed that threshold.

Dynamic stabilization, then, has to deal with what Rosa calls *desynchronization*. The need for speed and growth can be so great that the human psyche, political system, economy, environment, and maybe even religion itself cannot respond. Desynchronization is the threat that growth is pushed so hard that it outraces the time necessary for crops to grow, information to be understood, and markets to be checked.[11] And, I would add, the human spirit to seek mystery.

This is the double bind of late modernity. There is no other viable societal option than dynamic stabilization (not yet, at least). Even with its threats of desynchronization, dynamic stabilization is the best we have. The late twentieth century has taught us that other systems are either obliterated by globalization or untenable.[12] Therefore, it would be deeply irresponsible from a societal perspective to pull the lever and halt late modernity's acceleration and destroy dynamic stabilization (the anarchy of *Mr. Robot* is not a good idea).[13] Unable to stop the machine, most of us agree there is something within the machine's very operations that is maiming us. The problem with an accelerated modernity and its dynamic stabilization is not only the worries of

11. For more on this, see Hartmut Rosa, *Alienation and Acceleration: Towards a Critical Theory of Late-Modern Temporality* (Malmö, Sweden: NSU Press, 2014), 70.

12. E.g., Soviet communism. I still believe we have much to learn from cultural philosophical forms of Marxism. But I am much less supportive of political and economic systems built on these tenants. Certain forms of soft Marxism I personally find helpful as cultural critiques. For instance, what follows, through Rosa, will echo some of the thinking of the Frankfurt School, showing that capitalism and its dynamic stabilization releases all sorts of forms of alienation. Its freedom is so laced with alienation that at times it feels very hard to call its free markets *free*.

13. I'm deeply intrigued by Dave Snowden's argument that anarchy and fascism always move inside the same currents, but anarchy always loses. He means that anarchy creates the conditions for fascism. We see so many young people with anarchist dreams, using the internet to fantasize about bringing down the system. But if Snowden is right, then this only makes the possibility of fascism more ripe. For a more concrete example of this, it's amazing the Venn-diagram-like overlap of Donald Trump and Bernie Sanders supporters. They're oddly very similar, showing how quickly the eagerness for anarchy can flip to fascism. Both Trump and Sanders are viable (even electable—or elected in the case of Trump) because of this anarchist/fascist sensibility that is moving across the West. Snowden has written very little but has a number of engaging lectures, such as "How Not to Manage Complexity," keynote speech at State of the Net 2013, May 31 and June 1, Trieste, Italy, https://youtu.be/gaFQJaQTXhY.

desynchronization but more directly (and immediately for congregations) the ways the continued necessity for acceleration produces alienation.

Alienation

In the continued thrust of dynamic stabilization, we find ourselves alienated from nearly everything. We're alienated from one another, from our own bodies, and ultimately, Rosa believes, from the world itself. We are moving so fast for the sake of the good of the new, which stabilizes our identities and institutions, that the world becomes dull and lifeless.[14] Trying to keep up, we become too tired to actually live. In exchange for a world that is mysteriously frightening but fully alive, modernity offers stabilization through dynamic (always speeding up) forms of growth.

Inside the never-ending need for acceleration, we discover we can't taste anything, as if our taste buds for life have been burned by the speed. We can't stop to smell the roses and pulsate with the gratitude that we have life. There is too much to do in life to feel alive. To even take the time to joyfully and even painfully remember that we are in the world seems a luxury. We sense that we're living more on the surface of the world, speeding past it, than living in it. People even talk like this: "What I really want is to be—to feel—alive." This is a common but odd statement, something our ancestors in Avignon, Rome, or Wittenberg could never have imagined. For them the world was so alive, teeming with invisible forces, that it was frightening.

Ironically, though most of us want to feel alive, we have little concept of what being alive would actually look like. We might feel a faint or strong pulsing for life, but the world feels far away. Maybe this is why airline commercials, like Delta's "Good things come to those who go," are so intriguing. We sense that we can reenter the world and live again, reaching into the world by going to it, by traveling.[15] But even this mentality assumes that we're *not already* in the world; our present is too flat and dull to matter. The real living is something we must speed up—at least to the pace of a jet engine—to find.

To find this living through the speed of going, we'll have to grow our earnings. We'll have to work harder to earn the credit card points we need to someday—in some future—live. We'll end up feeling more disconnected from the world in front of us so we can someday travel to the world that Delta has curated for us. The late-modern crisis is that we are moving so fast,

14. See movies such as *American Beauty* and *Brad's Status* for examples of this.
15. Zygmunt Bauman has discussed this travel phenomenon in his small but important book, *Globalization: The Human Consequences* (New York: Columbia University Press, 1998), 92–98.

keeping the dynamic stabilization going, even in our own family economies and subjective experience, that we are alienated from relating to the world and being truly alive.

What this alienation looks or feels like is irresponsiveness. Karl Marx is right about modernity producing alienation but wrong about the nature of alienation. We are alienated not just from the means of production but from an open sense that the world (or some personal force within it) is speaking to us. Our longing may be for the future, but we're still breathing in the present world. Our being is in the present, working for our future dream. And this world we inhabit in the present seems frighteningly quiet. There is nothing discernible in the ambient noise of the speed of modernity. Rosa says, "Alienation . . . is a particular mode of relating to the world of things, of people and of one's self in which there is no *responsivity*, i.e., no meaningful inner connection. It is . . . a relationship without (true) relation."[16]

Of course, there is no way to breathe and act without some kind of relationship with the world. We are not beings in *Matrix* pods or brains stuck in vats. But this is what makes this alienation so hidden and yet heavy. We are still relating to things, people, the world, and ourselves. But the acceleration of late modernity, and its hypergood of dynamic stabilization for the sake of speed and growth, turns all these relations into "causal and instrumental connections and interactions."[17] Mystery, the fullness of time, and transcendence are beat out of our relations.[18] This move to reduce all our relations to causal and instrumental ones gets us stabilization, technological advance, space for identity innovation, and an overall ability to do more in less time.[19] But for these gains, the world itself is deadened, made into an object. Everything in the world becomes an object, and so our own subjectivity is made to feel meaningless and empty.

As Rosa says, in these conditions of an accelerated late modernity, "the world (in all its qualities) cannot be appropriated by the subject, it cannot be made to 'speak,' it appears to be without sound and color. Alienation thus is a relationship which is marked by the absence of a true, vibrant exchange and

16. Rosa, "Two Versions of the Good Life," 13.
17. Rosa, "Two Versions of the Good Life," 13.
18. We lose the hypostatic nature of our being and of the world itself. I discuss this hypostatic nature in relation to human beings and God's revelation in volume 1, *Faith Formation in a Secular Age: Responding to the Church's Obsession with Youthfulness* (Grand Rapids: Baker Academic, 2017), chaps. 8 and 9. I discuss it in relation to the natural sciences in my book *Exploding Stars, Dead Dinosaurs, and Zombies* (Minneapolis: Fortress, 2018), chap. 10.
19. I've been working on this problem since my first published article and then book. I framed this inside the practice of relational ministry, but the same problematic is what I'm discussing now through a full-blown articulation of modernity.

connection."[20] We get stabilization through growth. We receive the freedom to live many lifetimes and always be chasing the new in a short present. We even get cheap flights to Jamaica. But for the sake of these gains our relation to the world, and to our very selves, has been flattened and muted. We need to become alienated from life itself for the sake of speed. We choose the safety of dynamic stabilization, even if it means we lose the world with it.[21]

Disintegrations and Erosions

This alienation from the world affects the congregation. Dynamic, accelerating growth achieves stabilization at the institutional level, but to do so it must mute the world. And this muting of the world imposes on us a disintegration that erodes commitment.[22] We're going too fast to maintain or seek an integrated life. Without integration, we become psychologically imbalanced (too disintegrated to be healthy).[23] But in our accelerated late modernity, the norm for all of us is to live at a constant level of disintegration. We feel a lack of coherence in our own stories. The happenings, occurrences, and episodes of our lives seem to be changing and shifting so fast that it's impossible for us to integrate them into a coherent life story. We have no time to really ask, What does this mean? Or, How do I make sense of my existence or my own self now that this has happened? The best we can say is, "So . . . *that* just happened!" Then we move on, feeling no necessity to make such a happening coherent with and integrated into our life story. "So *that* just happened" functions as a verbal delete button, releasing us from having to turn an experience into a story. This phrase allows us to quickly move on, acknowledging the disruption but without the necessity of narration.[24]

20. Rosa, "Two Versions of the Good Life," 13.

21. This is to echo Bonhoeffer's essay on safety and peace. See "Address to the Fano Conference: English Transcription," in *Dietrich Bonhoeffer Works*, vol. 13, *London, 1933–1935* (Minneapolis: Fortress, 2007), 307–9. Bonhoeffer doesn't believe that safety and peace can coexist. You cannot have true peace without risk, without being unsafe. But this is worth it, Bonhoeffer believes. Late modernity, especially in the post-9/11 West, however, has taken a different stance. We have chosen safety over peace, and because of this we need to talk constantly of freedom (convincing ourselves we still have some)—but worse, we have lost the world itself for the sake of freedom. We are safe but unable to live.

22. For more on this, see Rosa, *Alienation and Acceleration*, 88–96.

23. It's often the case that, to move back into some kind of level of healthy integration, you need to find a therapist who will engage you in articulating the narrative-shape of your affect.

24. Admittedly, this isn't true for everyone. Some use the phrase to start a story or locate an experience as weird enough to do something with. But for most people it seems to be a way to not get tripped up by an occurrence.

Yet Taylor has taught us that the good life (whether subjective or objective, personal or cultural) demands narrative. You need a story about what makes life good to have an identity. It's never enough to ironically brush off happenings, keeping them at arm's length. We need a story. And this story must cross some threshold of coherence. I must be able to produce an integration that informs me of who I am, giving me continuity over time.[25]

Rosa's point is that time itself is moving so fast that it becomes a difficult task for us to put our happenings, occurrences, and episodes into a narrative arc. Things are coming at us faster than we can integrate. The rapid-fire experiences, actions, positions, and overall information of dynamic stabilization *can* overwhelm our ability to sketch out some coherent life story.[26]

Because we need an integrated story to have some connection to the good life, we find that this imposed disintegration has the effect of eroding our commitments. It's easy to be committed to something when it is deeply integrated into your story of the good life.[27] It's almost impossible for you to know yourself and to be living a good life if you refuse your commitments to these things and those persons (such relationships are much more than instrumental). If my commitment in such a relationship comes undone, that commitment didn't just erode; it was a direct violation. I've acted against my committed story of the good. I've hurt someone I love, violating their humanity as much as my own person, because I've denied the commitments that my life story and overall narrative of a good life demand I keep. Sin and grace are intelligibly rich visions and necessary operations when life stories are integrated. In this living world to which we are connected, we sin by denying a word (or Word) that is spoken to us.

But in the secular age grace and sin have been eclipsed. They are unnecessary categories when acceleration alienates us from the integration of our stories and the world becomes mute. This turns our failed commitments from violations of the good to just something that happened—just an erosion of our attention. It's much harder to label that erosion sin, necessitating the grace of restoration back into the story, when you never had a story of the good in the first place, and your breach of the commitment just kind of happened.

25. For a rich discussion on Taylor, identity, and narrative, see Andrew O'Shea, *Selfhood and Sacrifice: René Girard and Charles Taylor on the Crisis of Modernity* (New York: Continuum, 2012), 205–20.

26. Andrew O'Shea offers this: "Hence, gaining orientation to the good through telling and retelling our stories becomes paramount to having an identity." *Selfhood and Sacrifice*, 132.

27. William T. Cavanaugh discusses the importance of story in *Theopolitical Imagination: Discovering the Liturgy as a Political Act in an Age of Global Consumerism* (London: Bloomsbury, 2002), 116–18.

Sin and grace are eclipsed because disintegration becomes a necessary norm of dynamic stabilization. How can you be committed to something if you don't have the time to know if it means something to you, to your story, to your overall sense of a good life? You don't have the time or integration to even refuse some commitments. Instead, most often you discover that the commitments you found yourself in have now just dissipated, eroded under your feet. You realize you never directly decided to *not* be in a relationship with that person or stop going to that church anymore. It just happened. Your commitment just eroded, and one day you realized it was over or it had been a very long time since you'd participated. There's no reason to continue or return, because you can't even name why you were in the relationship or part of that congregation in the first place. You have no sense of why it mattered, because you had no time to integrate it into your life story. You just stopped showing up—you stopped living, alienating yourself from the relationships—for no direct reason other than that the relationship or congregation had never been integrated into your story of the good in the first place.

I recently heard the story of a woman who was part of a small church. She'd been committed to the congregation, teaching Sunday school and deeply part of the lay leadership. After her oldest two children left home and her own life story became fragile and fragmented, she decided one Sunday not to go to church. That one week turned into ten. Soon she realized she could never go back. When she finally met with the pastor over a year later, she explained that there was no real reason why she stopped coming, no direct sense for why she lost commitment. It just happened. It eroded. She experienced disintegration, the loss of her life story. Her narrative of the good (now that she was no longer parenting children in her home) allowed her other commitments to just slide away. The pastor lived under the burden that the congregation had done something wrong, that the woman had stopped coming because of a failure of the pastor's own leadership. But it wasn't her pastor's leadership or the congregation. It was the disintegration of an accelerated modernity that eroded the woman's commitments.[28] In talking to many pastors, this is a common story today. My wife and her friends even have a name for it: congregational ghosting. People who seem committed and happy just one day disappear and never return—they were neither angry nor upset, just absent.

This disintegration and erosion of commitment reshapes the inner life of the congregation as it remakes the inner life of persons who make up

---

28. We could say that the pastor needed to more directly front the journey of narrative integration, helping her people wrestle with their stories and competing versions of the good life. All these stories needed a structure that connects them with the life story of Jesus Christ. This kind of work can become the locale of revelation.

our congregations. Rhonda and the pastor in North Dakota got caught in a resource mentality. They felt the burden of the loss of time. They found themselves in a time-famine because of alienation. Their alienation made them wish they could keep their people committed. Rhonda, particularly, felt an erosion of commitment in her small congregation. To overcome this erosion she nearly burned herself out, finding herself on the same jagged path as my college friend in Kansas City. Rhonda imagined that if she could just give her people enough resources they'd stay committed. Yet inside this discussion of alienation we can begin to see that eroding commitment has nothing directly to do with an excess of resources, a surplus of encouragement, or even an understanding of the mission. It has a much deeper source. Commitment is eroded because the overall lives of late-modern people are fundamentally disintegrated. The acceleration of dynamic stabilization alienates them from the world.[29]

Alienation, the Big Challenge for the Church

What puts the local congregation in a crisis, I believe, is not necessarily that congregations are losing pace to dynamic stabilization (which is often how consultants and denominational officials frame it). Rather, the deeper issue is not only that people lack the time and energy for community, practice, and substantive moral traditions but that they're living alienated from the world. This means that any sense that a living God is moving in the world becomes unbelievable (after all, modernity obscures revelation). Our experience of the world is deadened; we are alienated from life itself. It becomes nearly impossible for people to have the ears to hear and the eyes to see the living God who comes into the world in Jesus Christ, speaking to us of life, rest, and mercy.

Leading a congregation is so difficult because the pastor not only has her own identity crisis to face but also needs to answer the question, How do I be a pastor when transcendence and divine action are doubted by me as much as by my people? (This is the central issue discussed in volume 2.) But before she can help her people discern the living, speaking God, she must find a way to connect her people to the world itself, rescuing them from the alienation of an accelerated modernity.[30]

29. Catherine Pickstock, in her influential book *After Writing: On the Liturgical Consummation of Philosophy* (London: Blackwell, 1998), esp. 145–50, provides some interesting thoughts about integration in relation to medieval experience and how the Reformation shifted this. She nicely teases out the implications. Her thoughts are worth exploring.

30. Above I've disconnected these two realities: divine action and an encounter with the living world. I've done this to make my point about the need to overcome alienation produced

Under the domain of Silicon Valley and the high good of innovating for the new, the world has become a dead instrument. The resource-rich church is a concession that the world is lifeless. Inside this lifeless world, the incarnation is replaced by what Taylor calls *excarnation*. Excarnation is the process, bound in modernity, wherein Christianity loses its sense of a living God who takes on flesh and lives deeply in the world in the body of Jesus Christ. And Jesus, who is true God of true God, begotten, not made, a creature who is nevertheless the Creator, calls us further into (not outside of) the world to receive and give ministry. In this giving and receiving we find the event of the very speaking of God. The Word comes to us not outside the world but deeply incarnate within it.[31] Excarnation is the opposite.[32] It is an alienated form of Christian faith that is disembodied (disintegrated) and de-ritualized (erosion of commitment), and therefore made into a flat belief system.

Inside the alienation of a deadened world, the congregation concedes that all it can provide is enough resources for people to stick around and maybe commit to a belief system that is ultimately absent any sense of encounter with the living God, absent any sense of a story that calls us to seek for life where there is death.

To avoid the excarnation intrinsic to alienation, religion must be freed from being another element in the acceleration of a person's or family's dynamic stabilization and instead be returned to an orientation to encounter a living world and the living God in the world. The congregation must forget about giving people resources. It must instead help them encounter the world, to return to life, to together seek for the good of being alive. The remaining four chapters of this book will explore this in detail. As we move into this constructive phase, we have to recognize that the congregation can so easily slide into *la fatigue d'être eglise* because an accelerated modernity has made the world flat and lifeless. The challenge is steep because modernity has not only disenchanted the world but also suffocated it.

––––––––––

I wasn't sure how this would go over. I seemed to be somehow holding my breath while speaking, not really fully grasping the implications of what I

––––––––––

by modernity. But I concede that to separate them is not how they function. Turning our people to a living God immediately draws them into living.

31. For a nice but overlooked discussion of this, see Ray S. Anderson, *Historical Transcendence and the Reality of God* (Grand Rapids: Eerdmans, 1975), 227–37.

32. Carolyn Chau, in *Solidarity with the World: Charles Taylor and Hans Urs von Balthasar on Faith, Modernity, and Catholic Mission* (Eugene, OR: Cascade, 2016), 69–73, provides some thoughts on excarnation that are worth exploring further.

was talking about. I hadn't had the occasion, like I've taken above, to craft my thoughts about disintegration and the erosion of commitment. I had only read some of Rosa's ideas and decided now to take the occasion to relate them to congregational life with a dozen pastors at a conference.

To my relief, it seemed to land. Most in the room nodded that this named their experience. But then a hand rose in the middle of the room. My heart quickened like that of a man finding himself standing on a windy ledge. I wasn't sure I'd be able to make the necessary connections.

The hand was attached to a woman in her early sixties. I'd met her a few other times. We'd talked casually, but I didn't know much about her other than her name. So gulping some air, I said, "Meredith?"

She launched in: "I'd say that I really felt this in my first few years at my congregation. I actually thought it was just me. I went into that call with a lot of doubt. I was one of those second career people in seminary, finally ordained three days before my fifty-eighth birthday. And I was soon floundering in my new call. There was just no energy in the congregation. I started to think, 'Oh, boy, I'm too old for this.' This church just wanted me to do everything and I couldn't keep up. And the more I tried, the less energy it seemed to create. I understood why they were so depleted. They'd been through two interims after a longtime pastor abruptly left after an indiscretion with the choir director."

I wasn't sure where she was headed. But she pushed on.

"So I was thinking I needed to quit. Or at least retire early. I was pretty sure I had misheard God's call. But then one Sunday something happened. Once a month before communion we invite people to come forward and speak their prayers. And this man, Henry, who's my age, surprised me by coming forward. He was more the silent type. He started to cry and said, 'My first grandchild was born two weeks ago. But right away they knew something was terribly wrong. Tomorrow she has surgery to repair a congenital birth defect. Something's wrong with her heart.'"

The whole room of pastors was now drawn in. I was no longer worried about where this story was going because it had already taken me somewhere deep. The world felt dangerous and tragic, but alive. Time itself shifted inside her narrative, as we not so much slowed ourselves in her story but found time full within it. We all felt, I imagine, drawn squarely into the present event of her narration, living this past moment now.

Meredith continued, "After he said this, everything changed."

14

alienation's other

resonance

"Everything changed for me, and more importantly, it changed for the congregation," Meredith continued. She had just stood up in a room of pastors and shared with us about Henry, a parishioner requesting prayer for his granddaughter who has a congenital birth defect in her heart. "I felt a warmness come over my body, I had goose bumps everywhere, and I almost laughed while crying as Henry shared this prayer request. Here I had been doubting my place and starting to resent this church, or at least questioning why God had sent me to this desert congregation. With these few words, everything came back to life. It was all clear. I could hear a calling. That's why I almost laughed."

"Like Sarah," I interrupted.

"Yes," she returned with a bright smile. "My first career was as a nurse practitioner. Before I retired I was the lead of an early childhood intervention team. We cared for children in situations like Henry's granddaughter. Of course, when you're caring for children under three who are experiencing disability, you're caring for their parents as well. You're teaching the parents how to care for their own child by caring for them. You're even teaching them how to care for themselves now that they're on this new journey."

Meredith paused. "I felt so alive doing that work. It was such a deep ministry. It's what led me to seminary. When I started in early childhood intervention,

I felt swept up into some mystery I needed to explore. Next thing I knew I was deeply involved in a church, became a lay leader, and entered seminary. With Henry's prayer it felt like things were all coming together in a beautiful and shocking way."

All of us in the room were now hanging on every word, not sure if five minutes or fifty minutes had passed. Meredith then said, "I knew the hardest part would be the first ten days at home, the period when things were supposed to return to normal but never would. The child still needs constant care, but the parents often have little help. It's on them to recognize problems and take steps to care for this little one. You leave with such self-doubt and worry. Added to all this, you're exhausted from the emotional toll of weeks of surgeries, hospital recovery, and reams of paperwork.

"So I gathered a team from our little church and we showed up. Henry's daughter and son-in-law weren't members of our church. As a matter of fact, we didn't have any families with children in our little congregation, a classic case study for mainline decline. We had tried everything to get families with children back in our church. After Henry's confession we decided to stop trying to get them to come to us. We would go to them and minister to these parents by caring for their little daughter. After all, if this little girl's grandpa was part of our church, asking for us to pray for her, then this little girl and her parents were in our community. When we prayed for a child, she or he became part of our church. We had dozens of children in our congregation: grandkids, nieces, neighbors! It was our responsibility to show up.

"So began our journey. From showing up for Henry's granddaughter, we as a church were called to care for other families and children facing similar journeys. Word spreads quickly across families with children with disabilities. Now we are journeying with anywhere from eight to a dozen children (and their parents). I guess my point is, I've discovered that it's really hard to be disintegrated as a congregation and experience the erosion of commitment when you're caring for children."

Alienation's Other

Over the last dozen chapters I've been framing the challenge facing congregations in modernity. We've seen from multiple angles that modernity is speed. It speeds up time. The church has always had something to say about time, often providing the practices, community, and moral traditions to seek (and experience) eternity in time. But time is conceived of very differently inside the accelerated (and continually accelerating) pushes of modernity. We live in a secular age because time no longer has direct correlation with the sacred. Time is free of transcendence and mystery. The present is made short, allowing us to live multiple lifetimes, making identity innovations essential. Our modern institutions are even stabilized by the speeding up of time for the sake of growth. It's through growth, which fetishizes the new, that institutions are stabilized and the good life always projected into the future.

This creates multiple challenges for the church, but none more acute than Hartmut Rosa's point that an accelerated modernity ultimately creates alienation—a fundamental (and haunting) alienation from the world itself. Modernity speeds us up to such a rate that it disconnects us from the world. Rosa says it this way: "Alienation thus is a relationship which is marked by the absence of a true, vibrant exchange and connection: between a silent and grey world and a 'dry' subject there is no life; both appear to be either 'frozen' or genuinely chaotic and mutually aversive. Hence, in the state of alienation, self and world appear to be related in an utterly indifferent or even hostile way."[1]

This entire three-volume series of books has argued that the challenge we face—whether in faith formation, pastoral identity, or the congregation—is the loss of divine action. Divine action is made opaque for many reasons, which Charles Taylor has helped us see.[2] But all these reasons rest squarely on Rosa's conception of alienation. If modernity creates the conditions for this alienation through continued acceleration, it's no surprise that, when alienated from a living world, we have no eyes to see a living God. Revelation is encountered in the world; it is the unveiling of God's eternal being in time. But if the world is deadened and we feel only a faint connection to it, then believing the immanent frame is closed is the only obvious choice. A grey, hard, inert world is our natural habitat.

We are alienated because of speed, which distorts our conceptions of a good life. And though speed creates the condition for alienation, slowing down is no way to respond to alienation. This late-modern alienation is too endemic, acceleration too tightly wrapped around the organs of the good life, to imagine that we could cut it out without nicking an artery. But then how do we respond? If alienation is the poison, what is the antidote? In other words, does alienation have an opposite? An other?

1. Hartmut Rosa, "The Mindset of Growth and the Resonance Conception of the Good Life," in *The Good Life Beyond Growth*, ed. Hartmut Rosa and Christoph Henning (London: Routledge, 2019), 46.

2. See volumes 1 and 2 for a full discussion of these reasons.

Meeting Bizarro Alienation

The third episode of season eight of *Seinfeld* is called "Bizarro Jerry." It's based on a theme in Superman (remember that Jerry Seinfeld loves Superman). In the comics, Superman meets his opposite other. Bizarro is the reverse-image twin of Superman. Where Superman is a hero, Bizarro is a villain. Even the *S* on Superman's chest and the curl of hair on Superman's forehead are reversed on Bizarro. In "Bizarro Jerry," Elaine's new boyfriend is Jerry's opposite. Whereas Jerry is impatient, sarcastic, and superficial, Kevin is forbearing, sincere, and thoughtful. Even Kevin's friends are the opposite of Jerry's. Bizarro George is calm and reasoned, and Bizarro Kramer, while tall and lanky, is cautious. Similarly, for Rosa, alienation has an other, a Bizarro if you will. Yet it wasn't a direct path for him to find it.

Rosa shows us that modernity means speed. And speed produces alienation. Yet Rosa's early work, which diagnoses the problems with modernity, didn't really offer a constructive vision beyond modernity's alienating problem. We were left with only the poison and not the antidote. Rosa tries mixing a medicine with a base ingredient of slowdown.[3] But he soon abandons this recipe. Looking further, Rosa discovers that the antidote to alienation isn't based in slowdown at all—that's not the good we long for. Slowdown might help us cope with the speed induced by modernity. But it can't fight the infection of alienation. To fight this infection, we need a medicine not based in slowdown but in what Rosa calls *resonance*. He makes this convincing case in his book *Resonanz: Eine Soziologie der Weltbeziehung* (published in English as *Resonance: A Sociology of Our Relationship to the World*).

In this massive work, Rosa explains that our constant pursuit of the good life cannot be answered by slowing down. Slow church won't be enough (especially not enough to lead people back into imaginations for encounters with divine action/revelation). Simple slowdown doesn't quite get at what we most long for and need.

What we seek, Rosa believes, is to be drawn into encounters of resonance.[4] Each of us has had at least an amuse-bouche of resonance.[5] We all have some

---

3. See, for instance, the five ways to slow down in *Social Acceleration: A New Theory of Modernity* (New York: Columbia University Press, 2015), 85–89, 301–5. Even here he's uneasy with slowdown being a response to acceleration, but he has not developed resonance quite yet.

4. Certain slowdown practices like meditation, silence, etc. can lead us into experiences of resonance, but we're seeing here that resonance is the end (though I'll need to define it more theologically soon). Silence and other movements to slow down are for the sake of resonance, never for themselves.

5. "Resonance" is the name for the expansive experience of attachment. We've lost something, feeling alienated in all directions, but what makes alienation so painful and depressing

direct experience with resonance. Resonance, while open to mystery, is never abstract but rather always concrete. Reading that poem, watching that movie, looking over that mountain vista, laughing and playing with that four-year-old. Such experiences are full. You feel a resonance between yourself and the world, a felt relationship that reverberates at the frequency of the good. You confess that such experiences really spoke to you, touched you. You weren't sure what you'd find when you started reading that poem, watching that movie, or making faces with that child, but soon you found yourself caught up in something, freely bound to someone, or opened to some way of seeing that made you certain you were inside a gift called life. You encountered a deep sense that life was calling out to you, seeking to include you. This is an event of resonance. In these moments of resonance you experience your own life teeming with meaning. This meaning seems to be coming to you.[6] It's an experience that seems to be full of time. Meaning is not just produced from within you amid the hurried pace to make something of your self. The world is animated. You sense that you're connected to something bigger than a container of resources. You're alive for something more than quickly seeking the new.[7]

Resonance is the only antidote to alienation.[8] Alienation is overcome when we find ourselves taken up and bound deeply in a *relationship* with the world.

---

is that we feel this lost reverberation of attachment, longing for what connects us back to our childhood moments of being cared for. Children, as we'll see, are so deeply treasured because of their ability to live in and through resonance, and to draw others into resonance. Sarah Hrdy says something similar: "Right from the first days of life, every healthy human being is avidly monitoring those nearby, learning to recognize, interpret, and even imitate their expressions. An innate capacity for empathizing with others becomes apparent within the first six months." Hrdy, *Mothers and Others: The Evolutionary Origins of Mutual Understanding* (Cambridge, MA: Belknap, 2009), 7.

6. Eberhard Jüngel claims that God's being is in becoming, in coming to us. He is pushing forward Karl Barth's actualistic ontology of revelation, claiming that the only God we can know is the God who acts for us. Therefore, our experience of God's being is always in becoming, always in coming to us. Like Rosa, Jüngel from a theological perspective is pointing to a reaching out that meets us in the world, primarily in the face of the risen Jesus Christ, who comes speaking. See Jüngel's *God's Being Is in Becoming: The Trinitarian Being of God in the Theology of Karl Barth* (Grand Rapids: Eerdmans, 2001).

7. Taylor offers his third way to fullness in *A Secular Age* (Cambridge, MA: Belknap, 2007), 10–12. This third way contains something from outside you calling out to you. This, to me, has a deep connection with Rosa's resonance. Taylor's third way of fullness seems to be a (perhaps incomplete) map to Rosa's resonance.

8. Christoph Schwöbel points to Rosa's work. I'm picking up and pushing forward, further into the context of ministry, the theological significance that Schwöbel sees in Rosa. "The German sociologist Hartmut Rosa has demonstrated the fruitfulness of such an approach for analyzing the human relationship to the world. It seems useful to recover the theological roots of the metaphor of resonance, which is particularly apt for exploring communicative relationships in

When bound deeply in the welcoming mystery of relationship, we feel full. We feel like life is good. We sense that we are relating deeply to the world, and the world to us. Resonance reverses alienation's toxin. When we sense that there is something in the world reaching out for us, pleased to join us, desiring to share in us as we share in it, speaking to us,[9] we encounter resonance. And we claim to find ourselves in something good.[10] Rosa explains that resonance "is a mode of relating to the world in which the subject feels touched, moved or addressed by the people, places, objects, etc. he or she encounters."[11] Alienation's other is resonance.

We feel most directly like we're living a good life, confessing a sense of fullness, when we find ourselves in these kinds of experiences of encounter. We feel not like we're speeding on the surface of the world but connected to the world and those in it. In these moments, time is felt not as accelerating but as full. Though never outside time, in our relationships and connections of resonance we sense something eternal in time. Time is no longer speeding past us, the currents of modernity forcing us out of the present. In resonance we rest in the good of the present. We rest in the good of just being alive, of having this full moment of feeling connected (to our own bodies, to a friend, to a God who sees and sends).

An Example: Resonance and *Being* Delighted

In Sofia Coppola's masterpiece film, *Lost in Translation*, she tells the story of two lost souls, two displaced vagabonds marooned by the acceleration

---

both horizontal and vertical dimensions. And this metaphor can be extended, as Rosa does, to help explore the embodied character of human relationships in the social world and the natural world." Schwöbel, "'We Are All God's Vocabulary': The Idea of Creation as a Speech-Act of the Trinitarian God and Its Significance for the Dialogue between Theology and Sciences," in *Knowing Creation: Perspectives from Theology, Philosophy, and Science*, ed. Andrew Torrance and Thomas McCall (Grand Rapids: Zondervan, 2018), 68.

9. This sense of sharing in and sharing with is to point to the theological commitments I've made in regard to *hypostatic* encounter in volume 1, *Faith Formation in a Secular Age: Responding to the Church's Obsession with Youthfulness* (Grand Rapids: Baker Academic, 2017), chaps. 8 and 9. See also *The Pastor in a Secular Age: Ministry to People Who No Longer Need a God* (Grand Rapids: Baker Academic, 2019). Resonance connects to the larger relational, incarnational, and personalist theology of ministry I've been developing over the last decade.

10. I'll have more to say about this soon, but the reader may notice that I'm persuaded by romantic philosophical leanings here. I cannot not be. Both my interlocutors—Taylor and Rosa—move in this direction. I'm also deeply influenced by Isaiah Berlin's *The Roots of Romanticism* (Princeton: Princeton University Press, 1999). Following Berlin, I think that romanticism is a legitimate and helpful (though not complete) response to modernity's rationalized pursuits of progress and reason (of speed).

11. Rosa, "Mindset of Growth," 47.

of time, in a five-star Tokyo hotel. Bob Harris (played by Bill Murray) is a washed-up, middle-aged movie star. He's in Tokyo to collect a paycheck. He's there to dispassionately shoot a commercial for Suntory whisky. He's lost in time because of jet lag. His days and nights are mixed up. But his real issue is the heavy alienation he carries. He is disconnected from his wife, from his purpose, from his work. The jet lag is a poignant reminder that he is alienated from the world itself. Time has passed him by, and the more he races to catch up, the more everything falls apart. Stumbling around the hotel, by happenstance he meets another lost and alienated soul: a young woman, half his age, named Charlotte (played by Scarlett Johansson). She too is fighting jet lag, displacement from time. And like Bob, she carries a deep sense of alienation. Newly married, trouble has already arrived. The connection her marriage promised is already lost as her husband races to make a career for himself as a celebrity photographer. His work is the reason she's in Tokyo. But even though she came along for the trip, she's left behind. She's alienated from the connections she longs for.

The film becomes an homage to alienated souls who long not for slowdown (both have an oppressive amount of time on their hands) but for connection. Through their friendship, Bob and Charlotte find connection that leads out of alienation. They begin to live again, to escape fatalism and embrace life, to taste again a resonance with the world. Their friendship and their many conversations become the events of resonance.

In one of the most moving scenes, Charlotte asks Bob what it's like to have children. She doubts she could do it and yet wonders if a child would bring her the connection she longs for with her husband. Bob's response is that, while it's never easy to be a parent, his experience is that to care for children is to be struck with delight. "They learn how to walk, and they learn how to talk. And you want to be with them. And they turn out to be the most delightful people you will ever meet in your life." With his children he experiences a fullness of delight.

Delight is the perfect description for the feeling of the connections that produce resonance. Delight is an encounter, a felt gift of being connected. Delight is never about resources and relevance. It can never be found outside the present. Delight always exists in the now, in the warmth of the gathered experiences of time. It is the result of being connected, being in relationship, experiencing a fullness that is the very Bizarro of busyness (and the alienation this kind of fullness produces). The fullness of busyness is frantic and stretching. The fullness of resonance is a delight in being.

Delight, then, is peace. It is enough, never a race to acquire more. Delight is an overflowing that never needs more because it never needs anything new.

It wishes just to stay a little longer in the now. Just to soak in being alive. Yet delight, and the now it accentuates, is not utopian. It's always overlaid with the tragic. As finite creatures, we cannot live forever in this now moment. Being full of delight is always bound to a certain event—this moment on this Monday with this little girl sharing ice cream and stories of pandas—and therefore promises to end. But this fleetingness creates all the more reason for resonance, to breathe in the delight of this moment in this full now. It's poignant to rest in the now of the chocolate ice cream running down her chin and the pained but beautiful vision that, though this moment will pass and she will never again be a chattering four-year-old, you're deeply *in* this moment. The event is filled with resonance because you're invited to embrace it all and be alive, knowing (more existentially than rationally) that it will give way. You find gratitude and joy from being with her, but also in how the connection with her brings the whole world around you into life, drawing you headlong into the goodness of being. Eternity itself reverberates at this dirty table at this nondescript Dairy Queen, because the relationship with her has taken you deeply into the world, soaking you in life. The connection has pressed in on your very being so deeply that it brings visions of the eternal.[12]

Two Dimensions of Resonance

It's difficult to analytically describe, piece by piece, resonance. It's impossible to dissect something that's living. It's like trying to scientifically articulate love. Love constantly slips from the grip of empirical science. Once it seems cornered by neuropsychologists, for example, it seems to disappear. The scientist's descriptions always seem to reduce love's inherent profundity.[13] At best, it gets us closest to what's true, to leave love to the rhyme and meter of the poet.[14]

12. This is how place-sharing, as I've developed in my earlier work, is connection not just to the cross but also to the resurrection, ascension, and glorification. Resonance must be seen as the inner dynamic of place-sharing. See volume 1, *Faith Formation in a Secular Age*, chap. 10.

13. I'm thinking here of Barbara L. Fredrickson, *Love: How Our Supreme Emotion Affects Everything We Feel, Think, Do, and Become* (New York: Hudson Street, 2013), in which the more she describes love scientifically, the more abstract and distant the reader feels from love.

14. Again, my argument—as well as Rosa's and Taylor's—is connected to philosophical romanticism. The German romantics asserted strongly that the mainly French empirical science could in no way fully describe the world and human experience in it. They showed that Enlightenment science could never really describe things like love, suffering, loss, and resonance. This is why Isaiah Berlin calls these German thinkers, like Johann Georg Hamann and Johann Gottfried Herder, Counter-Enlightenment thinkers. Taylor borrows this phrase from his teacher, but he often wields it more for figures like Nietzsche—who can't be understood outside this romantic opposition but who has a much more combative edge to his thought than Hamann and Herder, for example. See Isaiah Berlin, *Three Critics of Enlightenment* (Princeton: Princeton University Press, 2013).

This difficulty in analytically describing resonance makes Rosa's *Resonance* a critically acclaimed bestseller. He succeeds where few others have, describing this encounter without reducing it. Rosa explains that resonance has at least two dimensions (with two elements inside each of the dimensions). We encounter resonance only when both of these dimensions are present.

Dimension One and Its Two Related Elements

The first dimension is the phenomenological dimension of resonance. As we've seen above, resonance is a *feeling* of fullness. To say resonance is phenomenological is to say it's bound in experience.[15] And experience is intrinsic to feeling. Resonance is inseparable from some bodily experiential charge. Resonance is never excarnational. Rather, it connects our minds with our bodies, drawing us deeply into the present.

For instance, in delight you feel warm and yet moved. In the beginning of this chapter, we saw that Meredith asserts that she got goose bumps but felt free. You find yourself crying at the final scene of the movie and yet exclaim that it was beautiful. Resonance is inseparable from some *feeling* of connection to something that speaks or calls out to you from outside your self.[16] Resonance, then, is *feeling* alive through encounter with this outside experience that is other. We taste a spirit of deep relational connection at the phenomenological level of resonance. "Thus, the capacity to feel affected by something, and in turn to develop intrinsic *interest* in the part of the world which affects us, is a core element of any positive way of relating to the world."[17]

---

15. In volume 2, *The Pastor in a Secular Age*, chap. 11, I sought to steer things away from religious experience. I stand by that critique here. Experience alone is never enough. However, as I've acknowledged throughout this series, experience has importance. My critique in volume 2 was simply that experience cannot stand alone. Rosa is making a similar point.

16. This sense of feeling shouldn't be reduced to typical functioning. For instance, people on the autism spectrum may have a hard time feeling (more rightly, showing) a resonance with other people. But this isn't because they're feeling nothing much (they're actually feeling too much, they're overstimulated). Yet such persons often feel a deep resonance in other ways, for example, with puzzles. There is a feeling of being connected in these different activities.

17. Rosa, "Mindset of Growth," 47 (emphasis added). I've added the emphasis because I think it's better for this to be "concern" than "interest." Taylor discusses the importance of concern for our sense of the good, and even for our identity formation. Concern leads to strong evaluation. And you need strong evaluation of phenomenological experiences to have a sense of the good (a good life) and even an identity. I discuss Taylor's thought on this more fully in my book *The End of Youth Ministry?* (Grand Rapids: Baker Academic, 2020). I'm also keen on shifting things away from interest. My own commitments to personalism have led me to have some suspicion about interest, particularly about defining people as

Meredith finds herself in what she describes as a mainline desert congregation. She describes it this way because there is no feeling of resonance. Of course, she feels something. She feels exhausted (alienated) because in the congregation's own *la fatigue*, they have lost connection with any form of resonance. They're alienated from a calling that is outside of them, beckoning to them. This is why theological reflection that continually seeks divine action and revelation is so important for congregational life and an overall practical ecclesiology. It's not just an issue of doctrine. Imaginations for divine encounter, asking congregations to interpret a calling or encounter from outside of them (as congregation or as selves), create the life and energy for the congregation itself.

When Meredith began, her congregation expected their new pastor to be a fountain of energy that would bring feeling back to the church. But this was impossible, because they assumed the energy would come from within her (or from within her drawing it out from within them). This only leads to burnout. The weariness comes as quickly as Meredith's internally constituted energy is depleted. The drive for innovation will deplete the congregation's battery, cutting them off from feeling.

My argument throughout has been that Silicon-Valley-style innovation is no solution to the problems congregations face. What we need is not innovation (because of all the mis-goods it delivers) but resonance. Innovation is just an energy drink that can get us up and running. Its allure is that it really can get us moving into action. But it's formulated with too many chemicals and preservatives—with too many goods of accelerated modernity and Silicon Valley—which eventually promise a crash. Seminaries, consultants, and denominational leaders would be better off focusing on resonance.[18]

Let me explain why by getting us back to Meredith. Her congregation's absence of feeling is not remedied by loud music, yelling, and cheering like in the Pentecostal church down the street. Exuberance does not necessarily equal feeling. Rather, what I think Meredith meant by calling her congregation a desert was that it felt absent of both affection and emotion. The phenomenological dimension of resonance has these dual movements of affection and emotion.

---

their interests. I discuss this at length in *The Relational Pastor* (Downers Grove, IL: IVP, 2013), chap. 6. I don't think Rosa means to connect interest to any philosophical or theological anthropology, but I only alert the reader that the idea of interest may have hidden assumptions on what a person is.

18. I say this because resonance, while not a theological category, has many more openings and links to a theological imagination—to revelation and divine action—than innovation as bound to the timekeeper of Silicon Valley can ever promise.

Two Elements of the Phenomenological

Rosa illustrates how these movements work by using arrows. He explains that the phenomenological dimension of resonance has a movement of af←fection (the arrow, in this case, pointing toward us or coming to us). Something from outside of us touches us, calling us to care for it. The phenomenological dimension of resonance starts with an experience of otherness— that is, with an encounter with something outside the self. For Meredith, this begins with a feeling of empathy for Henry.[19] She almost forgets they're in the middle of the service. The anxious pull of acceleration, to get through the practice and onto something else, disappears. Rather, she's taken by the practice into affection for Henry and his experience. She's affected by his confession, encountered by something outside her self and even outside her maintenance of the religious activity.

And she's not alone. The whole gathered congregation feels it. They're drawn into affection for Henry through the event he is living through. The congregation's affect for his lived event becomes the congregation's own event of sharing in Henry. They're awakened by the affection for Henry and his granddaughter's personhood. Affection always calls for connection.[20] When we feel moved by affection we seek the stories and events that give coherence to our affection or, better, take us deeper into affection. Affection is always experienced inside of story, or at the least it longs for story. This is because affection moves out from our selves, out of a dead world. Feeling this affection, we are compelled, as language animals, to story why we've moved from outside ourselves, and our old ways of feeling and living, to have affection for something other than us. Affection is central to our personal and communal identities because it demands story. To encounter an event in which you find yourself moved by affection necessitates that you story why it is this person or experience draws you out of yourself and into this other to love. Meredith can only share her experience of affection for Henry by telling us the story.

Henry's crying is rain to an affection desert. In this case, it wakes the congregation to move out to him.[21] To move out to him to share in him through

19. For more on empathy in theological/ministerial view, see my *The Relational Pastor*, chap. 7.
20. This echoes a point stretching back to Augustine. James K. A. Smith devotedly works from Augustine's thought that "we are what we love." Our affections are inseparable from our spirituality, from the very core of our faith life. To place Augustine in conversation with Rosa, we can't find resonance (divine encounter) without examining (and re-forming) our affections. See Smith's *Desiring the Kingdom: Worship, Worldview, and Cultural Formation* (Grand Rapids: Baker Academic, 2009); and *You Are What You Love* (Grand Rapids: Brazos, 2016).
21. It is also possible that his crying leads not to affection and a moving toward but a retreat into self and resentment that he made them feel something, calling them out to him. Depressed congregations, or people for that matter, at times attack those who call to them, resenting that

affection means they'll need to connect their stories with his, even find a new story to live out of together. This linking of stories, initiated by affection, is a much more potent reviving force than innovation, because it longs for a connection with a fullness that is outside of us (as opposed to leveraging the resources we have to grow more resources). Affection is the antidote to their congregational alienation and depression. Henry's confession reaches out to the whole congregation. His granddaughter's suffering serves as an outside experience that encounters Meredith and the congregation, shaking them free from the dead world.[22]

As Henry continues to narrate this experience, giving testimony through prayer, Meredith feels warm and yet gets goose bumps because an uncanny connection is made, taking her into the second movement: emotion.[23] Meredith gets goose bumps because the phenomenological dimension of resonance is also dependent on e→motion (the arrow, in this case, pointing away from us or coming out of us). Feeling affected by an encounter, feeling affection for something other than us, "we answer by giving a response and thus establishing a connection."[24] This e→motion is what we mean when in popular parlance we say, "I'm feelin' you." This popular slang saying has the sense of "I understand you," but it points to something deeper. It intends to communicate that your experience has called out to me, awakening me, moving me into affection for you and your experience. To feel, not just to understand, is a leap forward into friendship, into participation. It's a witness that you've been taken into an event of affection that is impacting you by drawing you out of your self. It's triggering emotions in you.[25] You cry hard when you watch the movie.

---

they were made to move outside themselves. There's no guarantee that his emotion will lead to affection. In some contexts (like upper Midwestern Scandinavian ones), emotion can be passive-aggressively punished. This doesn't upend my point but just reinforces how important it is, and nevertheless how sin and brokenness can attack this necessity.

22. There is a lot here that could be mined. For instance, I think Luther's assertion in the Heidelberg Disputation that God meets us primarily in suffering has a lot packed within it. For instance, this is an epistemological or hermeneutical statement about how Luther reads Paul but also an epistemological or hermeneutical statement about how he understands revelation. If one were careful, a case could also be made that the *theologia crucis* is also a mode in which feeling and experience are ordered for Luther. Suffering awakens us to otherness, and therefore the *theologia crucis* may indeed have a practical phenomenological element to it. I've tried to work from this commitment in my works like *The Promise of Despair* (Nashville: Abingdon, 2010).

23. We discussed uncanny connections and divine action in volume 2, *The Pastor in a Secular Age*, chap. 12.

24. Rosa, "Mindset of Growth," 47.

25. Of course, this is not to say that everything I feel is real or true. Emotions can lie. But nevertheless I cannot have affection without emotion. And these are to be ordered and open to critique. For an example of overcommitting to emotions without any reflection on the depth of an affection that calls you out of yourself, and how a fear of a extrinsic affection leads

You're flooded with emotion. Though your eyes are swollen from sadness, you relay to your friend that you loved it. It connected you to something that resonated with your very being. The film was great because both af←fection and e→motion were present.

Both of these movements of af←fection and e→motion have to work together to draw us into the good of (into the good life bound in) resonance. We have to remember, as Rosa says, "Resonance is not an emotional state, but a mode of relationship."[26]

For example, anyone who's worked with middle-school-aged young people knows it takes very little to trigger emotion. Enough blood and torture wrapped in rejection, when discussing Jesus's crucifixion, will cause a room of middle schoolers to sob sorrowfully. But fifteen minutes later, it seems all forgotten. Part of this is just developmental. But I believe a broader explanation is that the crucifixion-talk triggered emotion but not affection. It drew the young people into themselves, into their own sadness, but it never moved them out to feel a connection to something beyond themselves, to love and then begin to narrate their own life story inside the story of Jesus's death and resurrection. Therefore, they had an occurrence of emotion but not an encounter with resonance, which reaches deep enough to reorder their very identities.[27]

Rosa's point, then, is that we encounter something in the af←fection movement that has its origin from outside of us. We feel something beyond or other than us. Resonance is never a self-enclosed reality. Taking us outside ourselves, it nevertheless affects the self. We feel goose bumps or a warm delight. Things

---

to many problems, see Greg Lukianoff and Jonathan Haidt, *The Coddling of the American Mind: How Good Intentions and Bad Ideas Are Setting Up a Generation for Failure* (New York: Penguin, 2018).

26. Rosa, *Resonance: A Sociology of Our Relationship to the World* (Medford, MA: Polity, 2019), chap. 5, sec. 3.

27. Rosa believes that this movement of affection and emotion is essentially dialogical. It is the nature and movement of discourse. Resonance is word and response. This connects to two major themes of my own work. First, it connects to Taylor's discussion on identity and our base as language animals. Taylor's discussions of identity are bound in dialogue. We have identity only through dialogue. For much more on this, see my book *The End of Youth Ministry?* Second, this connects to the neo-Barthian elements that are fundamental to my work. Ray S. Anderson, inspired by Barth, taught me long ago that God is a minister who moves in the world (revelation) as word and response. See Anderson, *Theological Foundations for Ministry* (Edinburgh: T&T Clark, 1979), 6–21. Grace is word and response. The inner life of the Trinity is constituted as a dialogue of word and response between the Father and Son in the Spirit. Therefore, whether or not I can adequately articulate this, I see resonance as a sociological/philosophical articulation of the phenomenological reality of grace and divine action itself. This line of thought needs more development. However, the space is limited, so it will have to be explored more deeply in another project.

feel lighter and yet fuller. Affection is inseparable from the emotions of connection. The emotions confirm our connection to something outside of us.

A good example of the two movements of affection[28] and emotion that make
up this phenomenological dimension of resonance is the classic Good Friday
hymn and African-American spiritual that predates the Civil War, "Were You
There?" The six verses of the hymn ask, "Were you there when they crucified
my Lord? When they nailed him to a tree? When they pieced him in the side?
When the sun refused to shine? When they laid him in the tomb? When he
rose up from the dead?" This is the narrative shape of the affectual. "Were
you there?" is not an empirical, historical question like, "Did you happen to
get in your time machine and go there?" Rather, it's the question of affection:
Do you have affection for this story? Has this story affected you? Pulled you
out from your self, out from a closed world, into something much bigger? Are
you resonating with it? You know you are if you feel it.

The emotional movement of the phenomenological dimension of resonance comes when the narrator of the hymn witnesses that indeed they have
been affected by this story: "Oh, sometimes it causes me to tremble, tremble,
tremble." Being pulled into this narrative of Jesus's death and resurrection
affects the narrator, bringing affection for the cross. The singer is resonating
with the narrative of deep meaning not only because they have affection for
it but also because it delivers emotions that confirm they are alive. They are
connected to a story that resonates with their being enough for them to feel
connected. (They're there!) They know their being is connected to something
other—their affections drawing them into a communion of story and persons—
because they tremble. The emotion is a response to a word that calls them out
to connect to something that is bigger than they are but fully includes them.[29]

28. There have been many mystics who have thought deeply about the affection of the cross,
or the spirit, etc. Affection has had a long history of spiritual resonance. Rosa is careful not
to mention too much of this, but it seems clear to me that resonance has a deep spiritual level
that correlates with many thoughts of the mystics.

29. We need to be careful here to hold both affection and emotion together. Emotion cut
free from affection can lie. It often does. Both Jonathan Haidt (*The Righteous Mind: Why
Good People Are Divided by Politics and Religion* [New York: Vintage, 2012]) and Justin Barrett (*Cognitive Science, Religion, and Theology: From Human Minds to Divine Minds* [West
Conshohocken, PA: Templeton Press, 2011]) have argued convincingly that emotions drive us
but that these emotions are often misdirected. Culturally we seem to be holding up emotion
(what we feel) over everything else, and it's leading to confusion (see Lukianoff and Haidt, *Coddling of the American Mind*). Emotion is important. We cannot have human lives of resonance
without it. But resonance is not just a feeling; it's a movement toward otherness in affection.
Affection conditions emotion. Instead of asking, How do you feel? (which assumes the answer
to be fundamental to a lived anthropology), we should be asking, What do you love? Affection
is more primary because it demands story. Emotion alone requires no story because it doesn't
demand an eventful encounter with otherness.

Meredith's congregation is transformed because Henry's story called them out in affection. And resonating with Henry's person, they feel something real. They begin to feel alive. The insecurity of being a little "dying" congregation gives way to being a little gathering of strange people who have together tasted a mystery, even felt eternity spilling into time. And this is enough. This is a delight that casts out all *la fatigue d'être eglise*.

The stage is now set for the second dimension of resonance.

Dimension Two and Its Two Related Elements

While resonance is fundamentally phenomenological, it cannot be only phenomenological. "Resonance is not just built on the experience of being touched or affected."[30] We need something more than just affection and emotion. It's not enough that the world is no longer mute. It's not enough that we feel a sense of belonging. Affection and emotion take us a long way, no doubt, but not far enough to defeat the toxin of alienation. They don't go far enough to free the good life from always being a future projection and to free resonance from being just a natural hit of a drug.

We need the second dimension of resonance: what Rosa calls *efficacy*.[31] In the phenomenological level of resonance we receive something: Henry's confession is a gift to the congregation. They feel awakened and connected through the encounter with affection and emotion. But another step is needed to take the congregation into resonance. From within the phenomenological they must feel *called out to act*. They must follow. This is what Rosa means by efficacy. Let me explain it further by framing this second dimension next to Dietrich Bonhoeffer's classic *The Cost of Discipleship*.

The German title for this classic is *Nachfolge*, or "follow." The book argues that the disciple is the one who follows. Bonhoeffer frames this, in part, through a reading of the rich young ruler text (Matt. 19:16–30; Mark 10:17–31; Luke 18:18–30). The rich young ruler came to Jesus with a question: "What must I do to inherit eternal life?" We are thrust into the territory of time in this text. In the midst of the dialogue, we're told that Jesus was struck with both affection and emotion for the young man. We can then assume that the rich young ruler felt the same. He was swept up into the phenomenological dimension, nearing an encounter of resonance. But before it arrived it was

30. Rosa, "Mindset of Growth," 47.

31. Rosa actually calls it self-efficacy, but I'm not sure the "self" part is helpful. Rosa seems to be echoing a psychological theory in doing so, but I feel like it will trip up my readers, giving ground back to self-focused innovation of acceleration. I've dropped it, but I've kept all the same sense that Rosa intends.

short-circuited. After the rich young ruler responded that he had kept the law since his youth, Jesus said, "You lack one thing: sell what you own; . . . then come, *follow me*." Jesus invited the rich young ruler to realize the fullness of resonance by adding efficacy to the phenomenological, to find his very person participating in the life of Jesus.[32] Discipleship is not just the feeling of affection and emotion but also a call to follow out into the world and act.[33] It is both to receive at the phenomenological level and to respond and participate. Resonance is both experience and action. We need to encounter eternity in time. Yet, though the rich young ruler could experience, he could not act and follow Jesus out into the world. Therefore, he departed sad.

To place Bonhoeffer in conversation with Rosa, the text teaches us that the resonance of discipleship not only is phenomenological but also has a deep sense of efficacy. To experience resonance, and therefore encounter a living world or, better, a living God in the world, we not only need to feel alive but also need to be called out to act in the world. This highlights the divide we see in American religion. To risk overstatement, evangelicals and charismatics have historically been better at the phenomenological level of resonance, stating affections and embracing emotion. In contrast, mainline liberals have spoken boldly of efficacy—of doing justice—but often absent affection and emotion. The missional church movement sought a way between by focusing on the efficacy of God's own mission—this is deeply helpful. Unfortunately, of late it has often been overtaken by missional entrepreneurship and missional innovation, which undercuts resonance and unknowingly perpetuates alienation.

32. A life that is given freely, but only in and through death. The *theologia crucis* is inescapable here. The young man must enter death, selling everything he has, not to render him actionless but to transform him and take him into the action of God through the cross of Christ. My working with Rosa and his more philosophical/social critical thought is not absent my long commitments to the *theologia crucis*. Rosa is very clear that resonance is not utopian, or just a feeling caught in an expressive individualistic net.

33. There is a much deeper theological conversation that connects to other parts of my work that I can only hint at here. This dimension of efficacy echoes Bonhoeffer's bold assertions about action in *Discipleship* (Minneapolis: Fortress, 2001). One can't miss the strong push for action. But Bonhoeffer believes Jesus is calling a person to come and die. See Bonhoeffer, *The Cost of Discipleship* (New York: Touchstone, 1959), 89. Therefore, there is a deep paradoxical sense of action and passivity in this conception. The cross and the form of discipleship it produces through justification renders us passive (on this point, see Tuomo Mannermaa's "Why Is Luther So Fascinating? Modern Finnish Luther Research," in *Union with Christ: The New Finnish Interpretation of Luther*, ed. Carl Braaten and Robert Jenson [Grand Rapids: Eerdmans, 1998], esp. 10–12), but again, paradoxically, this passivity gives us direct action, a movement into efficacy. This efficacy is not our own; it is to follow the person of Jesus through our own impossibility to participate with him in ministry. Ministry is an action—an efficacy—that is built within impossibility (a sense of passivity) that nevertheless moves us out into action.

A disciple is one who not only feels near the living God but acts in participation with the life and ministry of this living God. Rosa explains, "In the social dimension, . . . efficacy is experienced when we realise that we are capable of actually reaching out to and affecting others, that they truly listen and connect to us and answer in turn."[34]

It's important to be clear: This acting is not just the actor's will being imposed on. That is not resonance; that is a way of being an instrument of further alienation. Rather, efficacy that produces the other half of resonance synchronizes our own actions with the world itself. It's almost as if the world, or the other we meet in the world, has been waiting all along for us to act. It's almost as if the world, or the other we meet in the world, is already longing for us to participate with an event. There is flow to it all, which means time feels gathered and full.

Rosa, in seven hundred German pages, constructs a full three-dimensional conception of resonance. It's an ambitious project. This leads him into discussing expressions of resonance that we don't need to concern ourselves with here, such as eating. Yet it might be helpful to show how efficacy is different from imposing a heavy will by thinking about two expressions: music and sport.

Rosa explains that we encounter this efficacy dimension of resonance in the social realm, which is mainly what we're concerned with in regard to congregations. But he also explains that efficacy stretches out beyond just the social realm. We might experience this when we feel like a piece of music is almost playing us as much as we are playing it[35]—or, when playing soccer or hockey, we feel the game slow down and become more full. In these times we find our own actions flowing freely within the game itself. Afterward we might describe this as being "in the zone." The zone is a space where time is full and gathered and our actions are in harmony with something greater and other than us. To be in the zone is to be wrapped tightly in the good. We have affections and emotions; we feel a love for the game and a calm, connected excitement. But these phenomenological experiences are fed by and feed on efficacy. We encounter a deep sense of resonance when we discover that our actions are the very response the world (or the living God) has been calling for. Indeed, we can see how resonance (as both phenomenological and efficacy) punctures the immanent frame.

34. Rosa, "Mindset of Growth," 47.
35. Rosa explains that resonance has three axes—the social, material, and existential. Meredith's experience with Henry is a social experience of resonance. Being in the zone playing basketball, or learning about painting, is on the material axes of resonance. The existential, Rosa explains, can be seen when German youth visit concentration camps. This sense of suffering, death, and history takes them into the world. Resonance need not always be a light or happy experience. Resonance might be heavy (even a judgment). Henry's confession is heavy; for him, it is in the existential axis of resonance—but the point is that resonance changes things. Even encounters at a concentration camp, though horrific, can awaken us from alienation, changing our lives and calling us into action.

When Henry makes his confession in prayer, Meredith's sleepy congregation is awakened. They're drawn into affection and emotion for Henry. But they've not yet entered resonance. In fact, the phenomenological experience hums at such an enlivened frequency, giving Meredith goose bumps, because she immediately knows what she needs to do—she experiences a direct call, a deeply animating purpose that infuses life into her and the congregation. She's essentially given a vision, a way of connecting her action with the world, drawing her deeply into the efficacy of resonance. She even experiences time gathered, her earlier life as a nurse reemerging, having prepared her and this congregation for this very moment. Past and future arrive together in the now of ministering to Henry and his granddaughter. Meredith has a sense that this call for action—this efficacy—gives coherence to the whole of her adult life. It's the very reason she was called to this church at this time, she now knows. Through the phenomenological level of resonance, she's taken into the efficacy level, hearing directly Jesus's call to follow, to move out into the world. Not just to feel it but to act within it. Everything is now alive because the little congregation not only feels but also has been given a mission or a ministry that draws directly from the ministerial being of God. Issues of budget, sustainability, and stabilization are still brute facts, but they no longer possess the power to alienate this little congregation. God has called out to them, sending them into the world. Meredith's little congregation is revived because it's called into the world for the sake of ministry.

Ministry, I believe, is the most potent form of resonance because it draws us into affection with the otherness of God's self in and through a concrete encounter with our neighbor. This encounter calls us deeper into life as we participate affectionately and emotionally with those who are up against a death experience. It is a concrete experience (phenomenological) of living out (efficacy) the narrative of cross and resurrection in our own bodies. Giving and receiving ministry through our own person, as a bond of care and a proclamation of hope that turns death into life, shatters alienation by the weight of a resonance of new (out of death)[36] life and community.

Two Elements of Efficacy

As with the phenomenological dimension of resonance (whose two elements are affection and emotion), efficacy also has two elements connected to it: transformation and elusiveness. Resonance is fundamentally inseparable

---

36. The new that Paul and the New Testament seek is not the new of innovation and Silicon Valley, which looks to technically solve the problem of death. The new of the New Testament is a newness born out of death, a much different sense of the new.

from transformation.[37] The rich young ruler cannot follow because he cannot bear the transformation his action will cause. Often the deadness we face in congregational life is due to a loss of the centrality of transformation. (To lose transformation is to lose a concrete vision for the efficacy of divine action.) Congregations experience alienation because transformation has become unbelievable. Congregations are then separated from the source of their life.

Innovation is a process of innovating. To be innovating is to be making changes to something established, most often through new methods, ideas, or products (or "programs," in relation to congregational life). Innovating is a way of changing, improving, or adapting what is. But transformation is the impossible giving way to new possibility. Transformation is an event of revelation that is wrapped tightly around the unveiling of personhood, moving from death to new life. It's the arrival of a calling from outside of us. It's an epiphany of an all-new plotline for the story of our lives, not just a revamping. We are transformed when we leave one story for a whole new story with new directions and calls for action.

This is exactly what Meredith experiences. The little congregation is transformed because caring for Henry's granddaughter gives them an all-new story to live out of. Too often congregations look to programs and strategies to change them. But this reverses things. Programs and strategies are best born out of a story of transformation. Congregations should yearn for a story, not just look for innovative programming. A story that connects their actions with purpose and meaning won't necessarily give them resources; instead, it will flood them with the good, drawing them into visions for how their own actions can participate in the mystery of ministering eternity in time. Meredith's little church indeed finds a whole new program, not because they were looking for new innovative strategies but because they were readied to encounter a new story. And finding themselves in this new story gave them a new way of concretely being in the world.

When we concede, explicitly or implicitly, that transformation is impossible (or unwanted) and that innovation is the best we can do, the world becomes mute, God seems to be silent, and our theological visions are rendered excarnate. Though few of us would directly advocate this excarnate

37. It would be an interesting project to connect Rosa with James Loder. Loder's Kierke-gaardian existentialism always made him suspicious of social forms of community life (he called these *socialization*). He always worried about socialization (see *The Transforming Moment* [Colorado Springs: Helmers & Howard, 1989]; and *The Logic of the Spirit: Human Development in Theological Perspective* [San Francisco: Jossey-Bass, 1998]). Yet Rosa seems to find a way beyond these concerns. Loder's work on transformation has been important to my work, and Rosa's assertion that resonance is fundamentally transformational is important to point out here, even if it can't be developed more deeply.

position, we have nevertheless exchanged transformation for stabilization and sustainability. When we adopt the innovation of Silicon Valley, we take with it the immanent-bound visions of a good life that exclude transcendence and perpetuate alienation by always reaching for acceleration. To free us of this, our deepest concern[38] with regard to the life of the congregation shouldn't be how we can dynamically stabilize congregations through innovation (bishops need to exorcise this from their imagination). Rather, we should ask, In what ways can congregations take on visions, practices, and identities of transformation, even in the inherited immanent frame of our cultural context? The congregation needs narratives of transformation more than it needs innovation. Congregations would be better off hearing stories of other congregations' experiences with transformation than going through direct processes of innovation.[39]

Meredith told our group that "everything changed" with Henry's confession and the congregation's response. The desert congregation became a garden congregation, resonant with life. Persons like Meredith and the little congregation as a whole were transformed—"everything changed." They had a new story and thus a new identity.[40] As Rosa says, "Only in such a mode of receptive affection and responsive efficacy are self and world related in an appropriative way: the encounter transforms both sides, the subject and the world experienced."[41] The world is made alive, and God is speaking in it, calling out for us to participate in ministry. The congregation, once too fatigued to be the church, is transformed and given new life as it follows the call into resonating encounters of otherness.

By rehearsing and retelling these tales of resonance through affection, emotion, and action, the congregation is revived. The life of the congregation becomes no longer dependent on its own innovative action, which seeks to speed them up. Instead, it's guided by remembering the gifts and promises of resonance, and narrating the encounter with something other and beyond itself. Meredith's story of ministering to Henry and his granddaughter is a different kind of story (a story of transformation) than the tale of a church that found the perfect innovation to grow its numbers, budget, profile, reach, or even sense of importance.

38. Our strong evaluation, as Taylor would say. See *Human Agency and Language: Philosophical Papers 1* (London: Cambridge University Press, 1999), 16–33.

39. Duke's online publication *Faith and Leadership* curates such stories. This is very important work.

40. Rosa discusses story and identity further in *Alienation and Acceleration*, 97–100. Here he pushes these ideas much deeper than I have space to explore. For even more on identity, see Rosa, *Social Acceleration*, 225–35.

41. Rosa, "Mindset of Growth," 47.

The second element of efficacy is elusiveness. We've already discussed the first element of transformation. But we've exchanged transformation for Silicon Valley's innovation because we're uncomfortable with the second element: elusiveness. Modernity makes the world controllable and disposable for the sake of dynamic stabilization. But resonance is uncontrollable, making it much different from the innovations of dynamic stabilization. Resonance is elusive because it's a true encounter with otherness. The congregation receives life not by hearing its own echo or by recognizing that it has more assets than it thought (this is what innovation seeks) but by encountering a call from the one who is truly other (the Spirit of the living Lord, the sobbing of a suffering grandfather). True otherness is always elusive and beyond our control (it's an event).

Silicon Valley's sense of the good aims for controllability, and it is always disposing of the old for the new in a shortened present. Silicon Valley innovates so it can control contingency and attain the acceleration that we need to produce growth. This desire for control has the side effect of deadening the world and therefore alienating us from it. Inside this logic of innovation, divine action is pushed far from the center of congregational life. This must be so because divine action can only be experienced as elusive, which cannot be tolerated by Silicon Valley. The human being or community never controls the Word of God. God comes speaking, in an interruptive and elusive way, throughout the biblical text (we explored some of these texts in part 2 of volume 2). To seek anything but the elusive nature of a speaking God is to desire an idol.

Meredith could never have manufactured this moment of confession from Henry. As pastor, she could only wait in anticipation for such an event. Though she had no control over when an encounter of resonance would come, she could ready her congregation for the moment. And she unknowingly did. She formed them in practice: they prayed. For months it was dry and dull, a weary little congregation stuck in alienation. Nevertheless, they practiced praying to the wholly other God, who acts as minister. Meredith also preached about this God who arrives speaking and calling, interrupting us with new visions of a good life. Then when they least expected it, God arrived, calling out to them through the tears of Henry.

In 1928, Karl Barth famously said, "You can't speak of God by speaking of humanity in a loud voice."[42] Barth wanted to remind the German liberal theological establishment that God is living and other, and therefore elusive.

42. Karl Barth, *The Word of God and the Word of Man* (New York: Harper & Brothers, 1957), 196.

We cannot be drawn into a resonant encounter with the living God unless, in opposition to the timekeepers of Silicon Valley (and for Barth, the state), we embrace elusiveness. Barth's point is that God's revelation is not a human echo. Rosa says the same thing about resonance: "Resonance is not an *echo*: it does not mean to hear oneself amplified or to simply feel re-assured, but it involves encounter with some real 'other' that remains beyond our control, that speaks in its own voice or key different from ours and therefore remains 'alien' to us." Rosa continues, drawing from Taylor: "Even more than this, this 'other' needs to be experienced as a source of 'strong evaluation' in the sense of Charles Taylor: only when we feel that this other . . . has something important to tell or teach, irrespective of whether we like to hear it or not, can we truly feel 'grasped' and touched. Resonance, therefore, inevitably requires a moment of self-transcendence."[43]

Resonance, then, is the faithful way forward for congregations living in a secular age. The congregation's life isn't in innovation but in being a people of resonance.

———

I thought back through my conversations with Meredith, my college friend in Kansas City, and the pastor in North Dakota; all three yearned for resonance as an answer to their alienation. And in different measure all three found this in and through the ministry of children. Back when Karl Barth made his statement about speaking of God in a loud voice, Dietrich Bonhoeffer was finishing his doctoral dissertation. In it he asserted that the practical form of the church community is to carry children. Now that we are deeper into modernity than Bonhoeffer could have imagined, his underdeveloped point may be a way forward for us. It seemed to be for Meredith.

To carry children is to be moved phenomenologically. It is to encounter affection and emotion as we give and receive care. But no one can carry a child in affection and warm emotion without efficacy. We live out our affection, giving shape to our emotion, by acting for children. To carry a child is to act for her, to receive her own action. My friend in Kansas City encountered this with his own children, and the pastor and I experienced it in that North Dakota church gym.[44] To carry a child is to be transformed by his or

43. Rosa, "Mindset of Growth," 48. To avoid distracting from my point, I omitted Rosa's parenthetical "(which can be a person, but also a piece of music, a mountain, or a historical event, for example)," but I add it here because it's an important parenthetical to understand Rosa's conception of resonance.

44. Alison Gopnik says something similar: "I don't know about the spiritual intuitions that accompany mystical experiences or religious ceremonies. But I do think that the sense

her story.[45] Often we are so transformed by carrying a child that our very descriptive name is changed—we become mom, dad, auntie, uncle, granddad, or Mrs. Madden. We now live with a story of this little one before us, deeply changing our sense of the good. And this child, if we really carry her, remains always elusive to us.[46] She is other, her own person, encountering us with the delight of thoughts, perceptions, and notions that awaken us to embrace the world, to feel connected.[47]

Without the context of some church setting, I had no clue who this person was. I knew that I knew her, but I doubted myself. I was in airport mode when she said, "Hello." I was only worrying about getting from one spot to the next, interacting as little as I could with what was around me. It all highlights Rosa's point. In anticipation for acceleration across space in a short time, I had some vague anxiety that this speeding up could be delayed and keep me from my goal. I alienated myself from my surroundings to survive the speed and the chaos of travel.

So when Meredith said hello as I waited to board my flight, just three months after she told her story to our group, I was caught completely off guard.

---

of significance that accompanies the experience of raising children isn't just an evolutionarily determined illusion, like the man in the moon or the terrifying garter snake. Children really do put us in touch with important, real, and universal aspects of the human condition." Gopnik, *The Philosophical Baby: What Children's Minds Tell Us about Truth, Love, and the Meaning of Life* (New York: Picador, 2009), 238. Tobin Hart adds, "Children help remind us that we live in a vast sea of wonder and mystery. . . . Children often experience interconnection as they resonate with the feelings or thoughts of other persons." Hart, *The Secret Spiritual World of Children: The Breakthrough Discovery That Profoundly Alters Our Conventional View of Children's Mystical Experience* (Maui, HI: Inner Ocean, 2003), 65, 80. The following quote from David Hay and Rebecca Nye also connects children with resonance: "Children's spirituality is rooted in a universal human awareness; that it is 'really there' and not just a culturally constructed illusion." Hay and Nye, *The Spirit of the Child* (Philadelphia: Jessica Kingley, 2006), 18.

45. John Wall connects time, narrative, and the child in *Ethics in Light of Childhood* (Washington, DC: Georgetown University Press, 2010), 50–66, 77–85.

46. Chris Jenks shows how the child gathers time: "When we talk of the child we are also talking about recollections of time past, images of current forms of relationship and aspirations towards future states of affairs." *Childhood* (London: Routledge, 2005), 10.

47. Lisa Miller reports, "More than 80 percent of respondents said they perceived becoming a parent as inherently sacred." *The Spiritual Child: The New Science on Parenting for Health and Lifelong Thriving* (New York: St. Martin's Press, 2015), 104.

15

when Bonhoeffer time travels

resonance as carrying the child

I returned her hello with my own a few notches higher in energy, to hide that I couldn't place her.

"Where're you headed?" she asked.

Still, I couldn't place her. I had shared her story a few times with students and pastors in the past months, but her face had morphed in my retelling. My mind was blank, but I played along, hoping that her name would come to me as I talked.

Lucky for me it finally clicked. I felt silly. Then I found myself asking, "So how are things at your church?" Now proud of myself for remembering, I assured myself that my direct question would silence any suspicion in her that I hadn't remembered her immediately.

"Good. It's lively. We have about five families we're journeying with right now."

"What stuck with me from your story," I said, "was when you mentioned that your community believes a child is part of your congregation when he or she is prayed for. That was really moving. I've shared that with other people. I've used it to remind small churches that there is no such thing as a congregation without children. Every congregation has some children they care about—nieces, grandchildren, or neighbors. And because congregations are made up of persons, and persons have their being in relation to others, we bring these children we care for into the life of the congregation. We're the kind of creatures who have our being when we're with and for others.

So there is no such thing as a congregation that doesn't have children deeply connected to it."

"I know we're an unusual congregation," Meredith responded, "but we're anything but unique. We're just living out of a story that started with Henry; we're a little church that cares for children."

In the previous chapter, I asserted that congregations would be better off (nearer to a sense of the good life that opens them to encounters of divine action/revelation) giving attention to resonance rather than to the relevance of innovation. As we've seen, innovation (without a careful reworking of its goods) is for acceleration and therefore inevitably produces alienation born from the conditions of *la fatigue* (weariness). Innovation becomes a tool that props up a closed immanent frame. It becomes a disenchanted way of finding meaning in the immanent frame, speeding us up so that we no longer have time to feel the flatness of our existence and the deafening silence of our world—until we inevitably do.

Resonance, on the other hand, is a journey of seeking a narrative of connection to the world and those in the world who call out to us. Hartmut Rosa's three-dimensional look at resonance leads him to organize resonance around two axes: one vertical and the other horizontal. The vertical axis represents things like religion, art, nature, and history. We often feel a transcendent call in these locales. These locales pull us out of ourselves to remind us that there is mystery and meaning in the world that we can share in.

There is also a horizontal axis made up of love (not just romantic love), friendship, and parenting/family. In these locales we encounter resonance through attachment. We discover that acceleration's gift of speeding us up for the sake of a freedom to be and do whatever we want, in the end, is unveiled (shockingly) as no freedom at all.[1] The closer we get to such "freedom," the more we're alienated from life itself. Rather, we discover life, to draw from Luther, not in being free from others but in the freedom to be with and for those we encounter in attachments of love, friendship, and parenting/family (care). After developing the vertical and horizontal axes, Rosa is able to place certain activities such as eating, music, and sport at certain locales on these two axes.[2]

---

1. For Charles Taylor, Isaiah Berlin, and even Michael Gillespie, modernity is the struggle to rework and make sense of freedom. See Taylor, *Hegel and Modern Society* (London: Cambridge University Press, 1979); Berlin, *Freedom and Its Betrayal* (Princeton: Princeton University Press, 2014); and Gillespie, *The Theological Origins of Modernity* (Chicago: University of Chicago Press, 2008).

2. His more developed position includes three axes: vertical (existential), horizontal (social), and diagonal (material). There is some nuance to how he uses the vertical and horizontal axes

This project would balloon if I tried to articulate an ecclesiology that intersected or interacted with the vertical and horizontal locales of resonances. This is indeed something that should be done, and in a future project I hope to take up this challenge. But for the sake of this work and its limited space, I'd like to focus only on carrying children.[3] More so than limited space, this decision is driven by my belief that carrying children links us firmly with all the locales of resonance that Rosa mentions (carrying children moves across the horizontal axis—parenting, friendship, love—and the vertical—children can open us to mystery of history, nature, art, and religion, all in and through personhood).[4] If we explore resonance through ministry with children, we're given a concrete application that can open our imagination to wider implications and visions.

If we follow Meredith's logic, then all congregations have children within them. But not necessarily as resources. Small churches with few resources are often quick to point out that they have no children in their congregation, adding to the vicious circle, because they have no resources that would keep children as a resource. These congregations often think, *If only we had a preschool, a flashy Sunday school program, or a vibrant youth ministry.* They long for children but rarely get them to stay, because they want them only as resources. Playing the resource game, they lose.[5]

If we free ourselves from resource obsession and see our congregations instead as made up of persons, we become aware that all congregations have children. Catholic theologians Karl Rahner and Hans Urs von Balthasar,[6]

---

and this third axis. But I won't clutter things by getting into it. For simplicity, I'll stick with just the vertical and the horizontal.

3. Hartmut Rosa discusses how children are resonant beings. See his *Resonance: A Sociology of Our Relationship to the World* (Medford, MA: Polity, 2019), 50.

4. For example, think about how the arrival of a child leads us into newly defined relationships with our history and lineage. Through their eyes we see nature in a different, more welcoming (and perhaps dangerous) way. Every child is an artist, and we fill our fridges and offices with their works. And according to Justin Barrett, every child is born a believer: see *Born Believers: The Science of Children's Religious Belief* (New York: Free Press, 2012). This causes even atheistic parents to confront the religious locale on the vertical axis of resonance. See Wendy Thomas Russell, *Relax, It's Just God: How and Why to Talk to Your Kids about Religion* (New York: Brown Paper Press, 2015) as an example of an atheistic parent who is confronted by belief and religion through her child.

5. We fetishize youthfulness in our resource obsession of an accelerated modernity. We explored a genealogy of this from the perspective of teenagers and young adults in volume 1 of this series, *Faith Formation in a Secular Age: Responding to the Church's Obsession with Youthfulness* (Grand Rapids: Baker Academic, 2017), part 1.

6. Karl Rahner, *The Content of Faith: The Best of Karl Rahner's Theological Writings* (New York: Crossroad, 1992), 120–99. Hans Urs von Balthasar, *Unless You Become Like This Child* (San Francisco: Ignatius, 1991). For more on Rahner, see Mary Ann Hinsdale, "'Infinite Openness

Orthodox theologian Alexander Schmemann,[7] and Protestant theologian Dietrich Bonhoeffer[8] have all asserted that children hold an important place in the Christian life and therefore in our practical ecclesiology.[9] For all four, children's important place is not because they are resources but because of the events of resonance they embody in our encounters with them.[10] Children hold an important place in the church because of their unique and free humanity that calls us to care for and love them. Therefore, for the remainder of this project, I have only one answer for how congregations can escape alienation for encounters of resonance: carrying children.[11]

---

to the Infinite': Karl Rahner's Contribution to Modern Catholic Thought on the Child," in *The Child in Christian Thought*, ed. Marcia Bunge (Grand Rapids: Eerdmans, 2001), 419–23.

7. Schmemann, *Celebration of Faith*, vol. 2, *The Church Year* (Yonkers, NY: St. Vladimir's Seminary Press, 2012).

8. I'm thinking here of Bonhoeffer's *Sanctorum Communio* (Minneapolis: Fortress, 1998); *Act and Being* (Minneapolis: Fortress, 1996); and a few lectures and sermons. I'll be in dialogue with much of this below. For much more on Bonhoeffer's thought in regard to children and youth, see my *Bonhoeffer as Youth Worker* (Grand Rapids: Baker Academic, 2014).

9. Of course, they're not alone: see also Marcia Bunge, ed., *The Child in the Bible* (Grand Rapids: Eerdmans, 2008); Bunge, *The Child in Christian Thought*; Bonnie Miller-McLemore, *Let the Children Come: Reimagining Childhood from a Christian Perspective* (San Francisco: Jossey-Bass, 2003); Miller-McLemore, *In the Midst of Chaos: Caring for Children as Spiritual Practice* (San Francisco: Jossey-Bass, 2007); and Amy Marga, *Heavenly Bodies, Earthly Bodies: Motherhood and the Maternal in Christian Thought* (Waco: Baylor University Press, forthcoming).

10. Modernity has been on a long process of developing its views of the child. Overall this has been a positive move, giving children rights and esteem. But there is always the risk of instrumentalization. For much more on this discussion, see such works as Philippe Ariès, *Centuries of Childhood: A Social History of Family Life* (New York: Alfred A. Knopf, 1962); Colin Heywood, *A History of Childhood* (Malden, MA: Polity, 2001); Hugh Cunningham, *Children and Childhood in Western Society Since 1500*, 2nd ed. (London: Routledge, 2005); Giovanni Levi and Jean-Claude Schmitt, eds., *A History of Young People: Stormy Evolution to Modern Times* (Cambridge, MA: Belknap, 1997); Linda Pollock, *Forgotten Children: Parent-Child Relations from 1500 to 1900* (London: Cambridge University Press, 1985) (this text opposes Ariès's perspective); John Wall, "Fallen Angels: A Contemporary Christian Ethical Ontology of Childhood," *International Journal of Practical Theology* 8 (2004): 160–84; Steven Mintz, *Huck's Raft: A History of American Childhood* (Cambridge, MA: Belknap, 2004); James Allison and Alan Prout, eds., *Constructing and Reconstructing Childhood* (London: Falmer, 1997); and John Cleverley and D. C. Phillips, *Visions of Childhood: Influential Modes from Locke to Spock* (New York: Teachers College Press, 1986). Though space doesn't allow a full genealogy of this, to understand the modern development (or genealogy) of the child, follow Jean-Jacques Rousseau and John Locke. For two strong biographies of these key thinkers, see Leo Damrosch, *Jean-Jacques Rousseau: Restless Genius* (Boston: Houghton Mifflin, 2005); and Roger Woolhouse, *Locke: A Biography* (Cambridge: Cambridge University Press, 2007).

11. Through our discussion of the good life I've pushed the moral to the central of this project. There is coherence with children because, according to John Wall, children push us into deep questions of the good. "Childhood is morality's most profound test. Children may be the most important reasons for moral reflection and practice in the first place. The purpose of thinking in light of children is to imagine a more expansively shared humanity." Wall, *Ethics in Light of Childhood* (Washington, DC: Georgetown University Press, 2010), 10.

Bonhoeffer Meets Rosa and Goes Back in Time

There are intriguing points of contact between the work of Rosa and Bonhoeffer. Though the two German thinkers are separated by nearly a century, and are operating from within two very different fields, there are nevertheless some interesting connections. In 1925, at the age of nineteen, Bonhoeffer started his PhD work in the theology department at Humboldt (University of Berlin). His dissertation would become his first book, *Sanctorum Communio*. In it Bonhoeffer seeks to provide an uncompromising theological argument for the concrete life of the church. But to make this argument, articulating how the church is inseparable from revelation itself, Bonhoeffer dialogues with social theory, including numerous interactions with Ferdinand Tönnies and Georg Simmel, to mention only two.[12]

In 1962, prominent American sociologist Peter Berger critiqued *Sanctorum Communio* for choosing the wrong sociological dialogue partners, having picked the Simmel path over a more classic Weberian one (i.e., Berger thought it better to follow Max Weber to Talcott Parsons to an empirically based sociology, a more American style). Berger points out that, though the subtitle of Bonhoeffer's text is *A Theological Study of the Sociology of the Church*, it contains no tables, graphs, and charts of percentages that are endemic to the work of sociology, as Berger understood it. Berger finds little in the book practical enough to be considered sociological, let alone helpful to congregations. Berger blamed this on Bonhoeffer following what Berger believed to be an outdated Georg Simmel.[13] Berger believed Bonhoeffer claimed a sociological place for his work that just isn't there.

Yet fast-forwarding eighty years, Rosa's work seems to be just the kind of sociological work that intrigued Bonhoeffer. Not only is Rosa much more philosophical than what Berger's American sociological framework could stomach, but Rosa even returns to the concepts and descriptions of modern society offered by Georg Simmel.[14] Like Bonhoeffer's *Sanctorum Communio*, Rosa's most influential books are absent the graphs and charts of other empirical sociologists.[15] Rosa is straddling a line between sociology and philosophy

---

12. Michael Mawson provides a helpful articulation of Bonhoeffer's use and interpretation of these sociological and social theory perspectives in *Sanctorum Communio*. See *Christ Existing as Community: Bonhoeffer's Ecclesiology* (London: Oxford University Press, 2018), chap. 2.

13. Peter Berger, "The Social Character of the Question Concerning Jesus Christ," in *The Place of Bonhoeffer*, ed. Martin Marty (New York: Association Press, 1962), 51–80.

14. Rosa cites Simmel more than twenty times in *Social Acceleration: A New Theory of Modernity* (New York: Columbia University Press, 2015).

15. I'm thinking here particularly of projects like those of Robert Wuthnow. This isn't a critique. Wuthnow's work as an empirical, survey-based sociologist is very important. Rosa's work just has a much different, more constructive/philosophical feel to it.

(he's a critical theorist), discussing the shape of modern society, with which the young Bonhoeffer wished to be in dialogue.

Then we could playfully ask, in the style of *Quantum Leap* or reverse *Outlander*: If Bonhoeffer were writing his dissertation in 2025, not 1925, might the young Berliner not draw from the Jena professor? It's possible that all Bonhoeffer's Tönnies and Simmel footnotes would be replaced by Rosa quotes.[16]

Bonhoeffer, Persons, and Resonance

Bonhoeffer's objective in *Sanctorum Communio* is to articulate how "Christ exists as church-community."[17] We could even say that Bonhoeffer is intent on exploring how a congregation such as Meredith's is moved into a resonant encounter with Jesus Christ. Bonhoeffer is uncompromising that it's revelation (God's own revealing action in Jesus Christ) that creates the church. Therefore, his project can only be done in the theological faculty. But because this revelation is the incarnate Christ, it's concrete. It's in the world (it arrives unequivocally through *Weltbeziehung*, "world relations," as Rosa would say).[18] Bonhoeffer's strong commitment to Luther's *theologia crucis* keeps him from any excarnation.[19] The whole of his theology is for living in the world, linking it to Rosa's thought and Meredith's experience.

The form of the church in the world, Bonhoeffer believes, is personhood.[20] It's only in personhood that the church-community can be the concrete locale of Jesus Christ. The church is the community of persons who encounter the personhood (hypostasis) of God in and through the Spirit of Jesus Christ.

16. I say this playfully, but I think it's true. Rosa's whole project is an articulation of a sociology of world relations. This sounds very similar to what Bonhoeffer was after in his unfinished *Ethics* (Minneapolis: Fortress, 2005). Bonhoeffer articulates that there are not two worlds for the Christian but one world where God is active (see pp. 71–73). It is only in the world that we can encounter the living God. It's in and through world relations. To me this is a generative connection that I'll seek to do more work on in the future.

17. Cardinal Avery Dulles discusses Bonhoeffer's and others' view of the church as a communion in *Models of the Church* (New York: Image Books, 2002), 40–53. For more on communion ecclesiologies, see Dennis Doyle, *Communion Ecclesiology* (Maryknoll, NY: Orbis Books, 2000), 6–12.

18. This will become broader and more full blown as Bonhoeffer's project continues into the 1930s and 1940s.

19. Of course, one of the ways we arrive at excarnate conceptions of Christian life is by flattening justification and making the Christian life into a belief system. However, I contend that this is a misunderstanding of Luther. Luther, as Mannermaa and Volf claim, is a theologian of love. And love is never excarnate. See Tuomo Mannermaa, *Two Kinds of Love: Martin Luther's Religious World* (Minneapolis: Fortress, 2010).

20. This was a central theme in the theological construction of volumes 1 and 2. I called this the hypostatic.

Jesus Christ exists, is concretely present, for Bonhoeffer in and through this sharing in personhood (through *Stellvertretung*, sharing the place of our neighbor in friendship, love, and care).[21]

Or we could say it this way: the church-community has its being only as it is being-in-Christ. And the church-community is in Christ by being a community of persons in relations—and resonance, to add a little Rosa.[22] These relations are never instrumental or for any purpose other than sharing in each other's lives as a resonant encounter with the living Christ. Bonhoeffer has no patience for making relationships into a third thing outside the two persons in relationship, which would make the relationship into an instrument or a means to acquire something else outside the relationship. For Bonhoeffer, instrumentalized relationships always produce alienation.[23] And Rosa has shown us how. The church loses personhood, and resonance (becoming alienated from life), when its relations are made into instruments for acquiring resources. And relationships that are made into instruments can be used only for accruing resources.[24] The church loses community when its relationships become instruments. When it loses community, it loses the resonance of revelation itself. It is no longer a living community (a life-community, a phrase Bonhoeffer uses that I'll unpack below) but is alienated from the world and therefore from the living God, who moves in the world as the minister of life. The points of contact between Bonhoeffer and Rosa (with a little of my own theological construction) become clear.

Of course, a congregation *can* grow by making all its relations into instruments of influence. But while gaining growth, the congregation loses life (as the history of most megachurches shows). Life and growth are not always complementary. The congregation becomes cancerous, misdiagnosing its growing tumors as signs of life. It should instead be the case that the phenomenological and efficacy (Bonhoeffer would call this responsibility)

21. *Stellvertretung* carries so much weight for Bonhoeffer that I can only briefly highlight it here, which doesn't do justice to the depth of the concept for Bonhoeffer. Even in *Sanctorum Communio*, *Stellvertretung* is inseparable from sin, suffering, and the cross.

22. This fundamental assertion about personhood means that when we say "church" we're drawn first and foremost not to hierarchy or institutional structure but to the community of persons. Therefore, the congregation is the most concrete but also the most faithful form of the church.

23. It's in discussing the lack of the third thing that Bonhoeffer most clearly shows that all church relations are communal and never instrumental (see *Sanctorum Communio*, 98–99). The third things, or influence, as I've called it, are relations that have been overtaken by acceleration. They are relations that can no longer lead us into the resonance of joy.

24. I've shown how this is so in the context of ministry in my books *Revisiting Relational Youth Ministry* (Downers Grove, IL: IVP, 2007); *Relationships Unfiltered* (Grand Rapids: Zondervan, 2009); and *The Relational Pastor* (Downers Grove, IL: IVP, 2013).

dimensions of resonance are imbued with the revelation of the living Christ through the relational encounter with personhood. We are made alive, and made church, when we minister to and receive ministry from our neighbor, person-to-person, who calls out to us as Jesus Christ himself.[25] When our relations are no longer instruments but instead events, we are invited deeper into resonance. In sharing in each other's death experience for the sake only of sharing in each other's personhood, we find the mystery of the new, out-of-death life. (This is just what Meredith's congregation does with Henry.) We find healing because we encounter the very person who calls himself "the life" in John 11. (Jesus says, "I am the resurrection and the life." Jesus himself is the fullness of resonance, for he is the second person of the triune God, who is the Lord of life as a relationship, or better, *the* relationship.)[26]

Bonhoeffer, then, goes to great lengths in *Sanctorum Communio* to discuss the shape of personhood by claiming that it's always both/and. Personhood is always both open *and* closed, fundamentally individual *and* relational, and both will *and* spirit. This articulation of personhood encompasses most of the heavy lifting of Bonhoeffer's project. In articulating the shape of personhood, Bonhoeffer asserts that something is fundamentally lost when the congregation evades a conception of persons. To see this again through Rosa, personhood is often obscured in the acceleration of modernity,[27] where the present is compressed, the future and its newness are our aim, resources are our obsession, and dynamic stabilization is our hope. Innovation risks an

---

25. Henri de Lubac points to the ministering nature of the church: "Israel was 'a kingdom of priests and a sacred nation.' The same holds true of the whole Church, for all Israel is summed up in Christ, and he is the sole true Priest, and all Christians are identified with him." *The Splendor of the Church*, new ed. (San Francisco: Ignatius, 2006), 134.

26. John 11 could be explored through the resonance perspective discussed in the previous chapter. The phenomenological dimension is there, as is the efficacy. Jesus has affection for Lazarus and his sisters, is stirred by emotion, and then calls out and acts (the efficacy), transforming Lazarus from dead to alive, and his sisters' mourning to joy. And it's all embedded in an elusiveness. Jesus himself is elusive. (He shows up late!) The text's major point is the proclamation Jesus makes about himself—he is the resurrection of life, he is life. This narrative wears all the marks of Rosa's resonance perspective.

27. Bonhoeffer is following a long line of thinkers before and after him who have made this point. Jewish thinkers like Martin Buber, Franz Rosenzweig, and Emmanuel Levinas, for obvious reasons, have particularly made this very assertion that modernity attacks personhood. There is a bent in modernity to seek out and destroy personhood. Personalism is an interesting philosophical position because it refuses to shy away from how modernity seeks to attack personhood, but it nevertheless escapes the temptation to seek the end or destruction of modernity. Rather, personalism actually believes that modernity *could* allow for a space for personal encounters if reformed and reordered in certain ways. Personalism isn't an anti-modern position, but it is one that points out the problematic of the modern project unchecked. This kind of personalism is central to all my work. For more on personalism in my own project, see *Christopraxis* (Minneapolis: Fortress, 2014).

attack on personhood, which cuts you off from the elusive transformation personhood brings. In the loss of personhood the congregation is no longer a church-community (no longer a *Gemeinde*) but becomes an institutional shell absent the revelation of Jesus Christ. Trying to innovate the empty shell, absent the Holy Spirit experienced in the spirit of personhood, is a deeply wearying and resentment-inducing operation, as many pastors in late modernity have experienced.[28]

Allow me to state this all more positively, and put it again in conversation with Rosa. Had he written his dissertation in 2025, Bonhoeffer might have argued that a true theological conception of persons that creates a community of persons allows for a resonance that is encountered as the revelation of Jesus Christ. This community is living a good life (it is a life-community), not because it has a storehouse of resources through speed and innovation but because it has the resonance of shared personhood. It has life in and through the unique cruciform shape of the good life, which leads us to share in the life of each other (and the world) in and through the death experience as ministers. We discover that as the congregation becomes a household of ministry,[29] a community of persons, it encounters the profound paradox of finding a deep resonance with life by sharing in death. Sharing in death—in the brokenness of persons' narratives, ministering to one another, as Meredith's congregation does with Henry—awakens them to life itself. The person-to-person attachment brings resonance born from the relational connection of ministry. When Meredith's congregation reaches out to Henry with affection and responsibility (efficacy), they discover a deep sense that they are now following the one who is the resurrection and the life (John 11). They feel overtaken by an event of life. They're alive, encountering resonance because they are encountering Jesus Christ in and through their connection to Henry and his granddaughter.

Bonhoeffer and Carrying Children

We should be honest: even reading *Sanctorum Communio* through Rosa's perspective and Meredith's congregational experience doesn't free Bonhoeffer's thoughts from appearing anything but practical. Berger's 1962 critique still seems right on. There appears to be little in *Sanctorum Communio* that

28. Michael Mawson discusses Bonhoeffer's view of the person in *Christ Existing as Community*, 66–81, and see esp. 83–84 for a discussion of the open and closed.

29. For more on the household of ministry and its practical form, see the conclusion of volume 1, *Faith Formation in a Secular Age*.

could be helpful to actual congregations. Berger's point, to give him Charles Taylor's language, was basically to assert that while Bonhoeffer's theology may not be excarnate (especially the later stuff), his ecclesiology most definitely is! It has no connection to real life. The *Wunderkind* in Berlin, Berger seemed to think, might have wished to have his feet on the ground, but he was really, in his dissertation, in intellectual outer space.

Many Bonhoeffer scholars have come to Dietrich's rescue.[30] They've spilled much ink showing that Berger is mistaken. But most have done so by ignoring one of the two horns of Berger's critique, choosing to deal with only the larger but duller of the horns—the assertion that Bonhoeffer is misguided in his social theory. The smaller but more piercing and therefore dangerous horn is that *Sanctorum Communio* is painfully impractical. But this accusation of impracticality (and the oversight or disinterest in this critique in Bonhoeffer scholarship) is only because the place of children in *Sanctorum Communio* has consistently been overlooked. Our own bias keeps us from recognizing that Bonhoeffer indeed gives us a very practical picture of what a sacred communion of shared personhood looks like. It looks like a life-community (one could say a community of resonance). The church-community becomes a community of resonance by being a life-community that concretely carries children.[31]

Volunteer-Societies and the Zombie Resource Feast

Bonhoeffer turns specifically to children in the middle of the project,[32] when he contrasts what he calls a volunteer-society with a life-community. Bonhoeffer sees a volunteer-society as the antithesis of a community of personhood. Meredith's congregation was a desert because they'd become a volunteer-society. Most congregations in late modernity teeter ever closer to *la fatigue d'être eglise* because they have become volunteer-societies. In volunteer-societies, a person's belonging and commitment rests almost completely on what they receive from the collective. A volunteer-society feeds on resources, and when those resources are scarce, it turns lifeless, sluggish. It goes into zombie-mode,

30. Some examples would be Mawson, *Christ Existing as Community*, chap. 2; and Clifford Green, *Bonhoeffer: A Theology of Sociality* (Grand Rapids: Eerdmans, 1999). Particularly, Mawson astutely deals with Berger's misunderstanding of Bonhoeffer's uses of social theory. He doesn't deal as much with Berger's critique of impracticality.

31. David Jensen offers a different perspective from Bonhoeffer, but nevertheless focuses on carrying children, in *Graced Vulnerability: A Theology of Childhood* (Cleveland: Pilgrim Press, 2005), esp. 47–50.

32. He begins talking about children on page 90 of *Sanctorum Communio* and then returns to discuss the child, volunteer-society, and life-community on pages 240–41.

seeking resources. The only supposed hope for a volunteer-society that loses its mojo, with its affections and emotions dried to a crisp, is innovation. But this almost always produces further alienation. Innovation seems to be the answer to the congregational funk, but it actually just adds to the problem. It never questions the imagined constitution of the congregation as a volunteer-society in the first place.

Even the congregation that knows itself to be a volunteer-society might be tempted only to instrumentalize its relationships for the sake of growth—even if just growth in energy. But this only pushes them further away from resonance. To seek innovation as the answer to the congregation's depression is to double down on the Silicon Valley assumption that all human collectives are best seen as volunteer-societies that exist only to assist us in being the self we wish and in chasing some undefined good life in some coming future.

A volunteer-society assumes only one side of the dialect of personhood that Bonhoeffer has explored (it loses the both/and). It assumes people are open without being closed,[33] individuals before relations, and wills absent spirit. A volunteer-society contends that *people are what they're interested in* as open individual wills. A congregation that has any meaning for such people can only survive by meeting these people's interests. Being only open individual wills (without being also closed relational spirits) makes us zombies for our interests.

The volunteer-society is a collective of alienated (or potentially alienated) people. The congregation becomes a collective of zombies seeking their wants. They're interested in feeding on resources. They even move in hordes as a way to get these wants. But zombies are alienated from life. They're dead (or undead), though in constant motion, never resting.[34] If people are interested in keeping up with the acceleration of the pace of life and chasing the undefined good life in some coming future, then the congregation must provide these open individual wills with the resources to meet their interests. The congregation must speed up to meet this constant motion. Innovation is the process needed to upshift.

33. Their openness is assumed to be bound in wants, but there is no closedness of mystery and otherness that would make resonance possible. Resonance is an encounter with otherness, and closedness is necessary for otherness. A relationship with otherness (one that therefore escapes instrumentality) requires closedness. Obviously we need openness to have relationship, but without closedness (without a sense that the other's being is closed, is mystery to you, or is "infinite" to use the language of Levinas) we'll always turn our open relationships into instruments for our own wants.

34. Rest was an important dynamic in my sketch of an ecclesiology of faith formation at the end of volume 1, *Faith Formation in a Secular Age*. See the conclusion for more.

How do you know if your congregation is a volunteer-society? Bonhoeffer says we'll know because a volunteer-society is not able to carry children.[35] A volunteer-society does what a horde of zombies alienated from life does. They encounter everything, even the personhood of their own children, *not* as open *and* closed, individual *and* relational, will *and* spirit, but as resources. The best a volunteer-society can do with children (and it's truly imagined as the best) is to push them out of the present and into an undefined future.[36]

Sadly, children have no concrete place in a volunteer-society's sense of the good life (even baptism is imagined for some future purpose). The volunteer-society can have no delight in children because it sees no use for them in the now. A volunteer-society sees children only as potential—potential members, potential voters, potential consumers, and potential denominational affiliates (baptism is for potential, and therefore loses its sacramental weight). Or it's possible that against this short present our sense of the potential turns existential. We see our children as potentially in crisis, potentially ruining their future, potentially walking away from the faith or just needing religious literacy to be a potentially good citizen. The volunteer-society's vision of the good life is so projected into the future that children can have value only outside the now, outside the life of the community as it is now. (Unfortunately, I believe American children's and youth ministry has been an innovation necessitated by the volunteer-society. It was only after the acceleration of late modernity that congregational youth ministry, for instance, appeared on the scene. It may be a concession to the congregation as a volunteer-society.)

Life-Communities and the Move into Resonance

Yet a life-community does something much different. A life-community can carry children.[37] What carries them is the community itself. The congregation does not seek resources in order to keep its children, nor does it see children as

---

35. See Bonhoeffer, *Sanctorum Communio*, 257.

36. This is where the analogy of zombies breaks down. I'm willing to say no (almost no) parent wants anything but the best for their child (congregations too). They're not mindless zombies willing to eat their own children. But this is where the good life is so defining. When the good life becomes only a dream-state in some undefined future, then even though we love our children we tend to be unable to carry them (especially as communities). Our anxiety is pushed toward the future, so we can't just be with them to carry them in their questions, pain, and searching. We go looking for answers, for fixing, so their future good life won't be in jeopardy. When the parent or youth worker or congregation is all about fixing, they aren't carrying, and the child can feel alienated from life.

37. Jacqueline Lapsley sketches out this sense of carrying children in the Old Testament book of Isaiah. See her "'Look! The Children and I Are as Signs and Portents in Israel': Children in Isaiah," in *The Child in the Bible*, ed. Marcia Bunge (Grand Rapids: Eerdmans, 2008), 100–101.

resources. Rather, the congregation that is a life-community sees its children as persons. It seeks to be a community that surrounds and carries them, not for some undefined future but in this now, in this broken and yet delightful now. Children gather time. By carrying them, we're moved deeply into the now.[38] This is their gift to us. It is not the resources of the congregation but the resonance of the community itself that holds up the child. To live in this spirit of personhood, the congregation needs (not *wants*) the child, because the child fundamentally moves in the world as a distinct other who nevertheless has his or her being in and through relationship.

The child became our pastor in the North Dakota gym. My friend's own children became his Sherpa back into life—not because these children were magically innocent (that would be to objectify them, turning them into resources) but because they lived directly as distinct others who nevertheless have their being in and through relationship. We experience the necessity of their attachment as a deep portal into the resonance of life. Life is full for children ("That was *great!*" the little girl said in the gym) because children *have their being* directly in and through loving attachments, and yet they encounter the world as other. They are persons encountering life as open and closed in affections and emotion, individuals and yet always relations in being. They are wills through an efficacy that brings the spirit of elusive (uncontrollable) transformation.

The child is the sign of a life-community, not because they are innocent or pure (or some other charmed object)[39] but because of the necessity of relationships of love, which gives them their being and carries them moment by moment, producing in them a deep resonance with life itself. Being a person who experiences affection as closed, as other—and therefore a unique individual yet nevertheless bound in relationships—opens you to the world. It allows you to willfully act within the world. When you do, you discover that such actions done with and for others make the world pulsate with a spirit

38. I do mean "now" in a more sacramental sense of shared life that brings together past and hope for a future (a future that is more eschatological). Rosa mentioned to me that he's uncomfortable with overly glorifying the now. In Germany there is a whole movement that focuses on this now moment, embracing the now as all there is. He doesn't think this is quite resonance. I agree. Now isn't YOLO ("you only live once"). That *seems* like living in the now, but it's really just a concession to a sense of a consumeristic good life that refuses efficacy and wants only sensations of fullness disconnected from something outside of feeling subject. It's emotion minus affection, transformation, and elusiveness.

39. Yves Congar offers something similar to Bonhoeffer: "A child receives the life of the community into which he enters, together with the cultural riches of the preceding generations (tradition!), which are inculcated by the actions and habits of everyday life." Congar, *The Meaning of Tradition* (San Francisco: Ignatius, 2004), 23.

that connects you. Children resonate with life because they are free—but never free-from, always free-for.[40] They hold together the dialectics of open *and* closed, individual *and* relational, and will *and* spirit.

Bonhoeffer's point is that children are a litmus test for the congregation. The child who is carried (and not as a resource or object) is other, but this otherness—this closed spirit, which has its own individual will—occurs through open encounters, direct efficacy (or responsibility) of (affectionate and emotional) attachment. The child is alive by sharing in being, by resonating with the whole of the world, as a representative of a history,[41] as a mystery of being,[42] as an embracer of nature, and as an artistic actor.[43] The child shares in being through giving love, being a friend, and receiving the delight of being parented (carried). A congregation that carries children, as Meredith's does, is a life-community, a community not hunting resources but encountering resonance. This congregation's life is not in its innovation but in its encounter with the concrete others whom it ministers to and is ministered by.

A practical ecclesiology for the congregation born from Bonhoeffer never asks, How can we survive? How can we grow? How can we innovate and be more relevant? Instead it asks, How can we care for and carry our children?[44]

40. I'm trying to be careful here not to idealize or essentialize children. There are thousands who find themselves in situations of abandonment. My and Bonhoeffer's point is only that children need life-communities. They show all of us our need for otherness and connection. Resonance is a connection to the world, and children seem deeply engaged in the world, I believe, because of this attachment. I'm following the distinguished social theory of Richard Sennett here: "Buried in all of us is the infantile experience of relating and connecting to the adults who took care of us; as babies we had to learn how to work with them in order to survive." Sennett, *Together: The Rituals, Pleasures and Politics of Cooperation* (New York: Penguin, 2012), 9.

41. John Wall means something like a history when he discusses children as a central ethical demand. See *Ethics in Light of Childhood* (Washington, DC: Georgetown University Press, 2010), 95–100.

42. See Martin Marty, *The Mystery of the Child* (Grand Rapids: Eerdmans, 2007). Douglas John Hall points to the importance of children when it comes to sensing the depth of existence: "Children, as Paul Tillich never tired of insisting, instinctively ask ontological questions. It is instinctual with them because, in their earliest stages of self-awareness, their very survival and growth depend upon their coming to terms with the consciousness of their own being—and with the prospect of not being. What Tillich called 'the shock of non-being' is perhaps a greater shock to the five-year-old than to the thirty-year-old, who has already learned subtle psychic techniques for repressing it. Very young children have been known to be so obsessed with death, despite the relative absence of actual death from their experience, that they could overcome it only with the help of skillful and sensitive adults." Hall, *Professing the Faith* (Minneapolis: Fortress, 1993), 315; see further 316.

43. Gareth Matthews discusses children and art in *The Philosophy of Childhood* (Cambridge, MA: Harvard University Press, 1994), 116–18. See also Erika Christakis, *The Importance of Being Little: What Young Children Really Need from Grownups* (New York: Penguin, 2016), 78–79.

44. And by "our" I mean all the children in our community, maybe even the nation and world.

It recognizes that it's Jesus Christ himself who is putting the child in our midst (Matt. 18), revealing himself through our call and connection to our children.

Our children, as Meredith has taught us, and Bonhoeffer's theology has witnessed, are all those who are connected to us as persons. When we pray for them, they are bound in the life-community of the congregation. Meredith's congregation finds resonance with life that is the living Jesus Christ when they decide to carry children as the doorway into being a community of persons in ministry. The good life is in the now, and time is gathered, as they share in personhood and experience the mystery of connection.[45]

Before I hurry myself onto my plane, I ask Meredith what they do each week when they gather to carry children. She looks at me and smiles. She is sure I won't think it's very profound. But I nonverbally assure her that I am interested.

"Well, every week we pray specifically for the children we're caring for. Then we ask the children present to pray for us. I always add a refrain I wrote, drawn from Matthew 18, that reminds us that Jesus beckons us to turn and be children. I try not to do much else than just remind us that we're all connected to children and that children are in our midst. This congregation first belongs to them, for the kingdom of heaven belongs to them."

We exchange nods and smiles, and say goodbye.

---

45. In volume 1, I articulated a pattern of formation embedded in Paul's conception of faith. I called this a movement from *kenosis* to *hypostasis* (or vice versa) to *theosis*. The astute reader will see how the placement of children and our call to carry them lives out of this pattern. It's a kenotic act to carry children as opposed to seeking resources. It's inextricably hypostatic—about persons. The child comes to us always as a revelation of personhood. As Meredith's congregation witnesses, it brings the transformation of *theosis*. To welcome the child is to welcome Jesus himself.

16

to become a child

Matthew 18 and the congregation that is carried

As I sit in my imposed slowdown for another flight, Meredith's comments about Matthew 18 ignite my imagination. I decide to pull out my phone and find it on my Bible app.

On December 11, 1928, the twenty-two-year-old Bonhoeffer gave a lecture to his congregation in Barcelona called "Jesus Christ and the Essence of Christianity."[1] About halfway through articulating the essence of Christianity, Bonhoeffer quotes Matthew 18:2–3: "Jesus called a child, whom he put among them, and said, 'Truly, I tell you, unless you change and become like children, you will never enter the kingdom of heaven.'"

Bonhoeffer then says, "For Jesus, the child is not merely a transitional stage on the way to adulthood, something to be overcome; quite the contrary, he or she is something utterly unique before which the adult should have the utmost respect. For indeed, God is closer to children than to adults. In this sense, Jesus becomes the discoverer of the child." He continues, echoing thoughts

1. This lecture appears in Dietrich Bonhoeffer, *Dietrich Bonhoeffer Works*, vol. 10, *Barcelona, Berlin, New York* (Minneapolis: Fortress, 2008), 342–59. See his note at the bottom of page 342 for some context, particularly how the title of the lecture points to Adolf von Harnack's *Das Wesen das Christentums* and Ludwig Feuerbach's book of the same title. Bonhoeffer is showing what he thinks of himself by giving this lecture—to this little congregation—such a title.

from his dissertation, "[Jesus] sees the children and wants to belong to them; who would block his path? God belongs to children, the good news belongs to children, and joy in the kingdom of heaven belongs to children."[2]

In the Midst

Bonhoeffer quotes from Matthew 18, but all three of the Synoptic Gospels have some version of this story (Mark 9:33–37; Luke 9:46–48). All three versions tell of Jesus calling a child and putting him in the disciples' midst (or at his side, in Luke). And for all three this is in response to an argument. The disciples are vying for who among them is greatest.[3] It's a real ego-measuring contest. They're positioning for who deserves the most, who among them is great enough to win the most resources for this coming kingdom. Jesus needs to show them that resource obsession stands in opposition to the kingdom of heaven. For the kingdom of heaven is one of life, of belonging and meaning, not of alienation. Therefore, Jesus calls the child to stand among these resource-obsessed disciples, and he says, "Unless you change and become like children, you will never enter the kingdom of heaven" (Matt. 18:3).[4] You must live for resonance, not for resources. Like a child you must meet a living world through relationship as gift. As Bonhoeffer says in his own exploration of this text, Jesus belongs (is attached) to children. You must be a person bound to others to enter this kingdom. This is a kingdom of resonance, not resources (and the alienation that resource obsession will inevitably produce).

As a matter of fact, two chapters later—showing that at least some of the disciples didn't quite get Jesus's point—Momma Zebedee comes to Jesus with a request (Matt. 20:20–28). She wants her boys to live a good life in a projected future. She's as intense in making a way for her children as any of

---

2. Bonhoeffer, *Barcelona, Berlin, New York*, 351. W. A. Strange adds, "But children did count for something in the ministry of Jesus. Children occur in several of the healings in the gospels. They also have their place in the teaching of Jesus. We find that Jesus was an observer of children, using the words of a child's game in one of his incisive sayings (Matt. 11:16–19). One of the distinctive features of Jesus' message and ministry was the significance he attributed to children." Strange, *Children in the Early Church: Children in the Ancient World, the New Testament and the Early Church* (Eugene, OR: Wipf & Stock, 1996), 38.

3. Hans-Ruedi Weber explains how the Roman world commonly saw children. See *Jesus and the Children: Biblical Resources for Study and Preaching* (Geneva: World Council of Churches, 1979), 33–35.

4. Judith Gundry provides very helpful insights on Mark's version of this text in "Children in the Gospel of Mark, with Special Attention to Jesus' Blessings of Children (Mark 10:13–16) and the Purpose of Mark," in *The Child in the Bible*, ed. Marcia Bunge (Grand Rapids: Eerdmans, 2008), 150–55. See also Adam Harwood and Kevin Lawson, eds., *Infants and Children in the Church: Five Views on Theology and Ministry* (Nashville: B&H Academic, 2017), 89–91.

the parents in the college-admissions scandal. She wants her boys to have accessibility, availability, and attainability (Hartmut Rosa's Triple-A), assurance that when Jesus enters his kingdom, her boys will get their dream and be living a good life.

She asks Jesus if her boys, James and John, might sit at his right and left hand when he enters the kingdom. Jesus's response is that his kingdom is not one of resources but of persons who suffer (Matt. 20:22–28). Therefore, to sit at his right or left is to bear the cross (*Is that really the good life you want for your boys?* Jesus essentially asks back). Jesus's kingdom will come through suffering, not because it's masochistic and therefore hates the world, feeling a deep disconnection from it. Rather, it comes through suffering because Jesus, as the Son to the Father, loves this world (John 3:16). Like Jesus, his disciples too will be called to share in the world not as untouchable celebrities but as a mother hen (Luke 13:34), friend (John 15:15), and bridegroom (Matt. 25:1–12).[5] The disciple will be called to resonate with the world, to minister to the world as he or she follows Jesus deeper into the world. The disciple must suffer and bear the alienation of the world, not as a punching bag but as one invested and attached in love for the world. Jesus binds the disciple to the world through the resonance of attachments of love, friendship, and care (the horizontal axis of resonances). We are Jesus's disciples only as we follow him into the world as ministers, attaching to the world for the sake of participating (being) in Jesus, who, through his Father, so loves the world.

The greatest among them must be like a child, attached to the world through love, friendship, and care. To enter this kingdom, they must all become resonating children—not experts, entrepreneurs, or disruptive innovators. The material substance of the kingdom that Jesus brings through his person and work is not made of brick buildings and streets of gold but rather of relationships of love, friendship, and care. The substantive structure of this kingdom is not in capitols and capital but in relationships. The joy of resonance witnesses to the fact that we are encountering the kingdom of heaven.

The Congregation as a Relational Space

The kingdom is a space forged by relationships for relationships.[6] Its tangible feel is resonance, because resonance is inextricably relational. Resonance is

---

5. This is to point to the three horizontal locales of resonance: parenting/family, friendship, love.

6. T. F. Torrance has discussed this in depth in his *Time and Incarnation* (Edinburgh: T&T Clark, 1997). He shows how space is a relationally constituted reality, exploring it particularly through the christological doctrines.

the joy of being connected to Jesus's own person through our personhood. It is like how a child experiences the joy of being connected to the personhood of her mother in and through the acts of giving and receiving ministry.[7] At its very core, the kingdom is made of the resonating relationship of the Father to the Son through the Spirit. The kingdom *is* the relational *koinonia* of Jesus to his disciples, whom Jesus sends into the world to love the world by being with and for the world.[8]

Because the kingdom is fundamentally and inextricably relational, its inhabitants are persons—its inhabitants are those who are open *and* closed, individual *and* relational, and will *and* spirit, both in church-community and in the world. The congregation that carries children, like Meredith's or so many others that in small ways invite children into the center of the community, receives the invitation to enter the world through affection, emotion, and efficacy. It finds an encounter of personhood that brings life and vision. It makes the congregation no longer relevance obsessed and resource obsessed but instead brings it into encounters of resonance.

When a congregation carries children, it is fundamentally orientated, without direct rational thought or effort, to a community of persons. Carrying children forms the congregation into a community of persons in relation. Carrying children reveals that a congregation is most fundamentally a relationship. The congregation is a distinct space, no doubt. But it is a space formed not through innovations or resources but through persons in relationship. The pastor doesn't manage the congregation's resources (building, organizational structure, programs). This is a recipe for depression, burnout, and alienation. The pastor tends the congregation's relationships.

A congregation becomes depressed when its identity continues to rest on its resources instead of its relationships. When a congregation's identity is in its resources, it is on an accelerating pace that alienates it from the world, making it excarnate in thought and practice. But even a congregation of persons in relationship ought not to be idealized. Such a congregation will *not* be free of conflict and discord. Bonhoeffer has reminded us in *Life Together* that a community of persons, a congregation that is a relationship

---

7. See Vasudevi Reddy, *How Infants Know Minds* (Cambridge, MA: Harvard University Press, 2008), esp. chaps. 2 and 3, where she articulates her theory that infants learn minds through second person discourse. It's a preverbal language event that develops very early. Reddy draws from personalists, particularly Martin Buber (as does Rosa), to develop this perspective.

8. For a helpful and congregationally focused discussion of *koinonia*, see Theresa Latini, *The Church and the Crisis of Community: A Practical Theology of Small-Group Ministry* (Grand Rapids: Eerdmans, 2011). See also Karl Barth's provocative statements about the church's need for the world as a counterpart in *Church Dogmatics* IV/3.2 (Edinburgh: T&T Clark, 1962), 828.

of persons, will not allow even the community itself to become an idol.[9] Persons in relationship will fight and disagree, hurt one other, and need to be forgiven. Even for those who carry children this is true; love/carrying and conflict go together, as any parent undoubtedly knows. But the relational congregation, and any parent, that encounters such conflict does not experience *la fatigue d'être eglise*. Instead, conflict is merely a sign that we are indeed in each other's lives, living in the world as persons attached through love, friendship, and care.

Bonhoeffer's point is that our primary step into being such communities is concretely to carry our children, recognizing that we all are persons who are open *and* closed, individual *and* relational, will *and* spirit. When we encounter others as person, we receive our own personhood; we come up against revelation itself (up against Jesus Christ existing as church-community, as *Gemeinde*, a relation of persons). When persons are bound to one another, we experience life. We taste a tangible resonance that leads us to embrace the whole of the world, giving and receiving ministry in and to the world.

The Three Movements of the Text

To move one notch deeper in exploring Matthew 18 and its relation to carrying children as the congregation's way into the resonance of revelation, we can see three different movements in these verses.[10] These three movements have a direct connection to the pattern of faith formation we saw in volume 1. And these three movements also graft onto Rosa's elements of resonance. Let's see how.[11]

In volume 1, following Paul, we asserted that faith formation begins with a death experience (the cross). Most New Testament scholars remind us when discussing this Matthean text (or its synoptic equivalents) that children had little to no value in the ancient world. They were nobodies, as John Crossan says.[12] Worse than nobodies, they were no persons.[13] For Jesus to put one of

9. Bonhoeffer, *Life Together* (Minneapolis: Fortress, 1996), 91–94.

10. Haddon Willmer and Keith J. White discuss these three movements in *Entry Point: Towards Child Theology with Matthew 18* (London: WTL, 2013), chap. 5.

11. Peter Balla, *The Child-Parent Relationship in the New Testament and Its Environment* (Eugene, OR: Wipf & Stock, 2015), 127–28, provides a nice discussion of this text.

12. Crossan, *The Historical Jesus: The Life of a Mediterranean Jewish Peasant* (San Francisco: HarperOne, 1993), 269.

13. For more on the cultural understanding of children, see O. M. Bakke, *When Children Became People: The Birth of Childhood in Early Christianity* (Minneapolis: Fortress, 2005), esp. 17–45.

these nobodies—no persons—in the disciples' midst is to make a big claim.[14] It is so big that Bonhoeffer is willing to assert that with this "placing in the midst" Jesus becomes the inventor of childhood. The death experience becomes clear. These creatures don't matter—it doesn't really matter to most whether they live or die. Yet Jesus tells his ambitious disciples that they must become like them. They must see and enter the death experience to find their way into the kingdom. It comes in this broken, backward, cruciform way. But how do we enter this way?

Movement One

This takes us to our first movement in verse 4. Jesus says, "Whoever becomes humble like this child is the greatest in the kingdom of heaven." This is obviously a direct call to humility. If you want to see the kingdom of heaven and enter its space, you must humble yourself like this child. You must humble yourself because to see and enter the kingdom is to find yourself in a relationship that is open *and* closed, individual *and* relational, and will *and* spirit. Because this kingdom is constituted as a relationship, you can only enter it in humility (not by status or power), positioning your body for a resonating encounter with another.

In volume 1 we called this the *kenotic*.[15] For a congregation to move into the kingdom of relationships of resonance that Jesus brings, it must start with the practice of humility. It begins with a willingness to see our own and our neighbors' death experience. Like a three-year-old who can't look away from the crying of a playmate, Meredith's congregation can't look away from Henry and the suffering of his granddaughter. As Rosa has so clearly stated, resonance is not harmony or utopia. It's a call to come and participate. Resonance is *not* devoid of suffering. When it's Jesus who calls, as Bonhoeffer says, it's the invitation to come and die.[16] We're invited to come and enter the death experience of our neighbor, not as experts with a utility belt of resources and strategies, but as a child, who sees, cares, and seeks connection.[17]

14. William Willimon discusses children in relation to burnout in *Clergy and Laity Burnout* (Nashville: Abingdon, 1989), 104–5. A. James Murphy offers an interesting counterargument about these texts. He holds that they're actually about upending the household, which happens in following Jesus. He summarizes this much more intricate argument in *Kids and Kingdom: The Precarious Presence of Children in the Synoptic Gospels* (Eugene, OR: Pickwick, 2013), 34; see also 102–3.

15. See *Faith Formation in a Secular Age: Responding to the Church's Obsession with Youthfulness* (Grand Rapids: Baker Academic, 2017), chap. 8.

16. Bonhoeffer, *The Cost of Discipleship* (New York: Touchstone, 1959), 89.

17. There is scientific research, of course, about this empathic move of children to see and draw near to those who suffer. See Michael Tomasello, *A Natural History of Human Morality* (Cambridge, MA: Harvard University Press, 2016).

Modernity has always had a problem with humility because it's always had a problem with authority (changing things that were once thought unchangeable has a way of quickly inflating your hubris). As a matter of fact, Adam Seligman shows how modernity sought to construct a human civilization built with no external authority that would demand obedience.[18] Modernity wagered that the only authority we needed came not from outside ourselves but from within each one of us. Our own selves becoming our authority.[19] This uneasiness with authority has made humility a degradable (at times despised) virtue in modernity (especially as authority has been further embedded in the self with the ethic of authenticity).[20] Without a proper relationship to authority, it's hard to understand humility.

Miroslav Volf has teased out these improper conceptions of humility in relation to Luther's understanding of nothingness.[21] He explains that to say "I'm nothing" is a social kind of nothingness, like a child in the first century. This is how the disciples understood the child in their midst, awakening them to the death experience. The child is socially nothing. This gets the disciples' attention but is *not* necessarily, if we follow Volf and Luther, the kind of humility that Jesus is calling them toward. It's not a proper form of humility to say, "I'm nothing compared to others." Such a form of humility will never lead us into resonance but only into counting and comparing, into resentment and alienation, pushing us from the world and our neighbor in it. This can't be the humility of the child because, though the society may feel this way, the child (especially a small one) is not cognitively aware enough to embody this misguided way of humility.[22]

18. Seligman, *Modernity's Wager* (Princeton: Princeton University Press, 2000); Alexander Schmemann adds, "When you say aloud the word 'humility,' you feel at once how foreign it is to the spirit of modern life. What humility can we speak of when all life today is built exclusively on self-admiration and self-praise, on enthusiasm for external power, greatness, authority and so forth." Schmemann, *Celebration of Faith*, vol. 2, *The Church Year* (Yonkers, NY: St. Vladimir's Seminary Press, 2012), 103.

19. Seligman gives a long discussion on Kant here, arguing that this was his project. See *Modernity's Wager*, chaps. 2 and 3.

20. For more on this, see Ryan McAnnally-Linz, *An Unrecognizable Glory: Christian Humility in the Age of Authenticity* (PhD diss., Yale University, 2016).

21. Miroslav Volf, "A Variation on Luther's Theology of Humility," in *The Joy of Humility: The Beginning and End of the Virtues*, ed. Drew Collins, Ryan McAnnally-Linz, and Evan C. Rosa (Waco: Baylor University Press, 2020), 48–53.

22. However, I should be honest, this is debatable. Erik Erikson and others have argued convincingly that even very young children have a sense, for instance, of what the larger society thinks of their caregiver. So maybe children would have a sense of their own societal location. But I still hold that this is too cognitive to be so. As noted above, Reddy, in *How Infants Know Minds*, shows that young infants do show cognitive abilities. They are very aware of minds. But grasping concepts like humility in comparison to others' social status is doubtful.

So this social form of humility is not what Jesus is after. Yet there is also a second improper form of humility. Volf calls this the existential form, which says, "I'm nothing compared to what I could or should be."[23] Clearly this is not what Jesus is saying. Jesus isn't saying here in verse 4, "Unless you become like a child—who should be so much more than this little snot-nosed brat is—then you can't enter the kingdom of heaven." This cannot be the meaning of Jesus's words, though this faux humility is endemic in an accelerated modernity. In the acceleration to maintain and innovate our identities, we're often tempted to compare ourselves to others, beating ourselves up and feeling deep stabs of guilt for not doing more, being better, or going faster. We look at those around us (peering at their Facebook pages) and see how much better they're doing than we are. Clicking through the pictures of someone from high school, we're pulled into a depressing "humility" that says, "I'm nothing compared to her."

This form of humility is false because it can never deliver resonance. As Søren Kierkegaard has taught us, there is no love in comparison because comparison is the counting of resources; it's the resentment that you don't have the same accessibility, availability, and attainability as someone else,[24] and beating yourself up for it. Comparison evacuates love, turning it into a relationship instrument, slaying resonance. Burnout and depression come with devastating force when we realize we can't be the selves we should be, especially compared to other fast-moving, innovative selves, and compared to other bigger, more exciting congregations.

For Volf and Luther, the proper form of humility is bound in an assertion like, "Along with all other human beings and the rest of creation, my own self is not the kind of [being] that could be something on its own."[25] To practice humility is to claim that you are the kind of creature who needs others, that you are ontologically in need of relationship. You are a person bound to others, therefore necessitating a level of humility to maintain your personhood. This is what Jesus means when he places a child in their midst. To be a child is to be a person who reminds us all that we are the kind of creatures who have our being in and with others. We are persons who need relationship in order to be.

This third kind of humility draws us into resonance. I become humble neither in believing that others are better than I am nor in thinking that I'm just nothing after all. Rather, I become humble when I remember that I'm the kind of creature who needs to find resonance with otherness. I'm a person who *is* in and through relationship. For the congregation to carry the child is to remember, in humility, that we are all persons. The child is greatest in the

23. Volf, "Variation on Luther's Theology," 50.
24. Kierkegaard, *Works of Love* (New York: Harper Torchbooks, 1962).
25. Volf, "Variation on Luther's Theology," 50.

kingdom because she is the kind of creature who needs others, who directly lives out of the resonance of a relationship with another. She is resonating with a depth of life itself in and through relationship. The phenomenological level of resonance, affection, and emotion is inescapable when we experience an ontological connection to a child. When we humbly stoop to play with him, we receive from him the gift of being with and for him.

Jesus is saying, "Unless you disciples recognize that you are the kind of creatures who need and therefore are bound to others, humbly giving and receiving love, friendship, and care, then you could never enter the kingdom of heaven. For the kingdom is the relationship of persons in giving and receiving ministry."

This takes us to the second and third movements.

Movements Two and Three

In verse 5 Jesus says, "Whoever welcomes one such child in my name welcomes me." To claim that humility is based in the confession that "I'm the kind of creature who needs others" is to assert that we are fundamentally hypostatic beings. In volume 1 we said that through a death experience we take on a kenotic disposition that moves us into an encounter with hypostasis, with personhood. In personhood we encounter the living Jesus Christ. Throughout volumes 1 and 2 I've claimed that Jesus Christ becomes present when we give and receive ministry person to person. Bonhoeffer can claim that Jesus Christ exists as church-community because the church-community is in the form of personhood, and Jesus Christ is present in and through personhood (this is deeply incarnational). Here in verse 5 Jesus says, "Whoever (whatever person) welcomes (gives love, friendship, and care to) one such child (who is so vividly a person in and through her relationships) in my (personal) name[26] welcomes me!" To welcome the child is to encounter the presence of the ministering Jesus Christ, for to welcome the child is to receive—resonate with— the child's humanity. In this encounter, we receive Jesus himself. Revelation comes in hypostatic union, and Jesus promises to be present in the resonant connection of receiving (ministering to) persons. Resonance is dependent on efficacy, and when we approach children in this spirit of efficacy, when we take responsibility for them, we encounter the living Christ.

This pushes us back to verse 3, "Truly, I say to you, unless you change and become like children, you will never enter the kingdom of heaven." This encounter with a child, calling us to come to children, is to be transformed.

26. I discussed the importance of personal names in volume 2, *The Pastor in a Secular Age: Ministry to People Who No Longer Need a God* (Grand Rapids: Baker Academic, 2019), chap. 13.

This is an encounter of resonance because it brings transformation. In volume 1, we called this *theosis*, echoing the ancient Eastern church's concept of transformation in the Spirit.

Much iconography in the Eastern church revolves around Mary with the child, *the* Mother caring for her little one. Jesus here in Matthew asserts that through humble encounters with the personhood of the child, we become transformed into children, recognizing that we too need to be carried in the arms of Mary. Carried in these arms, we recognize that we're persons inseparable from our mothers or from some other person who loves and cares for us. To be with Jesus, to become Christ (to be so in Jesus that we no longer live but Christ lives in us, Gal. 2:20), is not to be a god or Übermensch, as *theosis* is often misunderstood to be by those in the West.[27] Rather, it's to become a child like our Lord, who is carried by the mother.[28] Salvation comes into the world carried in the arms of a teenage mother. The God of the universe, as Luther never tired of reminding us, comes as a baby child who is carried.[29] To be *in* this Jesus, transformed into his very being, is to have his life in us. And to have his life in us is to be a child who is carried.[30]

This is the elusive transformation of resonance that Rosa points to. We cannot make ourselves into children. We can be turned into children only when we are willing to be vulnerable in our personhood enough to *need* to be carried by another.[31] You find yourself transformed into a child when you confess

27. Jaroslav Pelikan and Beverly Gaventa discuss *Theotokos* in Pelikan, *Mary through the Centuries: Her Place in the History of Culture* (New Haven: Yale University Press, 1996), 55–58; and Gaventa, *Mary: Glimpses of the Mother of Jesus* (Minneapolis: Fortress, 1999), 15–20.

28. Bonhoeffer essentially makes this same argument, though without the hint of Mariology or directly connecting it to *theosis*. At the end of *Act and Being* (Minneapolis: Fortress, 1996), 157–61, however, he claims that the child is the eschatological form—that is, being a child is the form of glorification. This is a strong connection, in my mind, to *theosis*.

29. For a superb piece on Mary and Luther, see Lois Malcolm, "What Mary Has to Say about God's Bare Goodness," in *Blessed One: Protestant Perspectives on Mary*, ed. Beverly Gaventa and Cynthia Rigby (Louisville: Westminster John Knox, 2002), esp. 131–35.

30. Hans Urs von Balthasar teases out this point, saying it so beautifully: "The Child Jesus reposed in his Mother's womb in 'archetypical identity' and came forth from it to have the experience of every human child as a result of Mary's turning in love toward him—the experience of being two in one, one with the Mother in her love and separate from her: such a union of love presupposes the otherness of each of the two loving parties. And we have shown how the horizon of all being opens up for the child in precisely this primal experience. But in the Child Jesus this experience, the basis for all that is properly human, must have been a direct transparency of his experience of being at home in the bosom of his Divine Father: separate from him as the Son, receiving his being as Son from the Father, but within this separation inseparably united in their common Holy Spirit." *Unless You Become Like This Child* (San Francisco: Ignatius, 1991), 30.

31. Vulnerability has been a hot topic since Brené Brown's TED Talks. See esp. Brown, "The Power of Vulnerability," TED Talk, June 2010, https://www.ted.com/talks/brene_brown_the _power_of_vulnerability. What makes them resonate with people is that she touches on reso-

that you are the kind of being who needs others. When we find ourselves in resonance, we often discover that we're being carried, that a relationship is holding and connecting us to something beyond us. Resonance, Rosa believes, is always an experience of being carried by some relationship. To put this together with Jesus's words, resonance means finding yourself transformed into a child as your person is connected to and by another.[32]

Carrying children, then, molds and shapes the congregation into a community that is positioned to see and experience the revelation of Jesus Christ, who comes into the world as a child. And this child, who is in the world as the world's very salvation, who is the resurrection and the life, is indivisibly the child who needs to be carried by his mother.[33]

---

nance itself. She responds to acceleration—and all the guilt it brings—by telling us to return to being a child, claiming our personhood, not by covering ourselves in resources but by no longer trying to do more things and instead just being our vulnerable selves. Her message is so powerful because it connects to the truth Jesus is proclaiming here, calling us to be vulnerable children. Again, Luther couldn't get past the thought that the holy God had become vulnerable in a manger. It means that justification and transformation can be connected. We are transformed not by our work or effort—this would be to accelerate our lives—but by being vulnerable children who need to be carried. This to me is what Tuomo Mannermaa means by the passivity of the Protestant/Luther perspective of justification (see note 33 in chapter 14 above). It's anything but a work, but nevertheless it includes me, even costing me something, to echo Bonhoeffer. It is formation, based not on acceleration but rather on participation, on resonance itself.

32. We might *find* ourselves in such a relationship, but we cannot *make* it happen. It's elusive, as Rosa says, and all theologians of revelation make this clear. But we can practice by taking on humility and caring for the children in our midst.

33. There is a whole Mariology that I'm tempted to delve into here. But unfortunately it would balloon this project. Following Catholic thinkers like Henri de Lubac and Yves Congar, we could make a connection between Mary, the church, and the call to carry children. The Protestant biblical scholar Beverly Gaventa has provided some very helpful discussions of the Synoptic Gospels. See Gaventa, *Mary: Glimpses of the Mother of Jesus* (Minneapolis: Fortress, 1999). Elizabeth Johnson's *Truly Our Sister: A Theology of Mary in the Communion of Saints* (New York: Continuum, 2003) is the most helpful theological text on Mary. Johnson pushes back against the liberation theology of Leonardo Boff in his book *The Maternal Face of God: The Feminine and Its Religious Expressions* (San Francisco: Harper & Row, 1987). Scot McKnight has offered a helpful "apologetic" for evangelicals on why Mary is important in *The Real Mary: Why Evangelical Christians Can Embrace the Mother of Jesus* (Brewster, MA: Paraclete Press, 2007). Kenda Creasy Dean and Ron Foster have provided a kind of Mariology for the sake of ministry in their important book *The Godbearing Life* (Nashville: Upper Room Books, 1998). I'm grieved I don't have space to flesh out this Mariology. However, the perceptive reader will see the links in and through the carrying of children. If the church carries children, the church cannot be conceived outside the ministry (and leadership) of Mary. Mary's resonance, as articulated in the Magnificat, is central for the practical life of the church. Bonhoeffer himself offered a sermon on Mary, making some of these connections. If readers had the patience for a five-hundred-page book, I'd be heading into this discussion now. Even for Protestants, Mary should be seen as the saint of carrying children as resonance. This carrying is foundational to the church itself.

There he was, Jesus being carried by his mother. I decide to take a picture, only to be gruffly scolded with harsh Italian words I can't understand. But the very large waving finger is clear enough. It communicates, *Put your stupid iPhone away*!

17

ending with a little erotic ecstasy

About six months after my encounter with Meredith at the airport, I am touring San Marco Cathedral in Venice, Italy. On this day, an equal measure of tourists and worshipers inhabit the beautiful Byzantine building of mosaics. My phone in front of my face gives away that I, unfortunately, am one of the tourists. I ignore a sign and walk to the left of the altar. There it sits: *Madonna Nicopeia*. This ancient icon, only about three feet by five feet in size, is now only a foot away, right in front of me. Legend has it that the *Madonna Nicopeia* was painted by none other than Luke the Gospel writer himself (talented guy, not only a doctor and a writer but a painter too! A real Leonardo, before Leonardo). Supposedly this icon was painted on wood from Joseph's workshop and received the thumbs up from Mary herself.

The icon depicts Mary carrying an infant Jesus, holding him in her arms. Her right hand just over the child Jesus's right shoulder is formed in the ancient sign of welcome, inviting the pray-er to join her in meditation and adoration of the child she carries. Even in tourist mode, I am pulled into Hartmut Rosa's horizontal axis of resonance—the history, art, religious spirituality, and natural beauty of the building is doing its work on me, connecting me to something full.

Whether the icon was truly painted by Luke can't be proven, but this icon has been a central piece of the Byzantine church's prayer life since the fourth century. Even on this day, as I sneak up to snap a picture, there are a dozen pilgrims sitting in chairs praying with the icon.

The big Italian man, who looks like an extra from *The Sopranos*, is reminding me with his waving single finger (which was the size of three of mine) that the *Madonna Nicopeia* is not in the Louvre or some other museum but in an active place of worship. I was invited to pray with, but not possess (even in a photo), the mother and her child whom he and I both call Lord.

––––––

We've seen in the last two chapters that one way for the congregation to shift from relevance and resource obsession to resonance is to follow Dietrich Bonhoeffer and be a community that carries children. Connecting Bonhoeffer and Rosa, we've claimed *la fatigue d'être eglise* is broken when the congregation is constituted in relationships of resonance. The congregation can only be in resonance when the congregation's relationships are freed from instrumentalization. Carrying children in love, friendship, and care is one (primary) way to avoid this instrumentalization. But to carry children means we must become children, affirming our personhood, remembering that we are the kind of creatures who need others. We all must be carried by another.

It's no surprise that Protestantism has been tempted to make its congregations into businesses, even glorifying innovation, wishing to be like little (or not so little) Silicon Valley start-ups.[1] Protestantism will always be susceptible to the temptation of instrumentalizing its relationships, because it has lost the place of the mother, of the Madonna. Losing the centrality of the Madonna in our imagination allows us to forget that we are children, persons, who need others in order to be. There is something profound about remembering that this Jesus who is our Savior is, as Matthew likes to remind us, "the child and his mother."[2] Children cannot be raised (loved, befriended, and cared for) in businesses or in any environment where personhood is lost in the instrumentalization of relationships for goals/objectives outside the relationship.

1. Of course, there are so many other reasons that Protestantism has found itself in a difficult position in late modernity. It would be too simple to say it's just the loss of Mary. I've tried to name many of these other struggles in part 1 of both volume 1 and volume 2. Brad Gregory, though at places overstating himself, offers a helpful articulation of this in *The Unintended Reformation: How a Religious Revolution Secularized Society* (Cambridge, MA: Belknap, 2012). But it also should be mentioned that this business drive in Protestantism is particularly endemic to American Protestantism, which has exported it to most of the rest of the world, affecting visions of ministry and congregational life from Taiwan to Australia to Scotland.

2. Beverly Gaventa adds, "The persistent use of the phrase 'the child and his mother,' however, should give us pause. While it is true that Matthew 2 refers to Mary only in connection with Jesus, it is also true that reference to Jesus almost always involves reference to Mary. With his consistent use of the phrase 'the child and his mother' Matthew reflects a powerful connection between the two. . . . In Matthew's story, the two belong together." *Mary: Glimpses of the Mother of Jesus* (Minneapolis: Fortress, 1999), 43.

(Businesses aren't wrong or evil, just not ideal, or even good, places to raise and therefore carry children.) Innovative start-ups, especially in Silicon Valley, are no place for a child. But the congregation is such a place, because the congregation is a community of persons who are carried by the very Spirit of Jesus Christ, who is the Son of God and the child of Mary.[3]

This has taken us pretty far, giving us at least some picture of how a congregation can find itself in resonance. (What this actually looks like for you is up to you to discover.) We've even explored how resonance can be imaged as revelation.[4] To conclude this project, we need to discuss two significant realities we've ignored in the last two chapters: time and change.

We've argued since the first pages of this volume that we find ourselves in *la fatigue* because modernity is the acceleration of time. Time is able to be accelerated because modernity shook itself free from sacred time. We imagine innovation and dynamic stabilization as the only hope for congregations to keep from decline and failure because we've conceded, as much as any secular institution, that time is absent the sacred.

We've also said little about change and resonance. Even while being carried by Mary, Jesus grows up. In Luke 2, we're told that after the twelve-year-old Jesus bailed from his parents' caravan returning to Galilee, to hang out with the teachers of the law, Mary found him and scolded him, and from that day he obeyed her and grew in wisdom (Luke 2:51–52). Thus to seek resonance and have deep concerns about innovation is not to be against change or even to be opposed to growth. But this change and growth must be set inside a much different vision of the good. Therefore, with this final chapter we'll explore time and change. To do so we'll turn and, like an icon, give our attention to the East, embracing the theological imagination of Byzantine (Eastern) Christianity, exploring the important, but little known in the West, thought of twentieth-century Greek theologian Christos Yannaras.[5]

---

3. The best way to get a handle on Mary is to follow Elizabeth Johnson, *Truly Our Sister: A Theology of Mary in the Communion of Saints* (New York: Continuum, 2003). As a Protestant, I see a need to recover Mary but want to avoid some of the glorifications like in Maximus the Confessor's *The Life of the Virgin* (New Haven: Yale University Press, 2012). I'm a big Maximus fan, though it is debatable whether he actually wrote this text or if it's just attributed to him. Regardless, I'm not a fan of its Mariology.

4. Of course, there is so much more to say, and therefore a full ecclesiology in discourse with resonance is necessary in the future.

5. I had come across Yannaras's name in my reading of Eastern theologians, but it wasn't until Rowan Williams's assertions in his book *Being Human: Bodies, Minds, Persons* (Grand Rapids: Eerdmans, 2018) about the importance of Yannaras that my own study began, particularly of his book *Person and Eros* (Brookline, MA: Holy Cross Orthodox Press, 2007). For those needing more context on Yannaras, I think it's fair to say that Yannaras is to Zizioulas as Jüngel is to Moltmann. Just as Jüngel and Moltmann were colleagues but Moltmann much better known

Person and Eros

Yannaras, in his prominent book *Person and Eros*, seeks to confront what he sees as a major error of philosophy. Like Martin Heidegger, he contends that philosophy has been overly concerned with knowledge (epistemology). This, he believes, turns all our relationships into instruments, alienating us from the world (to give him a little of Rosa's language). Yet unlike Heidegger, and like a good Orthodox theologian, Yannaras shows this by contemplating the Trinity. Starting with the trinitarian reality and working out, Yannaras asserts that to understand God is to *never* see God as an atomistic being. To do so will lead us to assume that God uses relationships for instrumental ends. Rather, starting with the contemplation of the Trinity, Yannaras reveals that this overconcern with epistemology not only has turned our relationships into instruments but has hampered us from seeing the base reality of the universe itself. What moves the world is not speeding up for the sake of getting more, but love itself. Love, he asserts, is the most central reality in the universe.[6]

Yet to say love is central is to affirm that the world is a place of motion. And so our opposition to acceleration and this call for the congregation to be careful with innovation is *not* to demonize motion and wish for inertia. Modernity is not wrong to see the world as dynamic, to even have an infatuation with motion.[7] The God of Israel who is lodged in modernity's consciousness, whether it knows it or not, is a God who moves. Motion is a good. And if motion is a good, then change can also have a place in the good life. As we showed in volume 2, the God of Israel is an arriving, acting God, a God who is satisfied to be known in historical events—the exodus and the resurrection.[8] This all presupposes motion. The God of Israel is not the Buddha, seeking to slide into being itself, escaping action. The God of Israel, rather, has being only in acts in the world.[9]

---

globally, with a smaller number of scholars finding Jüngel's thought to be much more rigorous, so it is with Yannaras and Zizioulas. Both Greek, Zizioulas is much better known than Yannaras across the globe. But for a small group of scholars, Yannaras's work is much more philosophically rich and overall more systematic than Zizioulas's. Zizioulas, though profound in his own right, wrote mainly articles, not long projects. Yannaras, on the other hand, has written over fifty books.

6. I think this is what Rosa is getting at through sociology and critical theory—which is an amazing accomplishment if you think about it.

7. I mean here speeding up and crossing space in production, travel, and communication. But modernity's infatuation with motion is also tied to scientific revolution and Galileo's, and then even more so Newton's, conception of physical bodies in motion. Central to all elements of the modern story is intrigue, even infatuation, with motion and speed.

8. J. C. Hoekendijk asserts something similar: "Our God is not a temple dweller." *The Church Inside Out* (Philadelphia: Westminster, 1964), 70, and see 70–80 for a discussion on the motion of God's act.

9. The God of Israel has a unique *Weltbeziehung*—a relationship of action with the world—to use a core word of Rosa's subtitle. This idea that God's being is known through God's act is

Again, modernity is not wrong to have an infatuation with motion. You can't have resonance through disinterest. The good life is not found in indolence. But when motion gets cut loose (for the sake of more motion) from a larger reality of love, it becomes a toothy gremlin, wanting to consume everything in its path. Motion for the sake of further motion leads only to the good of faster and faster acceleration.

When modernity wants this good of accelerated motion, it will take it at the cost of personhood (producing alienation). When personhood is consumed by acceleration, the motion of the world becomes something distinctly other than love. Love is dependent on persons (this is why "*Person*" comes before "*Eros*" in Yannaras's title). To lose our personhood for the sake of exponential increase in the speed of motion is to give us growth in impersonal realities at the cost of personhood. Modernity has succumbed to the temptation to choose speed and growth over personhood. American Protestantism, whether in megachurch or mainline form, has done the same. This is not an insignificant choice. Choosing speed and growth over personhood[10] allows our relationships to be instrumentalized. Relationships are used as instruments to attain something other than relationship. When this happens, love is lost. We've chosen the ability to accelerate but at the cost of a resonance with the world and the God who is moving in it. Motion is a good, but only when a higher good (Charles Taylor would call this a hypergood) conditions it.

Love, a Hypergood

Love is this hypergood that must condition motion. But Yannaras wants to be more specific about it. This hypergood that is love is not just a generic rom-com kind of love. It is Eros. Eros is a love that is on the move. It's a going-and-sharing-in kind of love. It's a love that has a passion for what is other, to resonate with another. Eros seeks to be with and for what Eros is not.

Yannaras's point is that the universe itself is in motion, because at its core is a relationship of loving Eros (the Trinity itself).[11] The universe is constituted

---

to echo Karl Barth's actualism. For more, see Barth, *Church Dogmatics* I/1 (Edinburgh: T&T Clark, 1936); Paul Nimmo, *Being in Action: The Theological Shape of Barth's Ethical Vision* (Edinburgh: T&T Clark, 2007); and Robert Jenson, *God after God: The God of the Past and the God of the Future as Seen in the Work of Karl Barth* (Indianapolis: Bobbs-Merrill, 1969).

10. I mean this at both the human and the divine level, even the natural level in a sense. See John Zizioulas, "Relational Ontology: Insights from Patristic Thought," in *The Trinity and an Entangled World: Relationality in Physical Science and Theology*, ed. John Polkinghorne (Grand Rapids: Eerdmans, 2010). Personhood is the reality that creates the current of love.

11. Yannaras says it like this, connecting it all to the good: "The erotic movement from God towards creatures, and from creatures back towards God recapitulates the mode by which what is is, and reveals the space of the whole universe as the unqualified and unmeasured how of a

through Eros because it is persons in relationship—as Father, Son, and Holy Spirit—who bring this world into being. The love of the Trinity is Eros. Eros is a love that is always on the move, bound in person-to-person relations. The Father moves to the Son in the Spirit, as the Son by the Spirit moves to the Father (John 10:30). From this Eros of the Trinity, God moves out to create a world in and through the resonating Eros of the love of God for Godself as Father, Son, and Spirit. What makes God *the* minister is God's deep Eros for the world. God's Eros for the world moves God to encounter and speak to persons in the world by moving to them, encountering them as friend and parent. It is Eros, not acceleration, that makes the world. If acceleration leads to alienation, as Rosa has taught us, then Eros leads to resonance. If acceleration inevitably produces alienation, and if alienation's other (Bizarro) is resonance, then what produces resonance is Eros.

Eros is essential to resonance. Resonance is relationship, and Eros is the force that sends us again and again to seek the other as open and closed, individual and relational, will and spirit. Eros desires the other, but always as a closed other. Eros is a love bound in persons in relations. It is the love of persons encountering, arriving, and coming to each other for the sake of sharing in each other's lives. Eros is impossible, Yannaras believes, outside of personhood, because Eros recognizes that we have our very being only in and through relationship.

A love in motion, then, is Eros. Existence itself, Yannaras wants to argue, moves at the speed not of acceleration but of Eros. This is its motion. Eros is always on the move, but never for the sake of more speed or to grow more impersonal resources. The motion of Eros is always for the sole good of personhood, of arriving in the life of another in order to love, befriend, and care for one another. Eros is the love of persons going to persons. Eros is the spirit (Bonhoeffer would call it the objective spirit[12]) of a life-community. The good life is fundamentally a life of Eros, a life of coming out of your self to meet and join another.[13] The love that carries children, and creates community, is Eros.

The Malformed

Because Eros only happens person-to-person, it is dependent on recognizing Bonhoeffer's both/and. Eros, when connected to personhood, recognizes that

---

loving communion—a space which can be understood only in poetic categories ('in the good, from the good, to the good'), only as dynamic disclosure 'outside God' of the mystery of the love of the Trinity." *Person and Eros*, 120.

12. See Bonhoeffer, *Sanctorum Communio* (Minneapolis: Fortress, 1998), 69–75.

13. Wolfhart Pannenberg built his anthropology around something similar. See his *Anthropology in Theological Perspective* (Philadelphia: Westminster, 1985).

we are both open *and* closed, individual *and* relational, and will *and* spirit. Eros, while passionately moving to another, always respects the boundary of the other. Eros is destroyed if it doesn't keep this boundary. It becomes something other than love. It may maintain its surge of emotion, but it loses its connection to the resonance of loving encounter. This happens because to violate another's closedness is to lose personhood, which *always* malforms Eros.

Yannaras's point—though it sounds odd to our ears—is that the Christian story is fundamentally an erotic one. He claims that God is erotic, for we know God through God's loving acts of moving (motion) toward us. This means that at its core the *Madonna Nicopeia* is an erotic painting.[14] It's a picture of the Eros of *the* Mother for *the* Child, inviting us to share in this Child's life by becoming children, remembering that we always need the Eros of another to be at all.[15]

Yet to say that the *Madonna Nicopeia* is erotic sounds odd to us, even dirty, because we've missed, and modernity has evacuated, how fundamental personhood is to Eros. There is no Eros outside personhood. For Eros to lead to resonance (a fullness of life and beauty) it must be bound inside person-to-person relationships that honor the mysterious boundaries of otherness. This is what makes it fundamentally erotic. The Christian story is the narrative of the triune God who passionately arrives and encounters persons, speaking to them, delighting in them, being made sorrowful because of them. But this is all for the sake of leading these persons deeper and deeper into the very life of this God by saving them from the forces that would smother their personhood (Hosea 11:1; 1 Kings 10:9; Deut. 4:37; 10:15; 33:3), even being willing, out of the ultimate act of Eros, to die for them so that they might live (Rom. 5:8).[16]

14. Graham Ward provides his own discussions of Eros in *Cities of God* (London: Routledge, 2000), 77, 121–56. For a project directed more immediately toward congregational life that also has a solid place for Eros, see Jacob Myers, *Curating Church: Strategies for Innovative Worship* (Nashville: Abingdon, 2018), 147–48. Henri de Lubac gives a beautiful articulation of Mary and her relationship to Jesus as love in *The Splendor of the Church*, new ed. (San Francisco: Ignatius, 2006), 337–38.

15. Catholic theologian Hans Urs von Balthasar discusses the place of the erotic as well in *Unless You Become Like This Child* (San Francisco: Ignatius, 1991), 47. "Famously, for Balthasar, the paradigmatic moment of experiencing personhood lies in the experience of an infant of her mother's smile. Importantly, Balthasar names love and not knowledge as the primordial experience of subjective consciousness." Carolyn Chau, *Solidarity with the World: Charles Taylor and Hans Urs von Balthasar on Faith, Modernity, and Catholic Mission* (Eugene, OR: Cascade, 2016), 143.

16. Eros is central to the being of God because each person of the Trinity is so deeply open to the other that the Son, for instance, is everything the Father is *but* (and this *but* is essential for it upholds the boundary of closedness and will) the Father. There is complete union in the triune being, but not at the swallowing of distinction and otherness. This allows for the continued motion of affection—of Eros.

When we say "erotic" in our common cultural language, we mean something very different. We might, for instance, say season one of *Game of Thrones* was so erotic, meaning there were so many nude sex scenes (and weird ones at that). Yet when we use "erotic" like this, we actually say the antithesis of what Eros means in relation to personhood. When we use erotic in relation to *Game of Thrones* or pornography, we actually mean that Eros has been destroyed and its empty shell has been made into something very different.

In such cases, Eros has been extinguished by making the good of sharing in another into just an instrument. It's erotic because it serves one instrumental purpose: to get you off. Its goal is to get you titillated enough to bend your spirit in a way it's not created for, to consume yourself (this is a deep alienation that is Luther's *incurvatus in se*). As late modernity creates more alienation, it's no wonder that addiction to pornography becomes more ubiquitous.

Erotica, like pornography, is a direct attack on Eros because it makes the relational motion of sharing in the life of another person into an accelerated instrument to get only your individual wants more quickly. Pornography is such an endemic evil because it attacks Eros by smashing personhood, falsely setting up the erotic in opposition to personhood.[17]

Our oversexualized culture, which wants sex fast and therefore free of personhood, has so perverted Eros that it's led us to assume that any relationship of friendship and care has a desire for sex hidden within it. We assume at some deep cultural level that human beings are not fundamentally persons needing the motion (acts) of love and participation but ultimately just selfish—Eros-absent—individuals on the hunt for something to bed. The false anthropology is that everyone is *not* driven by the Eros of shared personhood in friendship and care but instead moved to possess someone by sleeping with that someone made into an object of want. The more erotic (in the malformed sense) the pornography, the more the persons in it are treated like disposable objects—making it more thrilling, allowing you to more quickly get off.

The *Madonna Nicopeia* is properly erotic because it spills over with the love of *the* Mother to *the* Child. If we maintained, as our culture does, the pornographic understanding of erotic, calling the *Madonna Nicopeia* properly erotic would be a perverted fetish. But the *Madonna Nicopeia* is properly erotic because it's a sign of free persons sharing in the life of one another. The *Madonna Nicopeia* is properly erotic because it is the resonance of love, friendship, and care. And it brings with it a communion of persons as Mother and Child. A sacred reality of shared life opens us to spirit, history, nature, and art.

17. For a theological perspective of sex, see Nicolas Berdyaev, *The Divine and the Human* (San Rafael, CA: Semantron, 2009), 116–20.

The Eros of *the* Mother for *the* Child, and *the* Child for *the* Mother, in the *Madonna Nicopeia* is a love that carries all who pray through the icon, taking us deeper into the resonating good of the world. It reminds us that at the center of the universe is Eros, the very mystery that holds existence in being. This Eros is most tangibly for us human beings when a chosen teenage mother responds to a speaking God (this is resonance). She responds that she indeed is willing to be the Mother of the church by carrying this Child in Eros (Luke 1:38). And this Child who is Immanuel (God with us) is the fullness of the ministry of Eros. This Child, who is carried by the Eros of this willing Mother, is the second person of the Trinity who will die and overcome death (by the act, Eros, of the Father) so that *all* persons, even all things in motion—which natural science has taught us is everything—can share eternally in the direct Eros of the personhood of the Father to the Son in the Spirit.

When Meredith's little congregation decides that they will carry children, they in turn decide that they will be children, as Jesus in Matthew calls his disciples to be (Matt. 18:3). They will be like this fifteen-year-old child, Mary,[18] who hears the calling of God choosing her, not through a sex act but by the very speaking of God, to bear and carry a child who will save the world by allowing the communion of personhood to never end (not even by death).[19] Meredith's little congregation is never more the church than when it carries children. They are never more like the Mother, whose womb and arms create the church by carrying *this* Child, whom Gabriel tells Joseph to name Jesus (Matt. 1:21).[20] By carrying children as the children of God, Meredith's congregation participates in the Eros of the Trinity by ministering to the personhood of children as a community of persons. What brings life to this little congregation, what renews them, is the resonance that comes from persons in Eros through the act of ministry.

18. There is some dispute on Mary's age when Gabriel arrived. Most scholars contend that she was between thirteen and sixteen.

19. Even in this text of calling, God upholds the open and closed boundary. Mary, it seems, is free to deny this calling. The Magnificat is such a powerful piece of Scripture because this young girl is given a vision, and out of her freedom she is so resonating with the world that she is willing to claim from her own closed, individual will, "Let it be with me according to your word" (Luke 1:38). The Magnificat is a deep text of resonance. Beverly Gaventa provides a rich articulation of the Magnificat in "'Nothing Will Be Impossible with God': Mary as the Mother of Believers," in *Mary, Mother of God*, ed. Carl Braaten and Robert Jenson (Grand Rapids: Eerdmans, 2004), 32–35.

20. Graham Ward adds, "The ascension re-establishes a new anthropology, a new way of being human as being *en Christo* as the Church. . . . The logic of the Ascension is the logic of birthing, not dying, or a continuation of the logic of opening-up. The withdrawal of the body of Jesus must be understood in terms of the Logos creating a space within himself, a womb, within which (*en Christoi*) the Church will expand and creation be recreated." *Cities of God*, 113.

Time and Persons

As we've argued throughout this project, modernity is fundamentally about time, about speeding it up. To speed up time, modernity needs to evacuate any sense of sacred time. We live in a secular age, inside an immanent frame, because this sense of time (and our cultural timekeeper) doesn't believe, even works to oppose the idea, that time itself has any sacred weight. To affirm that time may have some sacred weight is to risk the need to slow down the drive toward acceleration and growth.

Yannaras reminds us that what makes time sacred is not necessarily the magical enchantment of a time before modernity. He is not, nor am I, calling for a return to Avignon and medieval Christendom. So we need to ask, Is there a way back to an embrace of sacred time other than returning to a world where devils and demons are everywhere and fate is our destiny? Or to ask it another way, not wanting to return to the magical medieval enchantment (I'm happy with no plague-carrying fleas!), Is there a way to encounter a sacred dimension in time?

Yannaras thinks so. And not surprisingly, considering where he has taken us above, this happens in and through personhood. For instance, you sense yourself being pulled into a sacred moment of delight at a nondescript Dairy Queen with your four-year-old daughter. Or time feels gathered when the preschooler says "That was *great!*" in the church gym. Or time feels full to bursting when a congregation gathers around the death experience of a grandfather and prays for his granddaughter. You sense this fullness of gathered time because of the encounter with personhood. Per Rosa, the answer to acceleration isn't slowdown but resonance. Resonance is the answer because slowdown alone allows time to remain free of the sacred. Slowdown concedes the definition of time to acceleration—just pumping the brakes on the speed. Resonance, on the other hand, recognizes that time itself has something inherently sacred within it. Time itself is a mystery.

For instance, in a deep conversation with a friend we might recognize that time flew by. It raced by not in the sense of acceleration, where we struggled to keep up, but in the sense of resting in the moment and feeling carried. You experience time itself running through you, warmly and fully including and welcoming you. You have no idea what time it is—you've lost track of the measurement of minutes and hours—but you do know your being has been in relation. There is something sacred about this. The event of encountered personhood is an experience of time that no measuring device can fully decipher, because it's the encounter of spirit. Such events of encountered personhood, through the Eros of friendship and care, are potent antidotes to *Zeitkrankheit*. You feel not a time sickness but a gift of being-in-time by being-with-others in love (Eros).

The experience of persons in Eros brings back into vision the sacredness of time by connecting us to something outside of us, giving us the resonance of being-to-being, unveiling that time itself is not free of the eternal. To push this a little further into human experience, time's sacredness is also experienced by being a person moved in Eros to create. When we find ourselves engulfed in a creative erotic act like painting, writing, or making music, time is different.[21] Time moves in different ways. A taste of the eternal is tangible in such moments. These creative acts connect us to our being, attaching us to something moving in the world, welcoming and holding in tension that we are open *and* closed, individual *and* relational, that we are free as will *and* spirit. In such moments, minutes and hours are more fluid and yet full. We feel time not running past us but gathered and carrying us. Persons in Eros experience time differently. They experience something sacred.

Yannaras's point is that personhood unveils that there is indeed still sacredness in time (though modernity asks us to ignore it, needing our relationships to be instrumentalized for the sake of speed). Modernity asserts that machines mark time and that time is stiffly objectified into seconds, minutes, and hours, into units as opposed to events. And with innovations, we can fit more action inside these units. It's the motion of impersonal *things* (like planets and particles),[22] and the machines that count them, that frame time for us. This makes these impersonal zones the caged location of our actions, blocking our vision of eternity in time. When our actions are caged in these impersonal zones, Eros is smothered and the sacred is abandoned. Eros is lost as the relational dynamic necessary for personhood. The Eros of persons in relationship is stripped for the sake of the innovation of instrumentalization. Things and machines, which are unable to be moved by the erotic, are what we concede time to (there is no modernity without the machines of production, information, and transportation, like steam engines, personal computers, and automobiles).[23] Modernity, through the machine, seeks to impersonally

21. George Steiner adds, "To ask 'what is music?' may well be one way of asking 'what is man?'" *Real Presences* (Chicago: University of Chicago Press, 1989), 6. Hans Boersma adds, "The purpose of life, according to Gregory, is to make music." *Embodiment and Virtue in Gregory of Nyssa* (Oxford: Oxford University Press, 2013), 70.

22. Though these are not as impersonal as we assume when looked at through a trinitarian perspective. For a discussion of how personhood and ministry move within all parts of the created realm, see my *Exploding Stars, Dead Dinosaurs, and Zombies: Youth Ministry in the Age of Science* (Minneapolis: Fortress, 2018).

23. For Yannaras's sense of technology and the impact of the machine, see *Person and Eros*, 103.

measure time so that more actions, cut loose from Eros, can be achieved inside these units of measured time. To make time measurable, the parts of it that are sacred, and therefore spill beyond the capacity of impersonal machines to measure, are ignored.

But to take this approach to time is to miss something essential. We overlook that these measuring and time-counting machines were made by persons. Machines never make machines. It is persons who, in erotic moments in the fullness of time (call this *eureka*!), found themselves discovering something profound—that electricity was light, that silicon could hold data. These persons found a way, through sacred moments of gathered time, to create a machine to measure time.[24] But once we make our machines, they make us. They turn time from the sacred, bound in personhood, to cold measurement. The machines that measure time are able to count the decay of motion but not the spirit of encounter.[25] In other words, these machines can count motion, but only motion outside of Eros. No machine can count love (counting love itself is an absurd notion). Modernity, as the era of counting and machines,[26] needs to accelerate as quickly as it can, because its machines have completely made time a race against the counting of decayed motion.

Getting Back to Sacred Time

Modernity is not all wrong in its obsession with time. Obliterating time, if this were even possible, is no way back to the sacred. The sacred will need to be found within time.[27] We need eternity in time. But if we acknowledge that eternity is in time, then time itself will need to be reordered. This is exactly what Yannaras is after. He wants us to see that because we act as and for

24. For this point I'm leaning on Michael Polanyi, *Personal Knowledge: Towards a Post-Critical Philosophy* (Chicago: University of Chicago Press, 1962). His point is that it is always persons who do science.

25. This is to point to Aristotelian physics and other conceptions of time, like Plato's. See Yannaras, *Person and Eros*, 131, 137.

26. Here I mean that modernity has its birth in philosophy's turn to mathematics, particularly René Descartes as the prime example (we call these thinkers he leads "the rationalists"). This turn is followed by industrialization and the creation of the steam engine. Or to put these together we could look at Blaise Pascal, who was a mathematical genius who even invented a counting machine. For a nice overview of his interesting life, see James Connor, *Pascal's Wager: The Man Who Played Dice with God* (Oxford: Lion, 2006). For a biography on Descartes, see A. C. Grayling, *Descartes* (London: Pocket Books, 2005).

27. Rowan Williams, connecting this to narrative, reminds us that our location is always in time. "Knowing God is bound to the passage of time in a new manner; so that to speak of God and the knowledge of God is always going to be in some way connected with narrative." *On Augustine* (London: Bloomsbury, 2016), 12.

persons, and because Eros is motion, time is necessary. You can't have Eros outside of time, because Eros is motion.[28] This is what allows Yannaras to get to his reordering. He asserts that time is ultimately the stage on which personal beings are disclosed to one another. Time is not the measure of impersonal motion but the encounter of personal relations.[29] Time, when not forcefully separated from personal relations, maintains a deep sense of the sacred. The sacred is encountered in and through the disclosure of persons acting with and for each other in and through Eros. Sacred time is the narrating of the moments of Eros (this is the ecstatic element of time that also orders change, which we'll get to soon).

To give these slippery thoughts some handles, think about Christmastime. What makes Christmastime so meaningful to so many people is that it's indeed a time—we call it Christmas*time*. But it's not just a time. What makes it an experience of resonance is that it's a time set within the horizon of personal relations. It's an event/time where persons are disclosed to one another and find connection. It's the relationship, the encounter with persons, that makes this time called "Christmas" so meaningful (so resonant). It's a time to share in each other's personhood, to act with and for each other in love. It's erotic (not in the sense of Santa dressed as a Victoria's Secret model but in the sense of the motion of shared personhood).

Personal relations can't happen outside of time. The motion of Eros, person-to-person, needs a time. We say things like, "Remember what you gave me for Christmas three years ago? That meant *so much* to me." Or "Remember on Christmas Eve 1998 when you told me you loved me for the first time?" There is no being outside of time, because there are no personal relationships outside of time. We need time because we need the motion of moving toward one another.

Yannaras's point is that the horizon of being (its range of experience and therefore its very constitution) is bound in the communion of persons. "The person 'defines' the *disclosure* of being, while time 'measures' this disclosure."[30] Again, someone at Christmas might say (not very romantically, but allow me to make this point), "Remember it was 1998, at your uncle's house, that you disclosed your being as in love with me. Remember that was over twenty years ago that our persons shared in each other's life in a new, ecstatic way."

28. "Eternity is not timelessness, but rather the fullness of time." Antje Jackelén, *Time and Eternity: The Question of Time in Church, Science, and Theology* (Philadelphia: Templeton Foundation Press, 2005), 224.

29. This is where, in Yannaras's mind, the Enlightenment and modernity as a whole—having followed Aristotle—went wrong.

30. Yannaras, *Person and Eros*, 131.

Time (in 1998) is the disclosure of persons ("I love you") acting with and for one another, directing their lives through personal relationships into a history ("that was over twenty years ago").

Yannaras is saying that personhood, and the relationships that make us persons, needs time. The temptation that led to modernity's infatuation with acceleration is the recognition that being needs time. This isn't the problem! The problem is that, recognizing the need for time and that time is motion, modernity became infatuated with making time its own horizon. It cut time loose from persons in relation (stripping being from relationality). Time is secularized and stands in opposition to a sacramental sense of eternity in time, when motion as time is allowed to have a horizon outside of personal relations.[31]

In turn, and most importantly for our project, we get back to some sense of the sacred in time not when we become timeless but when we live and move as persons in relation. When we have concrete experiences of resonance in and through Eros, the eternal is unveiled in time. For example, in the following story told by early childhood educator Erika Christakis in her book *The Importance of Being Little*, notice how motion (a moving toward) for the sake of sharing in personhood (for Eros) is so clear. In this story it's hard to miss that the sacred is still in time and that we can spot it and therefore participate in it inside the resonant experience of relationships of Eros. Christakis is telling her reader about being at a conference in which she was introduced to a program created by Dr. Rick Solomon to help parents connect with their autistic children. Solomon's program is called the PLAY Project. Christakis says,

> In one PLAY Project video I saw, a father was shown dressed in a bed sheet like a zombie, leaping boisterously from behind a door in a game of hide-and-seek with his young son. The father's demeanor was purposely exaggerated, like a clown on steroids. . . . This is a game the little boy really loved, and as soon as he showed the first inkling of a response, such as a flicker of eye contact or a muffled giggle, the father had been coached to pull his son into another bear hug, complete with exuberant sound effects and giant belly laughs. The whole play sequence was repeated again and again, and with each repetition the child participated more purposefully, and with greater affect, interest, and affection for his father.

31. Again, I'm channeling Michael Polanyi, *Personal Knowledge*, whose point is that it may be that planets and particles are in motion outside of personal relationships, outside of personhood (though Zizioulas, in "Relational Ontology," makes an argument that this isn't the case). Even so, it is persons who observe, describe, and come to knowledge of this motion. There is no described experiential motion in existence that does not come to us in and through personhood. All knowledge is personal knowledge, because it's persons who count and measure. And because it's persons, there is always a story that accompanies the measuring.

We can see all the dimensions and elements of resonance in this little story of persons reaching out to one another, connecting in Eros. Christakis continues, "With video feedback and coaching, parents in Dr. Solomon's practice are trained to recognize these tenuous signs of emotional connection, and to reward them immediately with a bespoke euphoria that's carefully fine-tuned to each child's unique quirks and amusements. The transformation of these disconnected, distant-eyed children into rollicking, roughhousing ones who could gaze into their parents' eyes for the first time was so striking that the audience literally gasped out loud."[32]

The audience gasps out loud not necessarily because they've found an instrument to solve an impersonal problem but because they've witnessed an encounter of erotic personhood. They've been given, in a flash, a direct vision of eternity still in time. When the father embraces his child and a connection is forged out of what seemed impossible, we're drawn directly into sacred time.[33] It's a sacred moment in that child's room, when the father's and son's eyes meet and their relationship is transformed, the death of disconnection obliterated in the encounter of persons. In such encounters, the sacred is still in time, because in time, in that room during that play therapy, the mutual being of son and father was disclosed to one another and shared in as love.

Concretely, we can say that eternity is encountered in time when we carry a child—talking with that four-year-old at Dairy Queen, praying with that grandfather, experiencing that child's joy as delight. The love for the child can't happen outside of time. But time is only the stage, the measured location of the encounter with the child.[34] Through deep encounters of love, friendship, and care, time is subordinate to the sacred action (motion) of the ministry of persons in relation.[35] Love is stronger than time, but love always happens

32. Christakis, *The Importance of Being Little* (New York: Penguin, 2017), 148. If you need another picture of eternity breaking into time, see Modris Eksteins's beautiful, moving, and spiritually weighty write-up of Christmas during World War I when German and English/French soldiers put down their weapons, shared a meal, and sang hymns. Eksteins, *Rites of Spring: The Great War and the Birth of the Modern World* (Boston: Mariner, 2000), 109–55.

33. Graham Ward adds, "The doctrine of participation, which is a doctrine of the Spirit, cannot be separated from a doctrine of time and a theology (which is also an anthropology) of desire. It is because the present participates in the eternal . . . that we who are time-bound, situated in specific temporalities or textualities of time, participate also in the eternal. But our participation is not simply formal. It is personal. For the eternal is not the endlessness of the infinite." *Cities of God*, 171.

34. Hans Urs von Balthasar discusses the way the child is open to eternity in time in *Unless You Become Like This Child*, 54–57.

35. David Jensen offers an interesting discussion of children in time: "Anyone who has spent a significant length of time with young children will recognize how quickly they subvert our linear understanding of time." *Graced Vulnerability: A Theology of Childhood* (Cleveland: Pilgrim Press, 2005), 130.

in time. And the love, friendship, and care for persons unveils that eternity is still in time. For eternity is most profoundly the person of the Father, Son, and Holy Spirit in relation. *The* Child is in time; he is in Mary's arms. But *this* Child is eternal, for he is *the* person in inseparable relation to God the Father. God is in time. God's being is known in the time of God's action (motion in the time of the exodus and the resurrection). But because nothing (not even death on the cross) can ever upend the erotic relation of the Father, Son, and Holy Spirit, God is eternal.[36]

By receiving the event of *the* Child's ministry for us—participating in it by ministering to our neighbor as a child—we are invited into eternity itself. We can recover, even in a secular age, a sense of sacred time (of the sacredness of time). And we can recover this not through innovation, which succumbs to making time its own horizon, but through the resonance of encounters of shared personhood. We can be a congregation like Meredith's that carries children, that gasps, as its worship, when it sees a sacred connection, testifying that eternity is in time, for death has been changed into life.

Now Concluding: What about Change?

To say that time is motion is to say that change is inevitable.[37] Even to properly order time as the measure of the disclosure of persons in relations is to make motion central. Eros love moves in (it is the motion of) passion for the other. To make these claims is to affirm the centrality of change. There is a movement from something to something else. This is change. Only a malformed Eros would never allow the person it supposedly loves to change. Love for something unchanging is a love not for a person but for an object.[38] God is never changing, in the sense that God is never something other than Person in Eros.[39] Yet, because God is Person in Eros, God changes. Because God

36. Kosuke Koyama adds, "Eternity is more than a time-concept. It is a love-concept. When love comes to transitoriness and embraces it, it is called eternity. Otherwise eternity is only an abstract concept." *Three Mile an Hour God* (London: SCM, 1979), 80.

37. See Yannaras, *Person and Eros*, 129.

38. What makes that kind of lover particularly frustrated (and often violent) is that he is trying to do something that can't be done. Persons can't be kept from changing. But this person can't imagine that the relationship would withstand any change, fearing that the other person will find someone new to love, and so he abusively demands that his partner never change. But he'll have to force something onto personhood to keep it from changing, therefore depersonalizing the other, oppressing the other's will and spirit.

39. As Barth would say, God is who God is in God's act. Or Luther would admit that God could be a monster, something other than person and Eros. God is free to be this if God wishes. But this is not what God has disclosed to us (a connection to Yannaras). Rather, Luther reminds

moves, as the Scripture says, God changes God's mind (Num. 14). Because God is in motion, calling Israel to repent, change, and return in Eros to God, change has a central place in a faithful conception of time. Change is a good. Resonance has a place for change, for resonance is inseparable from relationship, and relationships are not possible without change. Sacred time is not unchanging, even if its concern for presence and practice demands a longer (less compressed) present than modernity desires.

With the above in place, we can say that relationship determines and conditions change. And the push for change is creating depressed congregations. It will continue to do so because it pushes us into weariness, into *la fatigue d'être eglise*. Yet what links weariness and change—threatening a depression that produces an alienation from the world itself—is the seeking for change outside the sacredness of time (outside the events of persons in relationship of Eros).[40] Change is a slave master when the sacred is stripped from time and we therefore live inside a closed immanent frame where relationships are instruments. Unfortunately, many congregations, as much as any other entity in late modernity, have sought change outside of sacred time by instrumentalizing relationships. We tell congregants to build relationships with neighbors to get them to come to church, or we imagine that young adults will come only if we use a relationship to secure their participation.

For change to remain properly ordered, and not become a utensil for weariness, it must be born out of ecstasy. Ecstasy, Yannaras believes, produces a proper change. But his use of ecstasy shouldn't be confused with just an emotional high. The goal isn't to be continually and always a seven-year-old on Christmas morning, bouncing off the walls. Rather, ecstasy is to have an experience that is ec-static (moving us outside of ourselves in motion toward someone else). It's an encounter that comes from outside of you that beckons to transform you. The ecstatic is born from hearing a call from outside of you (as individual or congregation), as Mary hears the call of God through Gabriel (Luke 1).

The change that congregations need can only avoid weariness if the change is born from the ecstatic, through the erotic. For Yannaras, the ecstatic is born from persons calling out for the motion of another to encounter, meet, and connect with them, like a father dressed like a zombie, playing with his

---

us that the only God we should contemplate is the God who comes to us in Jesus Christ. This is a God who is never something other than person and Eros, but is moving and acting and therefore changing.

40. Chris Green provides a nice discussion about persons and event in discussing Robert Jenson's theology. See *The End Is Music: A Companion to Robert W. Jenson's Theology* (Eugene, OR: Cascade, 2018), 17–18, and see 54–55 for more on Jenson's conception of time.

autistic son. The father does so not for the sake of instrumentally healing his son but solely to connect with him (which is the more profound sense of healing). The encounter with him is ecstatic, bringing the fullness of time. It changes them both by drawing them deeper and deeper into each other's personhood. The change that comes into their lives is never wearying (though the jumping and noisemaking might get exhausting), because the ecstatic encounter of personhood produces its own energy.[41] The father would say, "I never get tired of it, because this is what I'm made for. I get tired of people misunderstanding him, I get tired of the extra tasks, but I never get tired of the hugs or especially the eye contact. It feeds my soul like nothing else."

Something very similar happens with Meredith's congregation. They are changed, not by the effort of innovation but by the disclosure of personhood. It's the beckoning to enter into sacred time, into a good life of resonance, that changes them. They're moved from doing something to doing something else by this calling born from the disclosure of Henry's person in and through the Eros for his granddaughter. In the wake of this encounter, the programs and activities of the congregation are radically shifted. It is a changed congregation. They do many new things that produce new directions. But the impetus for the new is not newness itself, nor the fear of living in a compressed present with a lack of resources for the future.[42] Rather, the impetus for change is the calling to share in the person of Henry (it's ecstatic).

Change happens through the force of the motion needed to respond to the disclosure of Henry and his granddaughter's personhood.[43] What pushes the congregation forward into change is not the need for more resources and the fear of waning relevance. It has nothing to do with the logic heralded by denominational leaders and consultants that says, "Congregations must change or die."

This focus on congregations dying will produce only dying. It saps the congregation's energy, killing the motion it seeks to multiply. Rather, the kind of dying that brings the change congregations need is ecstatic. It's the calling

41. It's an energy bound spirit-to-spirit, in the Spirit, to echo James Loder, *The Logic of the Spirit: Human Development in Theological Perspective* (San Francisco: Jossey-Bass, 1998). Loder contends that human spirit is made for the Holy Spirit, meaning it finds a continued energy in its union. My point is that human spirit is inseparable from personhood, so the disclosure of personhood for events of sharing produces its own energy—as long as Bonhoeffer's *both/and* is upheld (open and closed, individual and relational, will and spirit).

42. Amy Plantinga Pauw makes a strong case for the church concerning itself with the present in *Church in Ordinary Time: A Wisdom Ecclesiology* (Grand Rapids: Eerdmans, 2017), 108–10.

43. Rowan Williams, discussing Augustine, highlights the dialectic I'm getting at here: "God alone is simultaneously work and rest, and his completely stable action, both restful and ceaseless, enables us to grasp something of what time and change are." *On Augustine*, 19.

to encounter persons through a death experience in Eros—it is the kind of dying that is costly grace. The change in Meredith's congregation was ecstatic because it came from within the event of the disclosure of personhood. Her congregation couldn't control this (resonance is always elusive), and if they tried to, they would exhaust themselves. They could only await the free disclosure of personhood by being present to one another, seeking a good life in prayer, peace, and storytelling. They could narrate for each other their experiences of resonance. Yet after this disclosure, the congregation is doing something new, and the energy necessary for this new thing is concordant with the congregation's own personhood and gifts.[44] Change was born from the good of resonance. In other words, Meredith's congregation has what they need to meet this call, because this call encountered their persons through personhood, a revelation of personhood directly to their own personhood.

In seeing and participating in Henry's death experience, embracing his person, a calling comes from outside the congregation to change and take on new motion in the world. They're called, not to feel alienated from the world in accelerating to find more resources, but to faithfully respond to *this* call for ministry. They catch a vision for the difference they can make, not because they've innovated into something new but because the Spirit of the living God has disclosed personhood, calling them into sacred time. Meredith knows this is the working of the triune God, because the energy comes not from her or from the congregation itself. It comes from the calling born from the event of the disclosure of personhood, and the Spirit, as on the road to Emmaus (Luke 24), continues to disclose the very person of Jesus Christ in their midst. It's ecstatic, because what pushes them into change is not the threat of loss but resonance. It's Eros as the motion in time that produces change. And it is Eros's continued encounter with sacred time through ministry to persons that renews the congregation's spirit.

If a congregation wants change, it will start not by being concerned with relevance and resources, but with the good life of resonance, seeking for the living Christ where Christ can be found, in the disclosure of personhood, where time is not made to accelerate but becomes full and sacred. Time becomes full and sacred through the continued disclosure of personhood in Eros, like watching a father embrace his autistic son, and the son gaze into his father's eyes. Witnessing such events of sacred time will produce ecstasy in the congregation such that they will together, out of the energy of the Spirit of

44. I discussed the importance of gifts and giftedness for the church in volume 1, *Faith Formation in a Secular Age: Responding to the Church's Obsession with Youthfulness* (Grand Rapids: Baker Academic, 2017), 199–211.

the personal triune God, act in the world. They will resonate with life itself, exorcised from alienation, by the calling of the living God who gives them life as ministers. The ecstasy of witnessing eternity in time, in such concrete ways as a grandfather's tears and a father's hugs, will ignite the good life of giving and receiving ministry in the world.

index